Memory and Methodology

Memory and Methodology

Edited by
Susannah Radstone

Oxford • New York

First published in 2000 by
Berg
Editorial offices:
150 Cowley Road, Oxford OX4 1JJ, UK
838 Broadway, Third Floor, New York, NY 10003-4812, USA

Berg is the imprint of Oxford International Publishers Ltd.

Library of Congress Cataloging-in-Publication Data

A catalogue record for this book is available from the Library of Congress.

British Library Cataloguing-in-Publication Data

A catalogue record for this book is available from the British Library.

ISBN 1 85973 296 8 (Cloth)
1 85973 202 X (Paper)

Typeset by JS Typesetting, Wellingborough, Northants.
Printed in the United Kingdom by WBC Book Manufacturers, Bridgend,
Mid Glamorgan.

Contents

Contents

Acknowledgements

This collection has, for a number of complicated reasons, and as many of those involved with it know only too well, taken an extraordinarily long time to reach the light of day. My contributors deserve thanks for their patience as well as for the quality of their individual contributions. Thanks are due to the department of Cultural Studies at the University of East London which provided me with a sabbatical that enabled much consolidation of this project to take place. For their particular roles in keeping me on track I also want to thank John Samuel and Julia Boutall.

Notes on Contributors

Peter Carrier recently completed a PhD on Monuments and National Memory Cultures in France and Germany at the Freie Universität Berlin, where he lectures part time in the department of Politics. He has published in the journals *Historical Reflections*, *Borec* and *National Identities*.

Mariette Clare recently took early retirement from working in adult and community education with a special interest in access and inclusive learning. She is currently training in psychodynamic counselling and trying to write science fiction. She lives in a complex household in Leicester.

Stephan Feuchtwang is Professorial Research Associate with the Department of Anthropology, London School of Economics. The project mentioned in his chapter joins his two previously separated research interests, on local politics and religion in China and on racism and government in Europe.

Frigga Haug is the author of several books including *Female Sexualisation: A Collective Work Of Memory*. She teaches at Hamburg University.

Richard Johnson teaches cultural studies at Nottingham Trent University. He spent most of his academic career at Birmingham University's Centre for Contemporary Cultural Studies. His current interests are the culture of death and mourning, political identities and methodologies of cultural research. He lives in a complicated household in Leicester.

Annette Kuhn is Reader in the Institute for Cultural Research at Lancaster University. She is the author of several books, including *Family Secrets: Acts of Memory and Imagination* and she is an editor of *Screen*.

Rodney Livingstone is a professor in the School of Modern Languages at the University of Southampton.

Chris Locke was until recently Rank Xerox lecturer in electronic communication at University College, London. He recently left higher education for a post in the private sector.

Susannah Radstone teaches in the Cultural Studies department at the University of East London. She writes about cultural theory and film and is the editor of *Sweet Dreams: Sexuality, Gender and Popular Fiction* and co-editor of *The Women's Companion to International Film*. She is also an editor of *Routledge Studies in Memory and Narrative*. She is currently completing a monograph, *On Memory and Confession* and has recently co-organised an international conference. 'Frontiers of Memory'.

Gillian Swanson recently moved to the University of the West of England, following ten years living in Australia and working at Griffith University, latterly in the Australia Key Centre for Cultural and Media Policy. She publishes in cultural history and cultural policy, specialising in urban consumption and sexual cultures, women's participation in the arts, and cultural and multimedia industry policy.

Amal Treacher is a member of the Psychosocial Studies Area at the University of East London. She is engaged in researching adopted and non-adopted children in order to provide a social and psychological framework for understanding childhood subjectivity.

Working with Memory: an Introduction
Susannah Radstone

Over recent years, and as others have noted (Carter and Hirschkop 1997: v), memory has become both a central and an organising concept within research in the humanities and in certain branches of the social sciences. Memory research is currently being pursued in philosophy, history, cultural studies, literature, film, media studies and psychology, not to mention archeology and architecture. As a result of these endeavours, conferences are being organised to disseminate work on memory. Amongst these, Southampton University's 'Cultural Memory' conference (1995), Lancaster University's 'Time and Value' conference (1997), the Victoria and Albert Museum's 'Material Memories' conference (1998), the Freud Museum's 'Memory in Dispute' conference (1998), Newcastle University's 'Refiguring History' conference (1999) and Lancaster University's 'Testimonies' conference (1999) as well as the 'Frontiers of Memory' conference (1999) which I co-organised, have all attracted large numbers of engaged and engaging papers and have exuded a real sense of intellectual excitement. Meanwhile, articles and monographs concerned with memory have flooded scholarly journals and the academic presses, while at least one new volume series[1] is concerning itself exclusively with memory research. Consequently, universities have begun to incorporate much of this work into their courses, even in some cases, constructing discrete courses around questions of memory.[2] My own recent experience of organising an international conference to take stock of these developments[3] has impressed upon me the vast numbers of scholars worldwide whose research is currently occupied, in one way or another, with the interrogation and analysis either of the conceptual and historical category of memory, or of individual or social/cultural memories.

This explosion of interest in memory begs several questions. On the one hand, it provokes questions about the reasons for this apparent convergence of interest in memory across the disciplines. On the other hand, however, it provokes questions about the extent to which this *apparent* convergence represents any more than a pivotal relation to a concept – namely that of memory. In other words, though the humanities have apparently witnessed a vast expansion in work on memory, it may be that this work has less in common than first appears to be the case. Do the disciplines working on and around memory understand that concept in similar ways? And how do their theories and methods construe their object of study? These are the questions that this introduction will address and that this volume's varied contributions will hopefully illuminate.

Memory's Ups and Downs

The contemporary academic fascination with memory exemplified by the essays collected in this volume is but one manifestation of a more general historical upswing – or what one writer has described as 'a...boom of unprecedented proportions'(Huyssen 1995: 5) – in memory's valuation. Histories of memory's vicissitudes emphasise the high valuation placed on memory by the ancient Greeks and the Romans. In ancient Greece, memory was held in the highest esteem and rigorously trained (Casey 1987: 11). For the Greeks, indeed, 'Mnemosyne, the goddess of memory, was also the goddess of wisdom, the mother of the muses...and therefore...the progenitor of all the arts and sciences', while the Romans placed memory at the heart of all teaching, learning and thought (Samuel 1994: vii). In the 1100s writing was still regarded as a mere adjunct to memory (Fentress and Wickham 1992: 8–9). It was memory, rather than writing, that is, in which authority was vested (Smith 1966), and in the thirteenth century the value of the art of memory (Yates 1978) was advanced, once more, by St Thomas Aquinas (Samuel, ibid). Since the Renaissance, however, which saw memory's 'last great flowering' (Samuel, ibid), memory's estimation has declined sharply (Casey 1987: 11).[4] Until recently, that is. For certainly since the early 1970s (Huyssen 1995) (though the moment at which memory's resurgence began is debatable) there has been a renewed interest in and a re-evaluation of memory.

Though accounts of the precise periodisation of memory's vicissitudes may vary, what seems indisputable is that *contemporary* societies appear fascinated by, if not 'obsessed by' (Hamilton 1994: 10) memory. A simplistic explanation for memory's dwindling and resurgent fortunes might align these shifts with the epochs of antiquity, modernity and late modernity. This explantion would align memory's fall from grace with the shift from antiquity's reverence for the past, for ancestors and for gods to modernity's emphasis upon futurity, progress and becomingness. Both technology and temporality might be (indeed have been) marshalled in support of such an explanatory framework. Thus Andreas Huyssen, for one, has linked memory's contemporary resurgence with both a turning away from modernity's faith in progress and with a 'fevered' mnemonic response to the threat posed to memory by a postmodern world of instantaneity and electronic communications (Huyssen 1995). For Huyssen, memory's contemporary revival of fortune is related to a crisis of ideologies of progress and of modernisation, as well as to technology's role in the collapsing of modernity's established temporal order. On this account, the work of Friedrich Nietzsche might be taken as exemplary of modernity's emphatic rejection of memory in favour of a forward-looking forgetting. However, the story, not to mention the work of Nietzsche is, I believe more complex than this narrative can allow.

Though there is little space here for a fuller exposition of the complex history of memory's fortunes, two points bear, particularly, on the contents of this volume. Firstly, an account that stresses memory's historical vicissitudes might seem to suggest that memory itself is unchanging, but that its value changes in different periods. This is simply not the case. There is a history of memory that exceeds its rises and falls from prominence (Terdiman 1993: 3). In short, 'memory' means different things at different times. This is clearly not the place to debate the meanings of memory from antiquity to late modernity. In what follows, however, my aim will be, in part, to throw a little light on memory's contemporary meanings – an aim whose fulfilment will require some historical comparison. Secondly, I want to contest an account of memory's changing fortunes which aligns these with too crude a mapping of epochal shifts, particularly that between modernity and late modernity.

It is tempting to map the contemporary cultural foregrounding of memory onto a 'postmodern' *overturning* of modernity's (blind) faith in futurity, progress, reason and objectivity. But such a move would paint too monochrome a picture of modernity and would establish an exaggerated opposition between modernity and the present. Yet any alternative account risks countering this narrative by exaggerating the continuities between, say, nineteenth-century and late twentieth-century understandings of and valuations of memory. At one level, any mapping of memory's recent vicissitudes hangs on an interpretation of memory's place in the works of Benjamin, Freud, Baudelaire and Proust – works which each, in their different ways, insist upon memory's 'fragile value' (Marcus and Nead 1993: vi). For Andreas Huyssen, these writers formed an

> intellectual trajectory . . . that articulated the classical modernist formulations of memory as alternative to the discourses of objectifying and legitimizing history, and as a cure to the pathologies of modern life. Here, memory was always associated with some utopian space and time beyond what Benjamin called the homogeneous empty time of the capitalist present. (Huyssen 1995: 6).

In this account, modernity's forceful wielding of a legitimising and objectifying history is counterposed to the alternative utopian force of modernism's deployment of memory. The two forces of modernity and of modernism are represented, that is, as oppositional. In what follows, however, I want to relate the late modern foregrounding of memory not to memory's *oppositional* status within modernity, but rather to memory as the site for a conjunctural, late modern working-through of what I understand, rather, as modernity's ambivalences and equivocations. In place of a full elaboration of this view of modernity's relation to memory, I'll simply offer two pointers towards that thesis. In place of accounts of modernity which emphasise objectivity, rationality and progress, Christine Buci-Glucksmann's *Baroque Reason* suggests, rather, that 'the origins of the modern and modernism may be derived less from...universalism, rationality and coherence than from the uncanny, weird principles of otherness, contradiction, ambivalence and catastrophe' (Turner 1994: 33–4). Buci-Glucksmann's modernity has its roots in the *irrational* and in the seventeenth-century baroque. According to this schema, Benjaminian memory operates not in opposition to the rigidities of modernity's over-rational and super-objective history, but in the service, rather, of 'an expanded and truly critical rationality' (Buci-Glucksmann 1994: 60). If nothing else, this alternative account of modernity cautions against any oversimplified binary deployments of memory as the other to the supposed dominance, in modernity, of a legitimizing 'history' aligned with 'reason', 'truth' and 'objectivity'.

Buci-Glucksmann's challenge to Huyssen rests on a rebuttal of his account of modernity, which aligns the epoch too simplistically with reason and objectivity. On Huyssen's account, the utopian memory of, for instance, Benjamin, is simply perceived in opposition to this over-simplified account of modernity's dominant discourses. Huyssen's account of memory as an alternative *utopia* to modernity's dominant discourses is also open to challenge, however. Like Andreas Huyssen, Richard Terdiman seeks to account for the 'urgency of concern' with memory in the modern period (Terdiman 1993: vii). However, while for Huyssen, writers such as Proust and Freud are associated with the production of modern memory as an alternative and oppositional utopian space, Terdiman produces a reading of this same intellectual trajectory – and of Freud and Proust in particular – which emphasises the *dystopian* anxieties at the heart of their fascinations with memory. For Terdiman, the nineteenth-century 'memory crisis' erupted in response to a profound sense of cultural and historical dislocation. In contrast to traditional societies, in which 'objects and people could be said to carry their pasts and their meanings openly', post-Revolutionary urban society was characterised both by an opacity that demanded an 'effort of memory' and by a preoccupation with the functioning of memory (Terdiman 1993: 5–7). The dominant trend in writings on memory exemplified by Huyssen, perceives the nineteenth-century preoccupation with memory in, say, Proust, Benjamin and Freud in relation only to positivity and to the desire to produce memory in the face of its modern perturbations. Richard Terdiman proposes, rather, that this alignment of modern memory with utopia must be tempered by an alternative view of modern memory as rooted in 'a century-long preoccupation with the malignancy of the mnemonic'. Writing specifically of Proust, Terdiman insists on an understanding of nineteenth-century preoccupations with memory that emphasise ' the pervasive and continuing perception at the heart of the memory crisis: that rather than being subject to our recapture, the past in fact malignantly captures us' (ibid: 225). On Terdiman's account, the works of Freud and Proust, in particular emerge less as celebrations of memory's liberatory potential and more as attempts to forge liberation *from* memory's tenacious hold. In short, then, the nineteenth-century memory crisis delineated by Terdiman has its roots in revolutionary dislocations and disruptions that severed the possibility of memory's transparent relation to the past. Once disrupted, memory was both lost and over-present. While the links to a familiar past had become irretrievable, memory arose unbidden and in uncanny forms – forms that demanded new modes of interpretation. Yet at the same time and as Terdiman shows, in the nineteenth century, the belief (or lack of belief) in a liveable, if not utopian future became tied to a struggle with the ambivalences sited within memory.

In place of stressing modern memory's utopian challenge to modernity's objectivity and reason I have offered pointers to an alternative account that might complexify that monochrome conception of modernity while positing an ambivalent valuation of memory in nineteenth-century culture. What I am suggesting, in short, is that we might understand modern memory as neither modernity's utopian nor its feared other, but rather as the site within which modernity's equivocations found their most pressing expression.

The atrocities of two world wars lie between the nineteenth-century crisis of memory and the late twentieth-century 'memory boom'.[5] The horrors of the two world wars and of the holocaust are of central significance indeed, in any account of memory's vicissitudes. In a famous and much-quoted dictum, Theodor Adorno wrote that '(A)fter Auschwitz, it is no longer possible to write poems.' (Adorno [1949] 1973: 362). This dictum might be taken to imply that such horror meant the end not only of poetry and creativity, but also of memory. The near annihilation of the entire European Jewry certainly constituted the near-annihilation of Jewish memory. The traumatic impact of the holocaust has also been linked to the impossibility of both representation and remembrance. Yet as Shoshana Felman has argued, Adorno's dictum did not imply that poetry could no longer and should no longer be written, but that it must write 'through' its own impossibility (Felman 1992: 34). If the entire field of representation was contaminated by this event whose incommensurability precluded adequate representation, then art was the only – albeit the *apparently* impossible – hope. Likewise, it might be argued that the holocaust spelled not the end, but the inauguration of new and even greater difficulties in the field of memory. Post-holocaust remembrance was freighted both with the irretrievable memories of the untold dead and with the unspeakable, traumatic memories of those who lived on. At the same time, and as Adorno insisted, even in entering into representation, memory entered into the world that had produced the holocaust. Yet there was no choice but to remember. This was, if you like the founding equivocation of post-holocaust memory.

This ghastly history has been sited at the limit of the nineteenth-century memory crisis, registering, that is, the attenuation of all possibilities for the continuation of tradition in the long dureé (but see Winter 1995). Alternatively, this long-drawn-out terror has been sited at the far edge of the contemporary memory boom, emphasising memory's relation not to history, community, tradition, the past, reflection and authenticity, but to fantasy, subjectivity, invention, the present, representation and fabrication. Without doubt, the impact of the holocaust has had a profound influence upon memory's resonances in contemporary culture. Yet rather than locating this impact in relation either to the 'memory' more usually associated with the late nineteenth century, or to the 'memory' more typically linked with late modernity, I would rather suggest that we see its impact as *deepening* those equivocations between community and subjectivity; tradition and invention; the past and the present; reflection and representation; authenticity and fabrication, that had their source in modernity, but which bear yet more forcefully upon the late twentieth century. In other words, what I am suggesting, here, is that the late nineteenth-century equivocations which superceded a less ambivalent and less problematised relation to memory understood in relation to community, tradition and the past deepened during this period.

But the question remains of the *specificities* of contemporary preoccupations with memory. While I suggested, earlier, that I see these preoccupations not as a break with, but as a more forceful bearing down of modernity's equivocations I also stressed that this must be understood in its full conjunctural specificity. As both Richard Terdiman and Andreas Huyssen helpfully remind us, the nineteenth-century moment of Benjamin and of the memory crisis is 'no longer our situation' (Huyssen 1995: 6). In the nineteenth century, it was the perceived discontinuities between the past and the future which lay at the heart of the memory crisis. In part, this was a crisis prompted by fears that the past embodied in cultural memory was irretrievably lost; in part, it was a crisis prompted by anxieties about the unbidden eruption of that past in the present's shaping of the future. Political hopes and fears were embodied in the memory crisis. For Benjamin and Adorno, for instance, the crisis of memory was embodied, most forcefully in its reification in commodity fetishism – a reification that could only be 'undone' through radical remembrance. Whatever the nuances of the various strands that comprised this crisis – strands far too complexly related to be summarised here – the most significant legacy of this moment was the perception that memory could no longer be understood (if it ever could have been) as reflection, as the transparent record of the past. From this moment on, memory came to be understood as actively *produced*, as representation, and as open to struggle and dispute.

This legacy has continued to fuel the hopes and anxieties worked through in the late twentieth-century memory boom. Yet this late twentieth-century preoccupation with memory must be differentiated, nevertheless, from the nineteenth-century memory crisis.

Their divergent temporalities constitute one significant difference between nineteenth- and late twentieth-century understandings of and preoccupations with memory. Whereas in the nineteenth century, it was the felt break with tradition and the long dureé which constituted the temporal aspect of the memory crisis, in the late twentieth century, that crisis is inflected, rather, by the experiences of immediacy, instantaneity and simultaneity.

This shift is related in no small part to the development of new electronic technologies that collapse the distance that previously separated an event from its representation (Sobchack 1996: 5). Huyssen understands the contemporary memory boom in relation to this collapsing of the boundaries between the past and the present: '(Memory) represents the attempt to slow down information processing, to resist the dissolution of time in the synchronicity of the archive, to recover a mode of contemplation outside the universe of simulation and fast-speed information and cable networks...' (Huyssen 1995:7). At the same time, the contemporary fascination with memory substitutes for nineteenth-century anxieties, hopes and struggles concerning the loss and eruption of memories embodied in objects and in subjects, a far more complex set of hopes and fears about the possible implantation, transfer and reprogramming of memories. These anxieties and fears are related, in no small part, to technological developments which can, to all intents and purposes, evoke experiences of unlived-through events (Landsberg 1995).

Perhaps the most commented upon examples of this evoking of the unlived through are the 'heritage' experiences which make use of the most advanced technologies to evoke an experience of the past. Visiting fabricated, or even virtual 'historical' streets, or factories, for instance, has become a popular form of leisure or education. The meanings and value of this heritage industry as well as of the wider culture of nostalgia of which it forms part has been much debated. Whereas, for Raphael Samuel, for instance, these practices and this culture represent a popularisation of the historical imagination that is to be welcomed (Samuel 1994), for others, it represents either the far reaches of commodity fetishism and the atrophy of 'real' history (Jameson 1991), or, rather, the retreat from a public world of uncertain futures into a private and familial space of retro-fashion and old movies (Shaw and Chase 1989: 3). Held in common, however, by the critics of heritage, is a sense that at the heart of the heritage industry and nostalgia culture lies the desire for immediacy in the 'experience' of the past. Perhaps this desire represents neither the optimism of Samuel's popularised historical imagination, nor the pessimism of Shaw and Chase's retreat into nostalgia, but, once again, a more equivocal relation to the present which expresses itself through memory.

Like the memory crisis of the nineteenth century, then, the late twentieth-century memory boom is arguably shot through by — indeed represents — those ambivalences and equivocations rather than oppositions which arguably characterise this late modern moment. On Huyssen's account, memory's value resides in its (attenuated) struggle to sustain temporal anchoring and the time for reflection. Overlooked in this account, however, are the accounts, by others, of the potentially radical implications of those very shifts defended against by the version of memory deployed by Huyssen. In my view, the contemporary memory boom, then, represents neither simply the last defence against instantaneity and the atrophy of authentic reflective experience, nor does it represent, on the other hand, simply the hopes vested in new forms of experience: forms of experience liberated from the shackles of 'truth', location and embodiment. The contemporary memory boom represents, rather, late modernity's equivocations and ambivalences concerning truth, embodiment, location and the temporality of hope, equivocations which had their source in the disruptions and discontinuities of post-revolutionary, urban society, whose force was deepened under the impact of the holocaust and which are now being worked through in the context of late modern technologies and temporalities. In short, what I am suggesting is that at the beginning of the memory crisis, the scales of equivocation were weighted towards tradition, the past and so on. Under the impact of the holocaust, the scales arguably swung to a terror-struck, frozen balance between tradition and invention, the past and the present, authenticity and fabrication. Now, in the contemporary memory boom, the scales of equivocation swing again, and now they appear to be weighted a little more towards a 'memory' aligned with subjectivity, invention, the present, representation, and fabrication. Yet our preoccupations with memory remain equivocal. Though the scales may swing between, say, invention/tradition and reflection/ representation, the 'fragile value' of memory resides in its continued capacity to hold, rather than to collapse these equivocations. It is this holding of equivocation, I want to insist, which guarantees the radical value of memory in our own times.

Memory in the Academy

The contemporary explosion of scholarly research concerning memory has emerged within the context of a more general cultural fascination with memory and at a time when memory's late modern associations with fantasy, subjectivity, invention, the present, representation and fabrication appear to outweigh its modern associations with history, community, tradition, the past, reflection and authenticity. At one level, these associations suggest an alignment between memory work and the theoretical perspectives that have arguably dominated the humanities and the social sciences since the early 1960s. For Richard Terdiman, indeed, the late nineteenth-century crisis of representation – the crisis that inaugurated a break with reflectionism and that problematised the seeming 'naturalness' of the relationship between sign and referent – was merely the flattened-out representation *of* the memory crisis (Terdiman 1993: 7). It is certainly the case that late modern understandings of memory may *seem* to bear out the 'anti-reflectionist' and anti-essentialist insights of psychoanalysis, semiotics, structuralism and post-structuralism. Indeed, at their least impressive, recent writings on and about memory sometimes appear to have been produced simply to 'prove' structuralist or post-structuralist theory. In these cases, memory becomes a limit-case for anti-reflectionisms of all kinds: if *even* memories which are felt to be indissolubly linked with an actual, verifiable past can be shown to be the products of signifying processes associated with the present, with fantasy, or with culturally determined rather than given meanings, then that surely proves the cases of semiotics, structuralism, post-structuralism and psychoanalysis. It would be a mistake to collapse together these approaches to memory. While structuralist accounts, for instance, would seek to substitute the *determinisms* of language and structure for memory's reflection of historical reality, post-structuralisms would seek to emphasise, rather, the fluidity and mobility, as against the constituted nature of memory's representations. Nevertheless, in each of these different cases, what is rebutted is an understanding of memory as the registration or recording of the 'happened'.

But there is another trajectory within the academic memory boom that focuses on memory not to 'prove' anti-reflectionism, or anti-essentialism but to retain and hold in tension both the insights of post-1960s theories of representation *and* a (historical) understanding of what Terdiman has called 'an order of the constituted' (Terdiman 1993: 346–7). The work contained in the trajectory to which I am referring contains tendencies which, to greater or lesser degrees lean towards memory either as 'constituted' or as 'constructed'. But in this work, a tension remains in play *between* these understandings of memory. It is the tensions and equivocations sustained in this work which constitute its radicality.

The recent history of this trajectory of memory studies – memory studies, that is, that eschews crude binaries between, for example, the 'happened' and the 'imagined' – incorporates new directions taken in many fields, not all of which can be summarised here. In oral history, which has trailblazed the importance of memory as an organising concept, certain historians have been struggling to hold in tension an understanding of oral history testimony that acknowledges its *relation* to 'happenings', to 'the constituted', to historical experience while developing an understanding of memory 'as an active production of meanings and interpretations, strategic in character and capable of influencing the present' (Passerini 1983: 195). In this research, memory is understood as 'a text to be deciphered, not a lost reality to be rediscovered' (King 1997: 62). The representations of memory are understood, that is, in relation to both cultural narratives and unconscious process. Yet in this work – and I am thinking here, in particular, of the seminal work of Luisa Passerini (Passerini 1987) – memory's imbrication with cultural narratives and unconscious processes is held in tension with an understanding of memory's relation, however complex and mediated, with history, with happenings, or even and most problematically, perhaps from a postmodern perspective, with 'events'.[6]

This productive tension in oral history memory work has its origins in the quest, by radical oral historians, for the traces of counter-histories in the testimonies of their interviewees. Yet under the impact of post-1960s cultural theory, it quickly became apparent that the memories transcribed by oral historians did not simply constitute the record of unheard histories of working-class, female or ethnic interviewees. Instead, what began to be recognised was the highly mediated nature of 'memory'. Memories were not simply counter-histories that could straightforwardly challenge the legitimizing force of 'H'istory. Instead, they were complex productions shaped by diverse narratives and genres and replete with absences, silences, condensations and displacements that were related, in complex ways, to the dialogic moment of their telling. Nevertheless what distinguishes memory work from the far reaches of post-1960s theory, is that memories *continue to be* memories. Although it is now acknowledged, for instance that memory's tropes – of metaphor and metonymy, for instance – may be similar to those of poetry, and although it is now recognised that memory's condensations and displacements are similar to those found in dreams, memory work does not reduce memory to fiction, to dream, or to poetry, for instance. Memories, that is, continue to be memories, and it is their relation to lived historical experience that constitutes their specificity.

Broadly speaking, it is a concern with memory's representation of lived *experience* which is driving the turn to memory in areas including oral history, literary and cultural studies, and anthropology. As I have already argued, the value of much memory work lies in its refusal simply to capitulate to the extremes of post-1960s cultural theories – a certain ahistoricity, a rejection of the conceptual possibility of 'the constituted' and an abandonment of 'the subject', for instance. Nevertheless those theories and, more importantly, the particular questions they sought to illuminate do lie at the heart of memory work. At one level, research on memory can be understood, then in relation to the continuing struggle to develop, move beyond or supercede work on ideology which failed to explain both the *relation* between dominant social ideas and their 'internalisation' and, as feminism argued so many years ago, how it is that subjects come to capitulate to their own subjugation. But though in postmodern cultural theory there is now a tendency to abandon 'outmoded' conceptual distinctions such as those between subjectivity and objectivity, the outer world and the inner world or society and the individual, memory work, tends, rather, to hold these terms in tension. Moreover, while theories of ideology took as their starting point 'society', and 'dominant ideas', and assumed a 'top down' model of ideological transmission, memory work's tendency, rather,[7] is to take as its investigative starting point the memories of groups or individuals and to ask how these might be related to the wider culture. In short, though memory research investigates the links between individual or group memories and the wider and more generalised domains of history, culture, and society, its starting point is in the local, in the subjective, in the particularity of memory itself. The consequences of this focus are too extensive to do more than gesture towards, here. Nevertheless, it should be noted that this scholarly shift *can* be conceived of in relation to what Stuart Hall recently described as a new vision of democracy which asks not how can the particular, the local, the 'other' be made part of the universal, but seeks rather, to forge something larger out of diverse particularities (Hall 1999).

Contemporary research on memory occupies a doubly liminal position. At the level of theory, it occupies the space between the extremes of post-1960s cultural theory and an unproblematic belief in the 'constituted'. Meanwhile memory work's object of study is constituted between the individual and the social; subjectivity and objectivity; the inner world and the outer world. There is another sense, moreover, in which memory work's position can be understood as liminal. At the heart of much memory work in oral history, anthropology and cultural studies lies a belief in the relationship between remembering and transformation. Thus at the beginning of the turn to memory in oral history, Luisa Passerini argued that '(I)t may be that our attempt to retrieve memories . . . can contribute to the emergence of freer cultural attitudes and the instatement of the problem of freedom at the centre of history' (Passerini 1983: 196). Researchers interpreting the memorial traces of individual or collective sufferings and abuse do so not only to honour history's victims, dead and alive, but in the hope that memory can vanquish repetition. Moreover, whereas books and bodies can, and continue to be burned, any attempt to distort memory arguably leaves its traces in the form of *interpretable* 'silences and forms of forgetting' (ibid) which, once seized, constitute the memory of and the grounds for resistance. In this sense then, memory work occupies the liminal space between forgetting and transformation. In some cases, however, memory work seeks to move beyond the analysis of testimonies or texts and the illumination of the forgotten experiences of others. In these instances, memory work's impulse is directed towards practices of collective and self-transformation in the present (see the pieces by Haug, Clare and Johnson, and Kuhn in this volume). In these cases, memory work focuses on the reinterpretation and re-contextualisation of memory, in the service of revised understandings of individual or collective selves. Such work acknowledges that memory is our core (Butler 1989: 12), that we are 'made of memories' (Casey 1987: 290), that memories 'remind us of who we are' (*Guardian*, 1993) and it acknowledges, also, that 'remembering transforms one kind of experience into another' (ibid: xii). Yet though individual and collective memory work of the kind I'm describing recognises that in remembering 'we are re-fashioning the same past differently, making it to be different in its very self-sameness' (ibid: 286) it does not, as some do, assimilate this understanding of memory to a notion of memory's autonomy or freedom (ibid: 280 onwards). Instead, this individual or collective memory work adopts a critical and self-reflexive perspective on memory's capacity to 'keep us afloat' (Fentress and Wickham 1992: 24) and sees memory as the raw material for further 'acts of memory' (Bal et al 1999; Kuhn 1995) or 're-membrance' by means of which an individual's or the collective's cultural and historical formation can be seized. Such acts do not bestow 'freedom': history's constraints and contingencies cannot be so easily sloughed off. Yet in illuminating aspects of individual and collective formation, memory work can bestow a historical self or group knowledge – a *felt* knowledge of one's historical and cultural formation – that can expand the field of choice. Such is its liberatory potential. In these contexts the liminal space occupied by memory work lies between identity and its transformation or 're-membering'.

Memory research arguably holds in tension, or equivocates between the extremes of post-1960s cultural theory and the retention of an area of 'the constituted'. Its theoretical position and its objects of study are arguably liminal. In what follows, it remains to show how, in the essays collected in this volume, contemporary memory work's equivocations and liminality shape its practices.

Doing Memory Work

Though their specific themes and objects of study differ, the essays written for this volume demonstrate that doing memory work of the kind I have described – work that occupies liminal spaces – demands liminal practices. What I mean by this is that each of the essays collected here is situated between disciplines and deploys not just combinations of, but, more accurately, hybridized methods. At the same time, these essays are all marked by the holding in tension of oppositions associated with memory.

Though all the essays collected here share some ground with each other, they do fall, nevertheless, into two groups. The focus of the first group of essays falls on models of memory and touches on questions of memory, history and nation. The range of these essays encompasses questions concerning the historical determination of *conceptions* of memory as well as on the cultural and national determinations of memories.

In the opening essay of the collection, Chris Locke returns to questions that have haunted cultural theory at least since the time of Walter Benjamin's seminal writings on memory and the media (Benjamin 1968), though arguably for far longer. These questions pivot on the relationship between conceptions of memory and technological inventions and developments, and on the relationship between technological developments and the form, content and experience of memory. Locke takes as his starting point the development of electronic, computerised information retrieval systems, from their beginnings in Vannevar Bush's early design for a Memex machine to the contemporary Internet and the world wide web. Locke argues that Bush designed his Memex machine to improve upon nature. Bush stated, that is, that he had modelled his machine on current understandings of human memory. But by contrasting contemporary psychoanalytic understandings of memory and the functioning of the psyche with writings about the Internet, Locke shows that understandings of human memory now appear to model themselves on the Internet and artificial intelligence agents. This innovative method that contrasts technological and psychoanalytic understandings of memory arguably produces an equivocal understanding of the relation between technology and memory. Locke's study suggests, that is, neither that technology is determined by or modelled on understandings of human memory, nor that understandings of human memory are simply derived from the historical development of technology. Instead, a more complex picture emerges of the mutual historical implication of models of memory and technological advances.

The contemporary worlds of digital memory and of the object-relational psychoanalysis drawn on by Locke are characterised by 'depthlessness'. Computers are designed not to forget and the model of mind constructed by object-relational psychoanalysis replaces the unconscious with internal, competing agents. Depthlessness, too, characterises the forms of late modern national memory catalogued by the French historian Pierre Nora, whose influential and controversial memory work is described by Peter Carrier in the second essay in this collection.

In the seven-volume *Les lieux de mémoire*, Pierre Nora provides a catalogue of those 'places of memory', which, he argues, now form the basis of French social memory. Nora's work constitutes a theoretical intervention concerning the contemporary relation between nation, identity and memory. *Les lieux de mémoire*'s volumes together constitute a vast statement, indeed, concerning a shift that has arguably taken place in France. In this shift, French national identity forms itself through 'places of memory' rather than through a concept of national identity understood in relation to the history of 'a politically determined group of citizens'. This shift comprises a 'culturalisation' as well as a 'spatialisation' of a previously politicised and temporalised national memory. Yet at the same time 'the Panthéon', for instance, continues to evoke 'the past' albeit a 'past' that is remembered through place and as a symbol 'of politically and historically inert memories'. The startling methodological innovation undertaken by Nora is the mapping of spatialised 'places of memory'. In mapping and cataloguing the mnemonic symbols of French cultural identity – from 'Vichy' to 'Coffee' – he produces an inventory that constitutes the elements out of which contemporary French identities are forged. The spirit with which Nora undertakes this project seems less equivocal than elegiac and backward looking. The shift that has substituted 'places' of memory for a national memory rooted in historical under-standings of French national history is aligned, by Nora, with discontinuity and the loss of tradition. Yet on Carrier's account, the memory evoked by Nora's *lieux de mémoire* emerges not *simply* as depoliticised images, but as a 'dialectical relationship' between a 'first degree' understanding of their original historic interest and a 'second degree' understanding of their retrospective 'sentimental and ethnological interest'. This second degree understanding of places of memory oscillates, itself, between an uncritical identification with them, and a critical interest in their deploy-ments in the production of contemporary memory.

Nora's places of memory emerge, then, as doubly liminal. Moreover the transformative 're-membrance' performed by *Les lieux de mémoire* is no less equivocal. For, as Carrier explains, the memory work practiced and advocated by Nora is neither simply 'sentimental' nor 'ethnological' but balances, rather, between these two forms of second-degree retro-spection, in order to construct the unfamiliar and deconstruct the familiar. In this way Nora's memory work moves beyond analysis to seize the opportunity for intervention – for 're-membrance' – offered by late modern places of memory.

Like Pierre Nora, the anthropologist Stephan Feuchtwang is concerned with the links between social memory and nation formation, but in place of *lieux de mémoire*, Feuchtwang's focus falls on lifestories of cataclysmic events. In his essay, then, he describes with precision the theoretical and methodological aspects of a planned research project to collect memories of such events. The significance of cataclysmic events resides in the 'totality' of their nature. But as Feuchtwang insists, the point of the project is not to show how such events bind the memories of individuals, groups and 'the nation', but to investigate, rather the complex forms of – and the politics of – memory *transmission* that are continually in play in the relations between the personal, the social and the nation. Feuchtwang's essay rigorously eschews any reduction of the complexities of memory transmissions. He emphasises the diverse levels of memory through which his project plans to navigate, as well as the 'different kinds of hegemony and their ambiguities within which memories are transmitted'. More than that, though, his project incorporates the equivocations and the transformative aim that is characteristic of the memory work this volume seeks to advocate. Positioned between understandings of memory that associate it with partiality activity, construction and fantasy and understandings of memory that align it, rather, with events and with history, Feuchtwang describes the process of maintaining a 'third position' that can place itself *within* the partialities and particularities of memory while it 'listens and hears sides split from each other *and hears and describes the split'* (emphasis mine). It is by means of this liminal practice of re-inscription – a practice that steers a path between the extremes of postmodernist theory and earlier formulations of memory's simple 'registration' of events – that Feuchtwang's anthroplogy contributes to the production of 'a more stable and less haunting past'.

Like Feuchtwang's, my own essay in this collection is concerned with national memory and the haunting past. The essay, which focuses on the cinematic remembrance of recent traumatic US history performs a liminal reading of *Forrest Gump*, as well as of reviews of the film. Understandings of traumatic memory have oscillated between its alignment with fantasy and with history. On Freud's earliest account, traumatic memory had its origins in the event of seduction. In his later revised account of traumatic or hysterical memory, trauma became aligned not with the event of seduction but with fantasy. More recently, however, (particularly in the US) and for reasons that I detail in my essay, understandings of traumatic memory have, once again begun to align it with history and with events, rather than with fantasy. But traumatic memory is, I argue, inextricably associated with both history and fantasy and there are methods of psychoanalytic interpretation that can illuminate their interplay. My essay, then, insists on an approach to traumatic memory that understands its relation both to history *and* to fantasy and my reading of *Forrest Gump* aims to demonstrate that only interpretations alert to the mediation of traumatic memory both by history and by fantasy are adequate to its complex meanings.

Gillian Swanson's essay is concerned both with the historical formation of memory and with questions of autobiographical practice. Her essay focuses on the historical formation of the modern subject beginning in the late eighteenth century and on the place of memory in that formation. The history she traces demonstrates the consequences for female subjectivity of the development of that modern subjectivity characterised by individuality and interiority. Having shown that modern subjectivity was inherently unstable: 'its constitutive features...act against the imagined unified persona of public masculinity, the citizen-subject', Swanson then argues that these disunifying elements became projected onto the feminine. At the heart of this modern subjectivity, argues Swanson, was a conception of subjective memory, in all its privacy and partiality. This modern conception of personal memory, argues Swanson, arises *from* the historical formation of modern subjectivity. Swanson's aim exceeds, however, that of establishing the place of memory within the formation of modern subjectivity. For a further purpose of her essay is to ask how this history of subjectivity and of memory might be put to use in the writing of female autobiography. Here, Swanson begins to share ground with the essays in the second part of this collection – essays concerned with autobiographical or collective memory work. Swanson imagines memory work as a self-conscious autobiographical practice alert not only to its constraints but also to its possibilities and she leaves us with a tantalizing question: how, she asks, can female autobiography remember the history of its own formation in the service of 'becoming'?

Like Swanson's, Amal Treacher's essay concerns itself with the relation between autobiography and memory, though the focus falls, here, on the specificities of children's memories. Treacher's essay describes an innovative pilot study aimed at researching childhood memories by eliciting and analysing the stories told by a group of young children. It is often supposed that childhood provides the raw material for adult memory. In childhood, memories are laid down; in adulthood they are remembered. Treacher's essay suggests, rather, that this understanding paradoxically risks both equating *and* drawing too sharp a division between adulthood and childhood. Her argument suggests, rather, a more equivocal view of childhood: a view that overestimates neither childhood's similarities with, nor its differences from adulthood. What is urgently required, argues Treacher, is research on the specificity of childhood and in her essay, she begins this task by investigating the specificity of childhood memory. Her findings are, once again, equivocal. Far from childhood constituting the 'raw material' for adult memories, children are actively producing memories from a very early age. But the task of their interpretation is by no means straightforward. On the one hand, childhood memories are overdetermined – by childhood fantasy and by childhood perceptions of social and cultural narratives and discourses. On the other hand, childhood memories are made by and make meanings for *children*. To what extent, then, does the interpretation of childhood memory by adults risk losing the specificity of those meanings? Though this is a question which no single essay can hope to resolve, Treacher's recourse to Christopher Bollas's writings points to an interpretation of the Oedipus complex that holds in mind both its meaning in relation to infantile sexual development – a retrospective interpretation – but also a more nuanced understanding of the experienced dilemmas of childhood of which it forms part, experienced dilemmas remembered by children. In this sense, research on childhood memory might be said to argue a position not dissimilar to the anthropologist's 'third position' advocated and practiced by Stephan Feuchtwang.

The final three contributions to this volume are too closely related not to be discussed together. The year 1987 saw the British publication of Frigga Haug's *Female Sexualisation: A Collective Work of Memory* (Haug et al 1987). This work introduced to a British readership the collective work of a group of German women who together had developed a practice they called 'memory work'. Doing memory work involved the collective writing and analysing of the group's individual memories – in this instance memories associated with sexuality. The aim of this practice was to move beyond 'top down' models of what was then termed 'female socialisation' and to develop in their place an understanding of 'the active participation of individuals in their formation as social beings' (Haug et al. 1987: 33). Memory work aimed, too, to move beyond the sometimes arduous practices of feminist consciousness-raising and to investigate, rather, the pleasures of memory. In so doing, memory work hoped to reveal, however, the remembered *minutae* of female sexualisation and, in so doing, to instate the possibility of transformation. In memory work, then, the group's aim was the revision of their combined memories.

In her essay for this volume, Frigga Haug provides, for the first time, a reflection upon and an elaboration of this influential memory work, as well as a description of the practice detailed enough for others to follow, if they so choose. Like the other contributors to this volume, Haug mobilises a liminal conception of memory: memory occupies the space between an imposed ideology, she argues, and the possibility of an alternative way of understanding experience. Like other essays collected here, Haug's conception of memory work or *re-membrance*, is a strong one, bearing associations not only with analysis but also with transformation. Like other contributors, too, she describes a practice of re-membrance that takes as its object not 'raw material' (for memory is always already revised), but the further remembrance of that which was already memory.

Annette Kuhn's 'A journey through memory' describes her own memory work, a practice which was informed, in part, by the example of *Female Sexualisation*. In her book *Family Secrets* (Kuhn 1995), Annette Kuhn wrote of her childhood – or, better put, of her memories of childhood. This writing, however, did anything but seek to re-evoke the experience of, or the immediacy of that childhood. Instead, in Kuhn's memory work, memories are actively staged, recontextualised and analysed in the service of revised, or even transformed productions of memory and of new and potentially therapeutic stories about the past. Like the memory work practiced by Frigga Haug, Kuhn's memory work is practiced *upon* memories. Its product, too is memory. Indeed, in the essay written for this volume, Kuhn produces a number of theses about memory texts gleaned from her own memory work practice. Kuhn outlines, that is, some of the defining characteristics and qualities of memory texts. But if memory work is practiced upon and produces memories, does this imply that the memory that is memory work's object is indistinguishable from the memory that is its product? This might constitute the unequivocal view of postmodernist theory. Yet I do not think that it is a position that follows from the essays of either Frigga Haug or Annette Kuhn. Both Kuhn and Haug acknowledge that memories make us. Yet though their essays confirm that memory is never raw material, it can, as Kuhn argues, be *taken as* raw material in the service of memories that we play a greater part in making.

In the final essay in this collection, Mariette Clare and Richard Johnson describe a collective attempt at memory work that was indebted to the work of the *Female Sexualisation* group. Following that group's example, Clare, Johnson and others at the Birmingham Centre for Contemporary Cultural Studies collectively wrote and attempted to revise memories not of sexuality, but of topics associated with conservative nationalism. Once again, the aim of this memory work was to illuminate and revise the relation between the personal, the social and the cultural. But the story Clare and Johnson tell is one of a project fraught with difficulty – a project, indeed, which, to all intents and purposes, failed. Yet in analysing the root causes of this failure, Clare and Johnson illuminate the relations between memory, identity and intersubjectivity. As they explain, their group's memory work became conflictual. Group members did not, that is, always recognise each others' memory stories in terms recognised by their tellers. Some revisions, that is, proved far harder to bear than others. At stake, here, was a struggle over identity. Clare and Johnson's essay shows, once again that memory's meanings cannot be fixed and it demonstrates, too, the transformative potential of memory work, though in this instance, what they show is that some transformations are far more welcome than others.

Notes

1. Routledge Studies in Memory and Narrative.
2. London University's Institute for Romance Studies is currently launching an MA in Cultural Memory, for instance.
3. 'Frontiers of Memory: an international conference' September 17–19 1999, Institute of Education, London.
4. Raphael Samuel's history of memory (Samuel 1994) seems to suggest, rather, a less discontinuous history for memory's fortunes. According to Samuel popular memorisation, which he counterposes to the less democratic practice of the 'legitimate' historian has been a more or less continuous though historically varied (and undervalued) practice in Britain, at least. Yet even if the practice has a long history, the question of its undervaluation remains.
5. For more on the impact of these events upon forms, understandings of and valuations of memory see, for instance, Santner (1990);Winter (1995); Young (1993).
6. Though postmodernist theorists such as Hayden White have usefully problematised the concept of 'the event', White himself nevertheless insists that his argument should 'not be taken to imply in any way that such events never happened' (White 1996: 20).
7. This is something of an over-generalisation that might fit oral history, literary and film studies better than it fits archeology or analyses of national memory such as Pierre Nora's *Les lieux de mémoire* (see Carrier in this volume). Studies of material memories, too, for example, might focus on the shared characteristics of, say, a nation's memorials.

Bibliography

Adorno, Theodor ([1949] 1973), 'After Auschwitz', 'Meditations on Metaphysics', in *Negative Dialectics,* trans. E.B. Ashton, New York, Continuum.

Bal, Mieke, Crewe, Jonathan and Spitzer, Leo (1999), *Acts of Memory: Cultural Recall in the Present,* Hanover and London: University Press of New England.

Benjamin, Walter (1968), *Illuminations: Essays and Reflections*, trans. Hannah Arendt, New York: Schocken Books.

Buci-Glucksmann, Christine (1994), *Baroque Reason: The Aesthetics of Modernity*, London: Sage.

Butler, Thomas (ed.) (1989), *Memory*, Oxford: Blackwell.

Carter, Erica and Hirschkop, Ken (1997), 'Editorial' in *Cultural Memory*, *New Formations*, Winter 1996.

Casey, Edward S. (1987), *Remembering: A Phenomenological Study*, Bloomington: Indiana University Press.

Felman, Shoshana (1992), *Testimony: Crises of Witnessing in Literature, Psychoanalysis, and History*, New York and London: Routledge.

Fentress, James and Wickham, Chris (1992), *Social Memory*, Oxford: Blackwell.

Guardian Education (1993), 'Memory', January 19, 16–17.

Hall, Stuart (1999), public lecture on race and ethnicity in the millenium, Institute of Education, July 1.

Hamilton, Paula (1994), 'The Knife Edge: Debates about Memory and History', in Kate Darian-Smith and Paula Hamilton (eds), *Memory and History in Twentieth Century Australia*, Oxford: Oxford University Press.

Haug, Frigga et al. (1987), *Female Sexualisation: A Collective Work of Memory*, London: Verso.

Huyssen, Andreas (1995), *Twilight Memories: Marking Time in a Culture of Amnesia*, London: Routledge.

Jameson, Fredric (1991), *Postmodernism, or, The Cultural Logic of Late Capitalism*, London: Verso.

King, Nicola (1997), 'Autobiography as Cultural Memory: Three Case Studies', in *New Formations* no. 30, Winter 1996, 'Cultural Memory', pp 50–62.

Kuhn, Annette (1995), *Acts of Memory and Imagination*, London: Verso.

Landsberg, Alison (1995), 'Prosthetic Memory: *Total Recall* and *Blade Runner*', in Featherstone, Mike and Burrows, Roger (eds), *Cyberspace/Cyberbodies/Cyberpunk: Cultures of Technological Embodiment*, London: Sage.

Laura Marcus and Lynda Nead, (1993) 'editorial', *The Actuality of Walter Benjamin*, *New Formations* 20, Summer.

Nietzsche, Friedrich Wilhelm, (1980) *The Use and Abuse of History*, Indianapolis: The Liberal Press.

Passerini, Luisa (1983), 'Memory', *History Workshop Journal* No 15 (Spring).

Passerini, Luisa (1987), *Fascism in Popular Memory*, Cambridge: Cambridge University Press.

Samuel, Raphael (1994), *Theatres of Memory*, London: Verso.

Santner, Eric (1990), *Stranded Objects: Mourning, Memory and Film in Post-War Germany*, Ithaca, Cornell University Press.

Shaw, Christopher and Chase, Malcolm (1989), *The Imagined Past: History and Nostalgia*, Manchester and New York: Manchester University Press.

Smith, Brian (1966), *Memory*, London: Allen and Unwin.

Sobchack, Vivian (1996), *The Persistence of History: Cinema, Television and the Modern Event*, New York and London: Routledge.

Terdiman, Richard (1993), *Present Past: Modernity and the Memory Crisis*, Ithaca and London: Cornell University Press.

Turner, Bryan S. (1994), 'Introduction', in Buci-Glucksmann (1994), 1–36.

White, Hayden (1996), 'The Modernist Event', in Sobchack Vivian (1996) (op.cit.).

Winter, Jay (1995), *Sites of Memory, Sites of Mourning: The Great War in European Cultural History*, Cambridge: Cambridge University Press.

Yates, Frances, (1978), *The Art of Memory*, Harmondsworth: Penguin.

Young, James (1993), *The Texture of Memory: Holocaust Memorials and Meaning*, New Haven: Yale University Press.

Part I
Conceptualising Memory

1

Digital Memory and the
Problem of Forgetting
Chris Locke

The History of Digital Memory and the Problem of Forgetting

The work of Franklin Roosevelt's chief scientific adviser, Vannevar Bush, has had a profound impact upon technology's incursions into society in the latter half of this century. As the founding father of the Advanced Projects Research Agency (ARPA), he created the grant-awarding body that moulded American science and technology research. Researchers working within the ARPA system were responsible for developing ARPANET, the first system that used 'packet-switching' to transfer computer information from one terminal to another, allowing more decentralised computer networking systems to evolve into what we recognise as today's Internet. Popular accounts of the history of the Internet refer to the function ARPANET had within America's defence capabilities – the system was supposed to have been developed to allow America's nuclear weapons stations to communicate within a decentralised network that would continue to function, even when individual sites were destroyed. The subsequent evolution of the Internet into a largely social communications system appears to represent the triumph of human social communication over brute, blind, militaristic technology. Technology once developed to facilitate nuclear missile launches now supports the Internet world's email, chat-lines, electronic commerce, porn, multi-user environments, academic discussion lists and even the PR activities of the Mexican revolutionaries, the Zapatistas. This popular account of the Internet's history figures Bush's ARPA as an instrument for social, as well as technological change.

Vannevar Bush's legacy includes not only his published research papers and the funding bodies that he created, but also the stamp his work has left upon contemporary understandings of the relation between computers and society. Most recently, the strength of Bush's retrospective fame has been fanned by the the Internet which appears to embody many of his key ideas. But the name of Vannevar Bush still carries none of the cachet of those of Alan Turing, Charles Babbage, or even Ada Lovelace. Though Bush's work is not accorded the social significance of, for instance, the Manhattan Project, the legacy of his research may well prove to be equally important. Apart from one recent biography (Zachary 1997), the recent groundswell of interest in Bush has produced few published reappraisals of his work. Yet his famous essay 'As We May Think' (1945) which described his proposal for a 'Memex' machine, appears in countless contemporary anthologies, contextualising subjects as diverse as technology and visual culture, digital libraries and cyberculture. Bush's work emerges, therefore, as a prefiguring of many contemporary developments in technology. As these technologies increasingly pervade our daily lives, the stature of Bush's work will inevitably increase. In retrospect, his name will be ranked alongside those of Alexander Graham Bell or Logie-Baird. Once the Internet has become the primary domestic communication system, Bush will be ranked alongside Bell – and as the technology of the telephone has reshaped our understanding of society, so will the technology prefigured by Bell.

Bush's Memex Machine

The Memex machine described in Bush's essay 'As We May Think' is doubly interesting. It describes a method of text-retrieval that implements text-linking, but it also offers a model of the workings of human memory. It is Bush's subtitle for the Memex – the 'Mind's Machine' – that is most telling. The essay offers the technological machine not just as a text-storage and retrieval system, but also as an extension of human memory. Bush's Memex claims to solve human memory's key problem – forgetting.

Bush describes the Memex with almost missionary zeal. In the post-war research environment, he suggests new objectives for scientists freed from their responsibilities to destructive projects – objectives which will harness the power of technology for the good of society. Technological information and knowledge management are identified as the next great aims for scientific research. These advances will harness the energies of the growing audience for scientific literature, creating an informed, empowered society. Bush proposes to achieve this by improving the tools we use to access the booming knowledge-base within a society: 'The summation of human experience is being expanded at a prodigious rate, and the means we use for threading through the consequent maze to the momentarily important item is the same as was used in the days of square-rigged ships' (Bush 1991: 89).

With a modernist faith in technological determinism, Bush imagined that teams of post-war scientists would now set themselves to the task of replacing these 'square-rigged ships' with new technology that would allow an individual to externalise their memory processes, encoding their memories as associative trails within a technological system. Bush's 'Memex' system was designed to achieve this task.

The Memex system uses microfilm to store and retrieve texts. Rather than relying upon external systems of cataloguing and indexing for the storage and retrieval of material, the Memex allowed the user to forge links *within* the text's content. Bush was no fan of library indexing systems since he found no correspondence between their rules of classification and processes of human thought. Bush believed that the 'unnatural' indexing systems used to classify knowledge made information retrieval difficult and time-consuming, since the user would have to learn the classification system before it could be used at any real speed. The delays caused by this incompatibility between artificial information-retrieval systems and human thought processes impeded the realisation of Bush's technologically advanced, more knowledgeable society:

> The real heart of the matter of selection, however, goes deeper than a lag in the adoption of mechanisms by libraries, or a lack of development of devices for their own use. Our ineptitude in getting at the record is largely caused by the artificiality of systems of indexing (Bush 1991: 101).

For Bush, the human mind functioned not by attributing classifications to areas of information – it is the alien nature of these classifications that make them so difficult to use. It functioned, rather, by finding *associations* between one item and another:

> The human mind does not work that way. It operates by association. With one item in its grasp, it snaps instantly to the next that is suggested by the association of thoughts, in accordance with some intricate web of trails carried by the cells of the brain (Bush 1991: 101).

It is this 'intricate web of trails' that characterises Bush's legacy to contemporary computer systems. Bush takes the model for his techno-logical system from the associative capacity of the human brain, yet Bush's Memex also aims to provide technological solutions to the design problems of the human memory. The Memex was designed to act as a supplement to human memory. Its information-storage and retrieval systems were modelled, therefore, on Bush's understanding of human memory. Bush replaced 'artificial' cataloguing systems with a dynamic, user-centred associative web of trails. But where the Memex beats human memory is in the permanence of this web of trails. Bush sees human memory's associations as merely 'transitory', whereas the trails that are forged within the Memex are stored within a technological system that is entirely permanent – a system that cannot forget. The Memex may not have had the size and speed of human memory (yet), but at least its memories were not transitory:

> One cannot hope thus to equal the speed and flexibility with which the mind follows an associative trail, but it should be possible to beat the mind decisively in regard to the permanence and clarity of the items resurrected from storage (Bush 1991: 102).

Though digital technology has now realised Bush's vision of the *Encyclopaedia Britannica* stored inside a matchbox, the manipulation of such bulky information within microfilm format was impossible. The insuperable problems entailed in realising the linking of microfilm on such a grand, rhizomatic scale ensured that Bush's Memex machine remained on the drawing-board. Bush's vision of a library in the desk could only have been actualised as reels of microfilm spooling around the ankles. His faith in the power of the individual user's memory was absolute, however. The Memex machine was to have provided the technology to allow the individual genius of a 'trailblazer' to be stored, repeated, used by others, and encoded and preserved for history.

The Legacy of the Memex

Analogue information is, by its very nature, difficult to manipulate and organise within a system based upon an associative web of trails. Since digital information does not suffer from this fate, Bush's ideas have been taken up by digital pioneers including Ted Nelson and Doug Englebart. Ted Nelson has done most to bring the Memex into the digital domain. He identified the possibilities of the Memex and figured them in his designs for a hypertextual text storage and retrieval system ambitiously named 'Xanadu'. Xanadu uses the Memex structure of associative trails, echoing Bush's belief in the workings of human memory, but uses the digital computer instead of microfilm as its storage device. Nelson coined the term 'hypertext' to describe a system of texts linked by associative trails that were structurally advanced from the sequential nature of the

Memex. As the Memex was based on analogue microfilm it was sequential in nature; but the digital, hypertext Xanadu software allows complete digital manipulation of textual information in an associative web that outweighs the complexity of those envisaged by the Memex.

> In Bush's trails, the user had no choices to make as he moved through the sequence of items, except at an intersection of trails. With computer storage, however, no sequence need be imposed on the material; and, instead of simply storing materials in their order of arrival or of being noticed, it will be possible to create overall structures of greater useful complexity. These may have, for instance, patterns of branches in various directions. Such non-sequential or complex text structures we may call 'hypertexts' (Nelson 1991: 253).

Nelson still clings to the value ascribed to associative paths by Bush – that they replicate the workings of human memory – but in its non-sequential nature, the hypertext Xanadu system takes a more dynamic view of the processes of human memory, based less on the authoring of single, concrete associative paths than on a complex, dynamic network of associations.

Hypertext offers valuable insights into the relations between the figuring of digital memory and understandings of human memory. In the mid-1970s, the introduction of hypertextual systems revolutionised the development of text-retrieval systems. Text database software systems which had previously relied upon classifying information according to subject fields, classes and categories became hypertext databases which allowed the retrieval of texts according to dynamic, authored associations *within* the textual content of the information. The notion of a storage system which used 'human' associative processes yet which would not forget was seductive, and has shaped the development of subsequent technologies, which have all inherited the notion that impermanence is an essential flaw in human memory.

Ted Nelson's beliefs in the social implications of Xanadu were on a par with Bush's expectations concerning the likely effects of his Memex machine. Both scientists shared a belief in the fallibility of human memory and both Xanadu and the Memex are systems which aim to mimic the processes of human memory with the additional benefit of permanence. In the Xanadu, digital systems realise Bush's dream of the 'Mind's Machine' that can store vast amounts of information in a very small physical space, allowing users to retrieve it in a manner that is familiar to them because of the system's use of a retrieval process which is, allegedly, so similar to associative human memory.

But both the Memex and Xanadu rely upon a human user or author to create these associative paths for the digital system. Hypertext is not then an autonomous, thinking agent but merely a hyper-efficient filing system that works according to a bespoke, individualised system. The user maps their own associative paths into the hypertextual system as a basis for the retrieval of information.

On the Internet, Hypertext is released from the solitary, self-enclosed nature of Bush's Memex machine, connecting individual trailblazers together in a complex network. The Internet is like a thousand Memex networks entwined – a network of collective memory trails without any global navigational system. Indeed, this lack of a universal cataloguing system is often raised as the Internet's primary problem. Navigating the Internet can be difficult as it is little more than a massive web of associative paths between texts authored by a million or more users. It is a chaotic memory system, the anarchic offspring of the Memex. There have been many attempts to classify the Internet according to a method other than that of associative paths, yet all have failed due to the essentially associative structure of the technological system it relies upon. In a system without a single author or a single authority, Bush's faith in the possibility of preserving human memory in technological systems becomes problematic.

The Internet presents a post-modern structure of memory – decentralised and chaotic. It is Bush's greatest legacy to contemporary society – the marriage of the decentralised information networking technology pioneered by ARPA with the associative paths of Bush's own Memex. No single individual can successfully navigate the vast spaces of the Internet's database. Instead, intelligent agents navigate and search that information space for their human users, using techniques modelled on the associative processes of human memory.

Artificial Intelligence and Intelligent Agents

It is ironic that the successful navigation of the Internet's associative networks depends upon intelligent agent software systems. Where digital memory refers to stored information in systems like the Memex and Xanadu, these memory systems are characterised by their inability to forget. Were either the Memex or Xanadu capable of forgetting, their function as information storage and retrieval systems would be fatally compromised. The problem posed by networks such as the Internet is that their users are unable to navigate information environments of such complexity. Designed not to erase information, but to endlessly connect and reconnect trails between nodes of information, the Internet becomes a space that is only navigable by a system that is able to swiftly select paths and trails from within this digital memory network.

An intelligent agent's ability to navigate an information space by blazing associative trails in a manner that replicates human behaviour, will be predicated upon that agent's ability to forget. If an intelligent agent is to truly mimic human memory processes in order to usefully navigate the information network for a human user, that agent must 'forget' unnecessary information, or information which is not useful to the individual goal it is seeking. Forgetting is not a useful attribute for a storage system. Indeed, the value of Bush's Memex system resided in its inability to forget. But forgetting *is* a useful attribute for an intelligent agent navigating such a system.

For Marvin Minsky, one of the foremost researchers in artificial intelligence, the success of intelligent agents is linked to their capacity to 'forget'. Inasmuch as intelligent agents 'learn by experience', they need to be able to select which information is essential to the task in hand, and reject the rest. Minsky characterises this forgetting as analogous to learning:

> We're still just beginning to make programs that can learn and reason by analogy. We're just starting to make systems that will learn to recognise which old experiences in memory are most analogous to the present problems. I like to think of this as 'do something sensible' programming. Such a program would remember a lot about its past so that, for each new problem, it would search for methods like the ones that worked best on similar problems in the past (Minsky 1990: 148).

Minksy is a firm believer in the possibilities of artificial intelligence and intelligent agents. He sees a technologically Darwinian future in which intelligent agents evolve by creating even more intelligent agents that replace the original agents because of their increased, and partially inherited ability to navigate the environments they inhabit. For Minsky, therefore, 'forgetting' constitutes those processes of selecting and discarding inform- ation that is not essential to the task in hand. Intelligent agents learn through these processes of selection and rejection of information. The evolutionary process figured by Minsky is a competitive one in which only the intelligent agents best suited to perform a certain task go on to spawn a next generation of agents.

Minsky's theory is best examined in relation to his understanding of creativity. Minsky understands creativity in humans not as something which is a factor of what we call 'genius', but an indicator, rather, of a human who has learnt how to learn better. The creative human, or genius, is to Minsky merely someone with acute skills in selecting and processing relevant information for a task. By learning to be better at this learning process, the individual becomes creative. Minsky's understanding of creativity allows him to argue that intelligent agents can become creative too:

> We still don't know why those 'creative masters' learn so much so well. The simplest hypothesis is that they've come across some better way to choose how and what to learn! What might the secret be? The simplest explanation: such a 'gift' is just some 'higher-order' kind of expertise – of knowing how to gain and use one's other skills. What might it take to learn *that?* Obvious: *one must learn to be better at learning!* (Minksy 1990: 150)

If creativity is just the process of learning to manage information, then intelligent agents, which are extremely adept at managing information are, to Minsky, creative. It is in Minsky's discussion of whether an intelligent agent can have a sense of self that we recognise how the related concepts of human and digital memory become circular. Bush replaces catalogued networks of information with associative trials, because he believes this to be the 'natural' way in which the human memory processes information. Minsky then suggests that intelligent agents, by learning to better process, select and discard information from within these associative trails, become capable of developing creativity and other human characteristics. Minksy supports his thesis by arguing that since digital memory and human memory are completely analogous, our notion of a singular self is an illusion that hides a complex network of information that accumulates to give the impression of a unitary self – a process repeatable by a computer:

> [. . .] it was only after trying to understand what computers – that is, complicated mechanisms – *could* do, that I began to have some glimpses of how a mind itself might work [. . .] how could we have expected, in the first place, to understand how minds work until after [we'd gained] expertise with theories about very complicated machines? (Minsky 1990: 160)

In this sense Minsky's hypothesis concerning the possibility of fully autonomous intelligent agents is self-confirming. Having argued that the human memory system is structured like digital computer memory, Minsky can then assert that the attributes of human memory can all be found in computer memory. Minksy does not merely attempt to map models of computer memory onto human memory. Rather, he argues that there is a fundamental relationship between the two systems that makes them analogous. Minsky does not set out to demonstrate that the intelligence of computers has now evolved to equal that of human beings. He argues, rather, that computers can now demonstrate to us the functioning of the human mind. Minsky's agents forget like humans do, and Minsky's humans forget like machines do.

Artificial Intelligence and Psychoanalysis

There would seem to be little common ground between artificial intelligence (AI) research and psychoanalysis. AI systems are preoccupied with what is, in its most elemental form, a process of developing a memory structure based upon rational and logical decisions, often using heuristic processes. Yet Minsky often supports his hypothesis by referring to Freud. It would seem an unlikely alliance, but it is one that is supported by Sherry Turkle.

Sherry Turkle's work (Turkle 1990) refers to AI research in which 'thinking' intelligent agents are defined as teams of agents accumulating the combined results from many smaller agents. Like Minsky, Turkle suggests that such systems resemble those of human memory. She isolates two branches of AI research: rule-driven and emergent. Rule-driven artificial intelligence is characterised as simple information processing according to a specific system of rules inputted by a programmer. Emergent AI is a form of artificial intelligence that learns by reacting to a digital environment and evaluating the outcome according to its predetermined goals – a dynamic process that creates its own set of rules:

> From this perspective, a rule is not something you give a computer but a pattern you infer when you observe the machine's behaviour, much as you would observe a person's. Its sustaining images are not drawn from the logical but from the biological. (Turkle 1990: 133)

Turkle supports Minksy by suggesting that emergent AI's learning processes resemble the processes of human memory described in object-relational psychoanalysis. Emergent AI systems that use many agents combined are like the object-relational psychoanalytic construct of the self, in which competing 'inner-agents' structure behaviour. Turkle goes on to describe the 'Perceptron' – a 1950s AI system for pattern-recognition that used many AI agents to create a decision-making process:

> So, for example, to get a perceptron to recognise a triangle, you show it samples of triangles and nontriangles and make the system 'guess'. Its first guesses are random. But the perceptron is able to take advantage of signals saying whether its guess is right or wrong to create a voting system in which agents who have guessed right get more weight. Perceptrons are not programmed, but learn from the consequences of their actions. (Turkle 1990: 135)

Turkle goes on to compare this teeming mass of small intelligent agents to the psychoanalytic notion of inner 'objects' that relate to each other. This object-relations school of psychoanalysis is then compared by Turkle to the object-oriented school of computer programming. Object-oriented programming is a method of programming systems that, like the perceptrons, behave according to their relationship with their environment. Programmed 'objects' are, in essence, small programmes that are instructed to test behaviours within their environments and then learn which behaviours are the most appropriate to achieve a certain goal. Object-oriented programmers are therefore capable of creating agents entirely composed of lots of small object-oriented programmes, all testing behaviours against each other and assessing which are capable of the successful achievement of their goals, and which aren't. Mapping this onto object-relational psychoanalysis breaks down the structure of the psyche into a dynamic system of diverse, non-hierarchical objects which drive behaviour:

> In classical psychoanalytical theory a few powerful inner structures – the superego, for example – act on memories, thoughts, and wishes. Object relations theory posits a dynamic system in which the distinctions between processor and processed breaks down. The parallel with computation is clear: in both cases there is movement away from a situation in which a few inner structures act on more passive stuff. Fairburn replaced the Freudian dichotomies of ego and id, structure and energy with independent agencies within the mind that think, wish and generate meaning in interaction with each other, much as emergent AI sets free autonomous agents within a computer system. (Turkle 1990: 140)

Like memory and inner objects, object-oriented agents and information environments are dynamic and relational. Agents don't forget. They compete, rather, to make their decisions count above those of all other agents Turkle borrows from connectionist theory – the AI theory which likens computer decision-making processes to neural networks. This move allows her to liken human memory to this dynamic, relational system.

According to Ted Nelson, the Xanadu creates a non-hierarchical hypertextual network in which information exists in a relational, dynamic network. A similar perspective informs Turkle's understanding of both connectionist memory *and* human identity. As emergent AI allows a computer system to develop in relation to its own digital environment, so object-relational psychoanalysis comes to view the internal development of human memory and identity in similarly relational and dynamic terms.

Object-oriented systems and AI are used to develop the intelligent agents that traverse the web. The information space in which these search agents are deployed is too vast for us to navigate alone. Instead, humans must make use of systems that are better than us at information processing, that can control teams of object-oriented agents to make decisions, and that can cope with information overload by deselecting agent decisions. Turkle recognises the consequences of the slippage between models of human and digital memory in object-relational psychoanalysis and emergent AI. Andrew Leonard has argued that:

> Turkle is an unabashed post-modernist [. . .] She attributes this new pragmatism in part to a sea change in the overall culture, the transition from a modernist age in which people believed in ultimate values to a post-modern age in which everything is relative and there is no foundation. (Leonard 1997: 67)

But these consequences have their roots in Bush's technological legacy, which has bequeathed us a society and culture that mimics the depthlessness of digital memory. It is a culture that bears the marks of Bush's mapping of a model of human memory onto a technological system that has echoed through contemporary AI research and that is evident in our use of agents to navigate the Internet. Agent systems become the trailblazers that have replaced the human agents in Bush's Memex. These agents blaze trails through memory. Vannevar Bush's Memex has ceased to be a technological system that supplements human memory. Instead, it has given birth to a system which is coming to *characterize* contemporary human memory. Ironically, a system that was intended to aid the fallible, forgetful human memory, has instead become a metaphor for post-modern definitions of human memory itself.

Bibliography

Bush, Vannevar (1991), 'As We May Think', in James Nyce & Paul Kahn (eds), *From Memex to Hypertext: Vannevar Bush & the Mind's Machine*, London: Academic Press.

Leonard, Andrew (1997), *Bots – The Origin of a New Species*, Harmondsworth: Penguin.

Minksy, Marvin (1985), *The Society of Mind*, New York: Touchstone.

Minsky, Marvin (1990), 'Why People Think Computers Can't' in Ermann, Williams & Gutierrez (eds), *Computers, Ethics, & Society*, Oxford: Oxford University Press.

Nelson, Ted (1991), 'As We Will Think' in James Nyce & Paul Kahn (eds), *From Memex to Hypertext: Vannevar Bush & the Mind's Machine*, London: Academic Press.

Turkle, Sherry (1990), 'Artificial Intelligence and Psychoanalysis: A New Alliance' in Ermann, Williams & Gutierrez (eds), *Computers, Ethics, & Society*, Oxford: Oxford University Press.

Turkle, Sherry (1996), *Life on the Screen: Identity in the age of the Internet*, London: Weidenfeld & Nicolson.

Zachary, G. Pascal (1997), *The Endless Frontier: Vannevar Bush, Engineer of the American Century*, New York: The Free Press.

2

Places, Politics and the Archiving of Contemporary Memory in Pierre Nora's *Les Lieux de mémoire*

Peter Carrier

The monumental seven-volume work *Les Lieux de mémoire* (Nora (ed.) 1984; 1986; 1993)[1] is a landmark in contemporary historiography: a comprehensive scholarly study of 'places of memory' or symbols forming the basis of social memory in France today. Having been developed as a seminar project by the French historian Pierre Nora during the 1970s, it brings together 130 essays by over a hundred historians on subjects as diverse and as apparently incongruous as 'Coffee', 'Vichy' and 'The King'. These thematic studies, headed 'La République', 'La Nation' and 'Les France', analyse the origins and evolution of the symbols of contemporary French identity: traces of the political and cultural construction of the Third Republic, of national unity and national division spanning fourteen centuries of history from 'The Franks and the Gauls' to 'Vichy'. Consistent with the diversity and conflict inherent in French history, *Les Lieux de mémoire* projects a pluralist understanding of memory; not collective memory, therefore, but a collection or constellation of memories which, in various combinations, constitute the memory of 'French' individuals. Paradoxically, however, while Nora's work testifies to the pluralist and fragmented nature of contemporary memory, it also projects a unitary 'total' history under the all-encompassing (though elusive) banner of Frenchness.

Although the symbols under discussion in these volumes are confined to the context of France, Nora's theoretical reflections on the relation between history and memory mark a valuable methodological contribution to the exploration of the historical and political role of memory in general. As a history of symbols tracing the evolution of the representation of events and cultural traditions rather than the events or traditions themselves, *Les Lieux de mémoire* has been described by one critic as a characteristically postmodern approach to history, one which 'reduces the memory of the past to the history of its images' (Hutton 1993: 22). However, *Les Lieux de mémoire* can be read not as a confirmation of history as an aesthetic phenomenon but as a conscious attempt to investigate the means by which residual collective images of this past have been constructed. In this way, it serves to expose the mechanisms of the social constructions of such images.

Nora's contribution to the debate over the politics of memory is twofold. First, *Les Lieux de mémoire* offers a structured analysis of the construction of French memory, a model method for the interpretation of historical symbols. Second, this work is itself a monument, a symbol and a *symptom* of the political role of social memory in France today, which both reveals and projects nationhood as cultural identity rather than as a politically determined group of citizens. The causes and implications of this specifically cultural understanding of Frenchness, including the political motives for the denial of French republican tradition, are the object of this essay.

An obvious example of the political function of memory which characterises the social context of and theoretical pertinence of *Les Lieux de mémoire* is the spate of fiftieth anniversary commemorations of the Second World War between 1989 and 1995. Commemorative ceremonies marking the beginning, end, and major events during the conflict underscored not only the media's readiness to evoke images of the past, but also the enthusiasm with which the public indulges in remembrance or, for those who have no personal memory of that period, in the construction of memory. Although the anniversary of the Second World War is not the only prompt for the contemporary fascination with the politics of memory, it provides an effective prism through which to examine the complex interaction of local, national, international and supranational politics in the construction of social memories. The intensification of commemorative events since the 1970s has generally taken place on a national scale: the staging of major bicentenary celebrations of the Revolution in France in 1989; the foundation of a Ministry for National Heritage in Britain in 1993; the readjustment of the national cultural landscape in Germany since reunification in 1990 (monuments, museums, street names, the national holiday (now 3 October), the seat of government, for example) which has been amplified by highly politicised controversies surrounding the commemoration of the assassination attempt against Hitler on 20 July 1944, echoing the 'historians' dispute' of 1986.

Despite the limited national scope of the studies in *Les Lieux de mémoire*, however, the concept of 'place of memory' has attracted international critical acclaim and inspired new fields of inquiry abroad. For example, the project to explore the history of Germany on the basis of places of memory, currently in progress at the Marc Bloch Institute in Berlin, is founded on an adaptation of this concept within a comparative Franco-German perspective (François 1995). The British historian Raphael Samuel rejects Nora's understanding of memory on ideological grounds, claiming that it is an expression of coercive national memory,[2] while Jay Winter, who also acknowledges the influence of Nora in his study of places of memory of the First World War (Winter 1995), chooses to challenge the notion of places or 'sites' of memory by examining them in a specifically international context. All three projects throw critical light on both Nora's work and the problem of commemoration in general. However, none explicitly probes the historical, historiographical and political assumptions underlying the notion of places of memory, and the reasons for writing a national history of France on the basis of its memorial heritage. In order to do this, one must first investigate the conceptual apparatus Nora uses to describe the role of memory today. *Les Lieux de mémoire* is not only an inventory of contemporary French memories, including such cultural landmarks as 'The Eiffel Tower' or 'Gastronomy', but a historical explanation of the state of contemporary memory in what Nora refers to as the 'age of commemoration' (Nora 1993d). Central to this explanation is the idea of rupture, or historical discontinuity, as the cause of radical transformations in collective consciousness: from historical memory to patrimonial, cultural, social, historiographical or archival memory – concepts which require closer examination.

The Functional Transformation of Memory: From Political to Cultural Consensus

Since its inception during the 1970s, Pierre Nora's notion of *lieux de mémoire* (variously translated as 'places' or 'sites' of memory) has almost become a commonplace in the everyday French language. It refers generally to the various symbolic 'places' or cultural expressions of collective memory such as geographical regions, monuments, commemorative ceremonies, well-known personalities, political movements, professional institutions or social habits described by Nora as the 'focal points of our national heritage' (Nora 1995: 83). A 'place of memory' may be loosely defined, therefore, as a cultural support for a particular collective memory. It is not necessarily a topographical place, however, like 'The Louvre', for it may be more loosely defined as a focal point of shared emotional attachment, such as 'Vichy' or 'Gastronomy'. In 1993, this term was even introduced into the *Grand Robert* dictionary, which defines a place of memory as a 'significant unit, either material or ideal, which the will of people or the effect of time have turned into a symbolic element of a given community'. The emphasis here on the signification pertaining to a 'symbolic element' of a 'community' brought about by 'will' or the 'effect of time' suggests that a place of memory is essentially a semantic element or tool which renders collective identity intelligible on the basis of historical origins ('will' or 'the effect of time') and contemporary political utility (the cohesion of a community). According to the definition, therefore, places of memory act as instrumental vehicles for collective memories underpinning social cohesion. Nora focuses not on the psychological mechanisms by which individuals adhere to places of memory, however, but on the *function* they have in sustaining French identity. It must be stressed, however, that though Nora attributes an instrumental or functional role to memory he does not interpret places of memory as forces capable of rallying communities in defence of minority or national rights. The object of *Les Lieux de mémoire* is not collective memory as such; the definition of memory as 'collective' suggests that a single memory is shared by a largely homogeneous community. (Likewise, the term 'identity' evokes a fixed stock of memories harboured by an individual or a community, while not allowing for the necessary complexity and instability of symbolic attachments within any society: attachments which are in a state of flux, and which command constantly changing degrees of emotional adherence (cf. François et al. 1995: 17).) Rather than promote a fixed collective memory or a closed sense of identity, Nora recognises the plural and composite nature of social memory. The French national memory conveyed by *Les Lieux de mémoire* does not imply homogeneity or coercion, therefore, but openness to new configurations and combinations of coexisting memories (cf. Namer 1987: 26). An individual may identify with any number of places of memory as diverse as 'Gaullists and Communists', 'The Industrial Age' or 'The King' without necessarily falling victim to a conflict of identity. Places of memory are, claims Nora, not a basis for a 'community of memory' (Nora 1993b: 964) and must not, therefore, be confused with the binding interests serving the cohesion of minority groups in contemporary Western societies, defined by race, religion or gender. Almost none of the places of memory in question ('Coffee' or 'The Forest', for example) could today serve to bind minority identities.

In addition to this pluralist interpretation, Nora identifies a qualitative change in French memory, where 'places of memory' serve as artificial props (though not substitutes) for a lost national memory. The very fact that places of memory such as the customs of 'Dying for the Fatherland' or 'Coffee' may today be perceived as *symbols* of national heritage makes them appear unnatural, for they can no longer be experienced without the awareness that they originally embodied meanings quite foreign to those they embody today. Places of memory are thus a symptom of rupture, an end of tradition-based continuity: 'There are *lieux de mémoire*, sites of memory, because there are no longer *milieux de mémoire*, environments of memory.' (Nora 1989: 7; 1984b: XVII) In the wake of the social transformations of modernity, broadly categorized by Nora as globalisation, democratisation, massification and mediatisation, *lieux* function as traces of such 'environments' in a society cut off from its past; society thus commemorates and monumentalises these traces as a means to perpetuate its lost tradition and maintain collective identities.[3] Even explicitly political themes such as 'Gaullists and Communists', 'The People' or 'Dying for the Fatherland' – once forces of social cohesion – are, as places of memory and objects of *study*, appropriated as politically inert forms of cultural heritage. Individuals may thus freely identify with any combination of places of memory at the same time, without the risk of one excluding the other on partisan grounds. Places of memory do not, therefore, function as a basis for consensus fusing or dividing community figurations in French society (Nora's system does not account for the problem of minority identities opposed to integration). Instead, they function as symbols of politically and historically inert memories – the prime example today being the French Revolution – which sustain contemporary French identity. The resurgence of revolutionary thought and activity culminating in the uprisings of 1968 was, asserts Nora, a form of symbolic celebration rather than effective political action, while the bicentenary of the French Revolution focused public attention on controversies over the commemoration itself rather than on the event being commemorated (Nora 1993d: 980).

If places of memory, including commemorations and the increasing monumentalisation of the past, are indeed symptoms of a politically inert past and radically pluralist identities, the dictionary definition of a place of memory as 'a symbolic element of a given community' is rather misleading, for it suggests that a place of memory is a force of homogeneous political cohesion. 'The Forest' or 'Coffee' are not likely to mobilise community identities, however. If they did, it is unlikely that either one could guarantee homogeneity or exclude any member of the community from simultaneous allegiance with other symbolic elements. Places of memory and community identities are not isomorphic. Each symbolic element underpins the identity of a community only in conjunction with other elements, or else in a hierarchical configuration, but only rarely could one element eclipse all others as the sole legitimation of a given community. The *Grand Robert* definition is in fact a misquotation from Nora's essay 'Comment écrire l'histoire de France?' in which a place of memory is defined more precisely as 'a symbolic element of *the memorial patrimony* of a given community' (Nora 1993a: 20 (emphasis mine)). 'Memorial patrimony' here points to a distinctive *quality* of contemporary memory associated with all memorial symbols rather than to the distinguishing contents of a specific community's memories or symbols. Nora's aim is not to oppose the different memories of particular groups, but to determine their common qualitative basis which, as 'memorial patrimony', is cultural rather than political, grounded in the 'collective heritage of the traditional aspects of memory itself' (Nora 1986b: 650). In other words, having lost their initial political pertinence, traditional divisions such as 'Civil France Versus Religious France' or 'Gaullists and Communists' are no longer experienced as exclusive social divisions, but as a cultural residue or heritage founded on memory alone, and therefore, paradoxically, as a basis for political consensus void of politics.[4]

The Historical Present: From Historical to Social Consciousness

Places of memory serve as a prop for memory, which in turn serves as a medium for the (subjective) sense of historical continuity. Paradoxically, however, this sense of continuity – the ongoing awareness, for example, of the historical significance of monuments or social customs such as the Pantheon or the 14 July celebrations – is undermined by a radical qualitative breach in memory itself, which modifies the moral and political value attached to the past. Memory, now dependent on external symbols or *lieux* and no longer transmitted naturally within social *milieux*, suggests that modern consciousness as such has also undergone a transformation, and that historians must therefore take account of the increasing influence of memory on public opinion, on the process of historical understanding, and on the historical discipline itself. Nora's notion of the 'historical present' is a response to this transformation (Nora 1993e).

It is a truism to state that memory functions in the present, yet Nora's insistence on the significance of places of memory as 'the presence of the past within the present' (Nora 1989: 20; 1984b: XXXVII) or that of memory itself as 'the administration of the past in the present' (Nora 1993a: 25) or as 'the medium for situating the past in the present' (Nora 1995) is indicative of an innovative legitimation of the present, and of the role of memory as previously neglected objects of historical research. A characteristic example of the rupture between the 'natural' *milieux* of memory and the 'unnatural' *lieux* or places of memory is provided by Mona Ozouf, who associates two such types of memory with the Pantheon: first, as a functional monument to sanction republican ideology, then as an inert symbol of a bygone age. The Pantheon, inaugurated as a sepulchre for the remains of French national heroes in 1791, is one of the key monuments to French national memory. According to Ozouf, however, it is now an anachronism. Its initial function as a prop to the cult of 'great men' instituted following the Revolution was not merely symbolic, for a place in the Pantheon was a reward to individual citizens – in the form of public memory extending beyond their lifetime – for services to the State, and therefore played a practical role by sanctioning both the political value of citizens and the democratic ideal of meritocracy as opposed to the earlier despotism of the *ancien régime*. In the political and historical environment of the 1980s and 1990s, however, the symbolic role of the Pantheon took precedence over its functional role, for the ideals it served lost their original pedagogical (and therefore political) function. For this reason, both the Pantheon and the values it represents have only a *memorial* role to play today, as archetypal places of memory (Ozouf 1984: 162).

Such genealogical investigations into the specifically contemporary significance of symbolic elements of French history pose a significant challenge to established methods of historiography. First, the focus on the present requires us to call into question standard periodisations, generally confined to the past, such as 'pre-', 'ancient', 'modern' or 'contemporary' history. Second, the study of the present renders consultation of documentary evidence practically impossible, and is therefore concerned less with establishing the veracity of historical facts than with the ways in which the past is understood and appropriated within contemporary consciousness. Nora responds to such challenges to established historiography by positing the 'historical present' as a branch of historical study in its own right. Unlike contemporary history, which analyses events and phenomena from the recent past (a period beginning with a given historical rupture such as a revolution or war, or a period measured according to the limits of living memory, for example), the historical present focuses strictly on current or *actual* phenomena (those acting or happening in the present). Its essential medium is therefore memory, an elusive support which lacks the historical legitimacy of documentary evidence available in the practice of contemporary history. Unlike oral history, however, which relies on memory as a means to unearthing or documenting a past event (with respect to the event itself), the historical present focuses on memory as an object of study for its own sake: the medium by which the past is rendered intelligible, and the resulting consciousness it sustains.

By laying emphasis on the present and on the *intelligibility* of the past in the present, therefore, Nora describes a fundamental change in contemporary memory, which is no longer a simple vehicle for a sense of historical continuity, but a medium fraught with critical detachment from the past. He claims that 'the solidarity between the past and future has been replaced by the solidarity between the present and memory' (Nora 1993d: 1009), and thus interprets this change in the experience of time in terms of a general transformation of 'historical consciousness' into 'social consciousness' (ibid.), while suggesting two reasons for this transformation. On the one hand, attention accorded to the present and the instrumental role of memory in the present is a consequence of pressing social and political changes and the economic crisis beginning in France in the 1970s (the departure and death of de Gaulle, the demise of French socialism, the end of the '*trente glorieuses*' and the rise of new political trends including the *Front National*, ecological and human rights movements) (Nora 1986b: 46). More fundamentally, however, the importance of the historical present is a consequence of the new collective apprehension of actuality *(l'actualité)* or current events triggered at the end of the nineteenth century by an increasingly effective mass media. The urgency of actuality is typically conveyed by 'live' transmissions and thereby engages the emotional involvement of the spectator in the present while preventing retrospection. The cultivation of public opinion via the mass media is therefore indissociable from the modification of people's awareness of time and space in the form of acceleration (acute awareness of the passage of time) and globalisation (the bridging of distances between events and spectators). 'Acceleration and globalisation,' claims Nora, 'have brought about a qualitative change to the present; they have democratized history itself, for history is no longer the privileged domain of the historian.' (Nora 1978: 470) The newly defined 'social consciousness' therefore corresponds to a displacement of the authority over collective consciousness from professional historians (via the medium of State archives, educational institutions, publications and the traditions they uphold) to journalists and public opinion, invited (via the mass media) to participate in the process of fixing the present as it becomes past. The effectiveness of the State and its institutions under the Third Republic ensured that collective memory reflected official historical interpretation; the relevance of past events in the future was thus sustained on the common assumption that history is governed by long-term linear continuity. This legitimation of tradition on the basis of history and 'historical conscious-ness' has thus been reversed by a new 'social consciousness' bound to events only insofar as they are of consequence in the immediate present and future. In Nora's system, memory therefore takes over from history as an increasingly autonomous dynamic force in society.

Nora considers the distinction between successive generations as one of the major causes of the increased political authority of social memory in the present and the sense of rupture between tradition and the 'historical present'. Each generation identifies itself in opposition to the previous or succeeding generation; indeed, the very existence of a generation is synonymous with an identity or collective memory which draws a temporal boundary between itself and both the past and the future. It is brought about by the natural succession of age groups, historic events and trans-formations in social conditions or political systems resulting in the intro-duction of new education programmes, for example. Categories such as 'the war generation' or 'the sixties generation' in the West are highly charged with meaning and presuppose a determining set of experiences and values common to a specific social age group. However, the cohesion of generational identity is, according to Nora, sustained by 'pure memory' where individuals are bound not only by common experience but also by a common reaction to something *not* experienced (yet associated with the previous generation). Hence the pithy but somewhat elliptical defini-tions of generations as 'the present as present' or 'permanent antecedence' (Nora 1993b: 948, 958): 'the generational rupture [. . .] essentially consists in "immemorializing" the past in order to better "memorialize" the present. In this respect, a generation is a powerful and even one of the chief sources of "places of memory", which constitute the fabric of its provisional identity and the focal points of its particular memory.' (Ibid: 959)

Generational consciousness, an expression of a broader social con-sciousness identifying with the present and firmly dissociating itself from the past, therefore plays an essential role in determining the nature and function of places of memory in the historical present. It fosters a form of collective memory whose collectiveness is based on its 'patrimonial' quality, not its force of cohesion or homogeneity. In this respect, genera-tional 'collective' memory had a decisive influence on the form and content of the very work *about* places of memory, *Les Lieux de mémoire:* the mere fact that historians choose to read or write about 'The Names of Streets' or 'Lavisse, a National Teacher' testifies to the relevance of these themes in contemporary France. Furthermore, the very act of focusing on the *actual* symbolic significance of places of memory as signifiers of the present (i.e. of contemporary French memory) automatically leads to the marginalisation or 'immemorialization' of the past as an anachronism, as in the case of the Pantheon. The place of memory most characteristic of generational consciousness is perhaps 'The *Ancien Régime* and the Revolution', for the very act of naming the Revolution, as well as the idea of revolution as radical change, tends to eclipse all that preceded it; the expedient term *'ancien régime'* likewise reduces ten centuries of history to an amorphous temporal block preceding the revolution (Furet 1993: 107).

Another aspect of generational or social consciousness, apart from its preoccupation with actuality, instrumentalisation of memory and marginalisation of the past, is its *provisionality,* resulting from the 'acceleration' of time and the constant flux of generations. In this respect, Nora's entire method, the foundation of a national history on places of memory, is itself provisional: all the authors of *Les Lieux de mémoire* are professional historians of a generation which experienced the economic, political and social transformations during the 1970s in France, as well as the challenge of the mass media. The choice of places of memory in *Les Lieux de mémoire* is therefore subject to criteria determined by this generation's particular symbolic attachments. These criteria are not definitive, but primarily subjective and 'social', determined by concerns of the present and the complex configurations of collective memories in contemporary France.

Archival Memory: From Historical to Historiographical Consciousness

The shift from historical to social consciousness, which displaces political authority from the professional historian to society itself, has coincided with a radical modification of the supports sustaining collective memory. Positivist historians in the nineteenth century had recourse to documentary evidence stored in archives in order to legitimate a specific reconstruction of the facts of the past worthy of social consensus or collective memory. Public opinion, on the other hand, legitimates or renders its understanding of the 'presence of the past in the present' intelligible by means of 'significant units' or symbolic places representing particularist, non-consensual interests or memories of an atomised society. The commemorations in France to mark the bicentenary of the French Revolution, the controversy over the inauguration of the Central Memorial of the Federal Republic of Germany in the Neue Wache monument in Berlin, 1993, or the international fiftieth anniversaries of the Second World War are remarkable examples of the dynamic social force of commemorative events, where the role of the media and public opinion are paramount, and where the historian's pedagogical role is reduced to that of a critic or moral guardian.[5] Places of memory therefore take over from documentary archives as *symbolic* archives supporting a type of memory which Nora describes as 'archival' – albeit not in order to compare memory itself to a store or data bank, but to underline its dependence on external recorded material foreign to the remembering organism: a 'prosthesis-memory' whose 'new vocation is to record; delegating to the archive the responsibility of remembering' (Nora 1989: 14, 13; 1984b: XXVIII, XXVI).

Nora not only expands the notion of 'archive' to include all objective or material representations which support contemporary memory, but also maintains that the shift from historical to social consciousness has resulted in a profound modification of the role of existing institutional archives, whose public historical utility has been progressively subsumed to the sphere of private memory. Public archives (institutional, national, supranational, etc.) are not only being extensively exploited for private purposes by genealogists and biographers, but are also receiving an increasing influx of documents from private or family sources, as well as from commercial enterprises or associations. In addition, public archives are today being rivalled by a considerable number of private archives fostering memories under the aegis of administrations which escape the monopoly of the State, such as companies, families, political groups and religious orders (Nora 1993c: 15). The rise of 'archival' memory has also brought about a radical modification of the forms by which memory is maintained and transmitted. Institutional archives are traditionally literal, classified chronologically, convey the authority of being given or 'found' rather than 'fabricated' items, and represent the interest of the institute in question. Places of memory or symbolic 'archives', on the other hand, are not necessarily literal, and may take any symbolic form, whether concrete or abstract: in Nora's terms, they may be 'immaterial' ('Heritage', 'History', 'Landscape'), 'material' ('Territory', 'State', 'Patrimony') or 'ideal' ('Glory', 'Words') (Nora 1993a: 12). In addition, they are not classified chronologically, but according to the politico-historical categories of 'The Republic', 'The Nation' and 'Les France', and according to symbolic types such as 'Monuments', 'Heritage' or 'Political Divisions'. Finally, they are generally 'fabricated' rather than 'found', and represent social rather than institutional interests.

The most significant aspect of Nora's notion of archival memory is the critical distance it introduces on the part of individuals towards the cultural tools traditionally used to maintain historical continuity. When Nora describes contemporary memory as 'archival', therefore, on account of its tendency to delegate the responsibility of remembering to objects or symbolic archives, he does not suggest that places of memory serve only as objects onto which individuals project a sense of belonging in order to construct an identity, but that they may also facilitate 'historiographical' consciousness by serving as objects for critical inquiry into the mechanisms by which their memories are constructed. It is for this reason that *Les Lieux de mémoire* includes analyses of some landmarks of French historiography: Ernest Lavisse's *Histoire de France* (P. Nora); François Guizot, the historian-statesman who promoted the French national archives and educational institutions under the Third Republic (Laurent Theis); the Annales 'school' of historians in the twentieth century (Krzysztof Pomian); studies of the national archives (K. Pomian), and the historical role of genealogy (André Burguière). These histories of historical writing inevitably entail an intellectual detachment from historical tradition: 'The fact that we study the historiography of the French Revolution, reconstitute its myths and interpretations, implies that we no longer unquestioningly identify with its heritage. By examining a tradition, venerable though it may be, we cease to recognize ourselves as carriers of that tradition.' (Nora 1989: 10;[6] 1984b: XXI)

The dissociation or 'disidentification' from historical tradition characteristic of archival memory is not only a consequence of analytical detachment, however. It is also a consequence of historical developments: the dwindling credibility of the State, which was formally guaranteed by such institutions as the cult of 'great men'; and the reduced pedagogical effectiveness of national symbolics. The efficacy with which the Third Republic guaranteed national cohesion was achieved not only by means of its educational institutions, but also by the effective use of public art and monuments in conveying republican ideology. Public monuments of the nineteenth century were, according to Ozouf, an expression of the 'faith in the spontaneous solidarity of aesthetics and morality, in the necessary docility of the public towards the lesson to be drawn from the senses and the efficacy of pedagogical art' (Ozouf 1984: 163). It is this contrast between the former pedagogical effectiveness of political symbols, sustained by public 'docility', and the relative indifference of the public today which characterises monuments like the Pantheon. However, public indifference to political symbols in the late twentieth century is only relative. Ritual and familiarity alter the relation of individuals to objects or symbols, but do not necessarily efface them altogether from memory. Places of memory such as 'The Pantheon', 'The Tour de France' or 'Gastronomy', for example, may continue to bolster a sense of national pride, for they are objects of ritual, habitual or even physical familiarity[7] acquired unconsciously during an individual's lifetime and reinforced by a passive solidarity with the habits of previous generations: of passersby (passing the Pantheon), cyclists (participating in or following the Tour de France) or eaters (of French gastronomy)! The historicity of such symbols does not presuppose knowledge of their history, therefore. Ritual, habit and familiarity, though not necessarily the products of ideological intention, inevitably foster a collective sense of belonging liable to conserve national heritage.

This ambiguity of archival memory, as a force of either identification or 'disidentification', is inherent to Nora's understanding of places of memory and national symbolics in general. In his first theoretical presentation of the project to found a history of France on the basis of places of memory, he asserts that 'we have to constantly detach ourselves from our familiar habits, experienced in the heat of tradition, and draw a map of our mental geography' (Nora 1984a: VII). However, he goes on to advise readers that although the ultimate purpose of a study of places of memory is to promote insight into the mechanisms of historiography and historical representations, they should, despite a 'risk of intellectual regression and the return to Gallocentrism', first seek 'pleasure and interest' via an 'innocent reading' (ibid: XIII). This ambiguity of memory as a medium for non-critical identification or critical 'disidentification' is particularly apparent in the case of the *Dictionnaire de pédagogie* (1882–7), a highly influential school manual during the Third Republic conceived by the educational reformer Ferdinand Buisson and modelled on a similar pedagogical encyclopaedia produced in Germany (1858–75). The pertinence of this manual today is not, according to Nora, determined solely by the insight it affords into the political or historical education administered under the Third Republic (Buisson's manual is founded on the concise ideological framework of the French Revolution, republican ideals, reason, democracy and education (Nora 1984c: 353)). Instead, its initial function, which Nora describes as 'historical and journalistic, corporative and universal', has given way to its role as a support for sentimental (emotional and uncritical) or ethnological (scientific and critical) memory:

> The *Dictionnaire* thus combines several types of memories: historical and journalistic, corporative and universal, sentimental and ethnological. The first two apply to the authors, the following two to the users, while the last two apply to contemporary readers like ourselves. What makes this work a place of memory is the effect of the first four on the last two, and the depth they acquire as a result. The *Dictionnaire* was intended to be a place of memory in its own day, for contemporary readers; however, on this first degree, its

meaning has been lost, along with the practices of its users. We see it as a place of memory only because we know that it was meant to be one in the past. It is this dialectic which, in our eyes, defines it as such [. . .]. (Ibid: 375)

The example of Buisson's dictionary leads Nora to define the memory fostered by places of memory in terms of a dialectical relationship between first- and second-degree understanding, between the original historical, journalistic, corporative and universal interests of their creators and users, and the sentimental and ethnological interest awakened retrospectively: an awareness of the rupture between their original and memorial functions. However, second-degree memory is itself prey to a dialectic operating between *sentimental* and *ethnological* memory, suspended between an uncritical indulgence in or identification with places of memory, and a critical interest in studying the very motives and mechanisms by which memory serves to build identity. Nora even defends such ambiguity as a characteristic of the method of *Les Lieux de mémoire*. Memory, a key medium for the transmission of tradition, is an instrument of both 'construction' and 'deconstruction':

> This process of deciphering determines the spirit of the whole undertaking. It is subject to two types of operation, however, which are different and even entirely opposed, involving either the construction of the object as a symbol, or its deconstruction. In the first case, we lend a voice to things which have remained silent, giving meaning and life to something which otherwise has neither meaning nor life. In the second case, however, we dispel the familiarity of something whose meaning is all too evident, and thereby restore the original strangeness to something which has been handed down as a ready-made legacy of the past. (Nora 1993c: 14)

The technique of constructing or deconstructing memorial symbols is most apparent in the third section of the volume *Les France,* subtitled 'From Archives to Emblems', where the relatively little-known archival mechanisms perpetuating social memory such as 'Archives' and 'Workers' Lives' are constructed as symbols or emblems, and the relatively well-known emblems such as 'The Eiffel Tower' and 'The King' analytically deconstructed.

The purpose of studying places of memory is not simply to define contemporary memory as a state of awareness of the rupture between historical and social consciousness, or between first- and second-degree meaning, between 'the milieux of inwardly experienced values and the places of their external commemoration' (Hutton 1993: 149). Instead, it is designed to 'lend a voice' to silent symbols or 'dispel familiarity' in the case of familiar symbols, and therefore *intervene* in the status and configuration of the symbolic framework of contemporary memory by highlighting less familiar places of memory and tempering the emotional appeal of more familiar places. In both cases, whether as a construction or deconstruction of symbols and their meanings, the notion of 'places of memory' serves as a heuristic tool for understanding the present-day political instrumentality of memory and, more importantly, for constructing a canon of the supports of contemporary French identity. Nora's primary concern is practical, not theoretical: the monumental seven-volume publication is itself a kind of encyclopaedic archive or inventory of French memories which therefore bears comparison with the monumental pedagogical works produced during the nineteenth century by Lavisse (Hartog 1995: 1228). The lapse in time between the publication of the first (1984) and last (1993) volumes even permitted their editor to remark, in the final volume, that *Les Lieux de mémoire* had already become a place of memory in its own right, before completion, on account of its widespread enthusiastic reception (cf. Nora 1993d: 977). The monumentality of this publication (containing contributions by the most reputed specialists of French history) and the force of its unorthodox title which, contrary to historical practice, denotes a historiographical method rather than its historical theme (French identity), have guaranteed its pedagogical aptitude as a scientific work of reference. However, *Les Lieux de mémoire,* as a 'symbolic element of a given community', does not conform to the doctrine of places of memory expounded by Nora. Whereas places of memory are the symbolic embodiments of archival or 'secondary degree' memory – formal cultural motifs of once politically dynamic 'first degree' memory – *Les Lieux de mémoire* projects a *third* degree of memory by projecting a new (pluralist and unitary) model of French memory. Although the notion of places of memory is open, and the selection of themes not exhaustive, this work nevertheless fixes the analyses within a tight literary structure based on the politico-historical categories of 'The Republic', 'The Nation' and 'Les France' (corresponding to the titles of the three respective volumes). The work itself is a construction, an *analytical* archive of symbolic archives, and therefore a projection (for the future) of a new form of French history. Its authors are historians who, by coming to terms with the role of memory in contemporary society, effectively reclaim political authority back from memory, from public opinion and the media, by offering a collective and global interpretation of the *idea* of France. The fragmented or 'atomized' configuration of private memories characteristic of social consciousness is hereby given a loose yet distinctly unifying form: the object of *Les Lieux de mémoire* is not strictly a national history, however, but the more elusive idea of national memory or identity, based on a collection of fragmented (not collective) cultural memories, which is defined openly within the three categories of the Republic, the nation and *les* France, yet which refuses to be reduced to any one to the exclusion of the others.

Rewriting French History

Historical rupture or discontinuity is perhaps the most decisive historiographical paradigm in Nora's writings on history and memory. The history of France traced in *Les Lieux de mémoire* is a history of national memory in a state of transition; a testimony to the process of coming to terms with and projecting a new symbolic role of memory, whether as an instrument for maintaining national heritage or 'patrimony', as the support of social rather than historical consciousness, or as the source of historiographical (ethnographical or sentimental) rather than historical consciousness. In all three cases, Nora's objective is to maintain a sense of historical continuity (ibid: 1012) by devising a new programme or method for the renewal of national history on the basis of symbolic places of memory (Nora 1986a: XX). The means for achieving this objective are not chauvinistic, however, but balanced between 'ethno-logical' or 'sentimental' retrospection. They are founded on a critical apprehension of the traditionally political legitimation of the French nation since the Revolution and therefore express a concern to reconstitute the nation as a cultural or memorial nation, involving 'the difficult undertaking of dissociating ourselves from the entire historical tradition of France while at the same time taking up the threads of this tradition anew' (Nora 1995: 89). This programmatic venture to rewrite French national history in terms of memory and identity raises two key questions regarding Nora's historiographical method.

First, on what historical grounds does Nora justify the necessity to rewrite French history on the basis of memorial rather than political or historical continuity, and to compensate for the end of two centuries of political tradition beginning with the Revolution by proposing to reclaim this tradition as cultural heritage? The ruptures in French history addressed by Nora are manifold, and include the rise of 'actuality' in the 1890s, 1918 ('disaster-stricken Europe'), 1945 ('the false victory'), 1962 ('the end of the global projection' marking the independence of Algeria after French colonial rule) (Nora 1993d: 1007), as well as the social, economic and political upheavals in France during the 1970s (Nora 1986b: 652). The most decisive rupture of all is portrayed as the consequences of the crisis of the 1930s: the end of the legacy of the Enlightenment, of political universalism, of historical progress, of the Revolutionary inheritance of the nation state and, above all, the demise of the Third Republic. For Nora, this rupture coincided with the end of the synthesis between historical practice and social memory (the pedagogical efficacy of history in ensuring social consensus), and therefore triggered the switch from the bond between State and nation (the ideological unity of collective memory) to that between State and society (an association of private memories) (Nora 1989: 11; 1984b: XXII). The consequent rise of 'archival' memory or 'historiographical' consciousness, dependent on memorial prostheses or representations such as commemorations, is therefore symptomatic of what Nora calls the voluntary, unnatural maintenance of memory in contrast to spontaneous, natural memory: *'Lieux de mémoire* originate with the sense that there is no spontaneous memory, that we must deliberately create archives, maintain anniversaries, organize celebrations, pronounce eulogies, and notarize bills, because such activities no longer occur naturally.' (Ibid: 12; XXIV) The distinction between unnatural and spontaneous or natural memory does not correspond to the difference between literate and non-literate 'oral' societies, between Western societies and some African communities, for example, or between official and clandestine factions of the French and German resistance during the Second World War, which avoided or destroyed written evidence. Nora refers rather to the distinction between 'spontaneous' memory preceding and 'unnatural' memory succeeding the crisis of the 1930s, before and after the crumbling of French republican tradition which had been upheld by the institutions of the Third Republic and effective historical education. The switch from natural collective memory as a support for national historical tradition to private memories supported by particular social symbols, from spontaneous to archival or 'prosthesis' memory, is expressed by Nora as a fall from the grace of consensual or collective memory, where history, via the historian 'half preacher, half soldier' (ibid: 11; XXIIf), played a sacred role in the maintenance of national memory. *Les Lieux de mémoire* is a response to this rupture, a recasting of national history as politically inert 'memorial patrimony'.

Second, what political assumptions underlie the conception and organization of memory in the 'archive' *Les Lieux de mémoire,* a wide-ranging collection of genealogical studies affording historical insight into cultural landmarks? Nora presents contemporary France as a purely symbolic reality, an open configuration of cultural focal points in an 'à la carte' France (Nora 1993a: 30), from which each individual may construct a personal 'menu' of memories. The very structure of the seven-volume publication therefore reflects Nora's political programme. Its sheer bulk (130 essays) surpasses the reader's capacity to gain an overview and renders futile any attempt to read this history from cover to cover as a narrative chronology. It therefore engages the reader in the active selection and construction of a personal palette of historical identities while maintaining a sense of mystique by obscuring the precise historical theme of the project behind a generic title indicative of method *(Les Lieux de mémoire)*, whose theme is therefore necessarily diffuse, a collection of particulars: plural, and therefore variable and inexhaustible by definition. 'Les France' is also plural, while 'The Republic' and 'The Nation' are historically determined, if not anachronistic, for they no longer fit Nora's conception of France as an expression of memory and identity. *Les Lieux de mémoire* therefore presents a radical attempt to dispense with traditional political categorisations of France, if not with definitions outright (ibid: 23). Nora rejects republican principles, is sceptical towards the 'authoritarian', 'unitarian', 'exclusionist' and 'universalist' (Nora 1984d: 652f) character of the Republic, and therefore subsumes political definitions of the nation, based on territory, universal suffrage and constitutional principles of citizenship, to the cultural dimension of memory.

Although Nora's pluralist model of 'national memory' is conceived as an alternative to coercive republican 'national history' (Nora 1993d: 1010), it nevertheless reflects the republican model of cultural integration. In spite of the radical qualitative rupture in memory, the criterion common to the memories projected in *Les Lieux de mémoire* remains the nation. According to Nora, memory is all-pervasive and neutralises division. 'Gaullists and Communists', 'The French and Foreigners' or 'Catholics and Laymen' are each presented as *single* places of memory, as cultural appropriations of a politically inert past. Some of the most stirring symbols of French culture during the 1980s and 1990s such as the 'Islamic veil' or the 'suburb' (resulting from controversies over Muslim schoolgirls claiming the right to wear the veil in secular state schools or over social unrest in the immigrant ghettos of large cities) (Gaspard & Khosrokhavar 1995) are absent from *Les Lieux de mémoire,* however. Their political pertinence has not been subsumed to patrimonial memory. These concerted expressions of post-colonial challenges to French cultural uniformity, like the broad *(infra-, inter-* or *supra*national) spectrum of symbolic events and commemorations such as those triggered by the fiftieth anniversaries of the Second World War, therefore challenge the conventional national boundaries of memory in *Les Lieux de mémoire.* Nevertheless, Nora's historiographical innovations – the implications of 'social', 'archival' or 'historiographical' consciousness and of the 'historical present' – provide remarkable insight into the mechanisms of contemporary social memory by which events from the past become part of the present.

Notes

1. For a selection of essays from this work in English, see Nora, P. (1997–) *The Realms of Memory: The Construction of the French Past*, New York: Columbia University Press (trans. Arthur Goldhammer) (three volumes: Volume I. (1997) 'Conflicts and Divisions').
2. Samuel bases his definition of popular memory as 'unofficial knowledge' on a critique of what he refers to as Nora's 'official' places of memory (Samuel 1995: 11). Although Nora's inventory of places of memory is indeed structured within the framework of French national memory, to call them 'official' suggests unfairly that they are imposed by dictate. Samuel's polarization of social memory into 'official' and 'unofficial' categories overlooks the liberal political convictions underlying Nora's insistence on the pluralist and fragmented nature of memories loosely classified as 'French'.
3. Nora's definition of *milieu* (environment) is founded on a sense of nostalgia for a time when history may have been experienced directly or 'immediately', i.e. without the medium of places of memory such as commemorations or museum exhibitions. For a succinct account of Nora's interpretation of the dichotomy between modern and pre-modern memory, see Wood (1994: 127). Patrick H. Hutton identifies a similar distinction in terms of postmodern and modern memory (Hutton 1993: 22).
4. Cf. Nora (1993a: 29): 'As if France ceased to be a history dividing us and became a culture uniting us [. . .].'
5. Organised by State administrations, these events sought to generate public consensus, yet often created division: paradoxically, they provoked and were occasionally overshadowed by particularist 'social' interests.
6. Translation slightly modified.
7. Cf. Paul Connerton's study of the role of 'bodily' or 'incorporated' social memory (Connerton 1989).

Bibliography

Connerton, Paul (1989), *How Societies Remember*, Cambridge: Cambridge University Press.

François, Étienne (1995), 'Von der wiedererlangten Nation zur "Nation wider Willen". Kann man eine Geschichte der deutschen "Erinnerungsorte"schreiben?', in E.François, H. Siegrist & J. Vogel (eds) *Nation und Emotion*, Göttingen: Vandenhoeck & Ruprecht, 93–105.

François, E. et al. (1995), 'Die Nation. Vorstellungen, Inszenierungen, Emotionen', in *Nation und Emotion*, 13–35.

Furet, François (1993), 'L'Ancien Régime et la Révolution', in *Les lieux de mémoire*, III. *Les France* 1, 106–83.

Gaspard, Françoise and Khosrokhavar, Farhad (1995), *Le Foulard et la République*, Paris: La Découverte.

Hartog, François (1995), 'Temps et histoire. "Comment écrire l'histoire de France?"', in *Annales HSS* 6, 1219–36.

Hutton, Patrick H. (1993), *History as an Art of Memory*, Hanover & London: Vermont University Press.

Namer, Gérard (1987), *Mémoire et Société*, Paris: Klincksieck.

Nora, Pierre (1978), 'Le présent', in J. Le Goff et al. (eds) *La nouvelle histoire*, 467–72.

—— (ed.) (1984–93), *Les Lieux de mémoire*, 7 vols.: (1984) I. *La République*; (1986) II. *La Nation* (1, 2, 3); (1993) III. *Les France* (1, 2, 3), Paris: Gallimard.

—— (1984a), 'Présentation', in *Les Lieux de mémoire*, I. *La République*, VII–XIII.

—— (1984b), 'Entre mémoire et histoire. La problématique des lieux', in *Les Lieux de mémoire*, I. *La République*, XVII–XLII.

—— (1984c), 'Le *Dictionnaire de pédagogie* de Ferdinand Buisson', in *Les Lieux de mémoire*, I. *La République*, 353–78.

—— (1984d), 'De la république à la nation', in *Les Lieux de mémoire*, I. *La République*, 651–59.

—— (1986a), 'Présentation', in *Les Lieux de mémoire*, II. *La Nation* 1, IX–XXI.

—— (1986b), 'La nation-mémoire', in *Les Lieux de mémoire*, II. *La Nation* 3, 647–58.

—— (1989), 'Between Memory and History: *Les Lieux de Mémoire*' (trans. Marc Roudebush) in *Representations* 26, 7–25.

—— (1993a), 'Comment écrire l'histoire de France?', in *Les Lieux de mémoire*, III. *Les France* 1, 11–32.

—— (1993b), 'La génération', in *Les Lieux de mémoire, III. Les France* 1, 931–71.

—— (1993c), 'Présentation', in *Les Lieux de mémoire, III. Les France* 3, 13–16.

—— (1993d), 'L'ère de la commémoration', in *Les Lieux de mémoire, III. Les France* 3, 977–1012.

—— (1993e), 'De l'histoire contemporaine au présent historique', in Institut d'Histoire du Temps Présent, *Écrire l'histoire du temps présent,* Paris: Éditions du CNRS, 43–7.

—— (1995), 'Das Abenteuer der *Lieux de mémoire* ', in François, E. et al. (eds) *Nation und Emotion*, 83–92.

Ozouf, Mona (1984), 'Le Panthéon', in *Les Lieux de mémoire, I. La République,* 139–66.

Samuel, Raphael (1995), *Theatres of Memory: Past and Present in Contemporary British Culture*, London & New York: Verso.

Winter, Jay (1995), *Sites of Memory, Sites of Mourning: The Great War in European Memory,* Cambridge: Cambridge University Press.

Wood, Nancy (1994), 'Memory's Remains: *Les Lieux de mémoire*', in *History and Memory* 1, 123–49.

3

Reinscriptions: Commemoration, Restoration and the Interpersonal Transmission of Histories and Memories under Modern States in Asia and Europe
Stephan Feuchtwang

This essay describes a comparative project whose aim is to deepen understanding of the link between social and personal memory as active processes. It is a project which I have designed but into which I would welcome others. The more case studies to compare, the better.[1]

The project will deal with the gaps and links between very different histories: the links between social memory, life history and nation-formation. Gaps of scale between the state system, the nation and family histories and possibly an incommensurability of concepts of personal identification and nation-formation are its problems, since the encompassing scale is sometimes sought as an authorisation of inter-personal memory.

Focus on Cataclysmic Events; Links between the Ordinary and the Extraordinary

One way of addressing the gap between the politics of nation-formation and life stories is to focus on what I call cataclysmic events. Cataclysmic events are a limit condition: the annihilation of history and the destruction of personality. Like all strokes of fortune and personal loss they invoke languages of sacredness surrounding death and discontinuity between the dead and the living. Languages and commemorations try to cross that discontinuity between historical and eternal time, across lives ended and beginning, but here across a massive discontinuity. The proposition which this project will explore and test is that such upheavals become points of reference for collective being, events which can be called 'total' in that they focus the attention of all biographies within a population however geographically defined – a large or a small place – studding its memories. Less destructive focal events are single deaths and funerals, such as the shooting of President Kennedy or the crash of Princess Diana. But wars, occupations and other occasions of mass slaughter or massive dislocation and destruction are arguably more potent focal events precisely because they are more destructive (as the Shoah has become a foundation of Jewish identity and of the state of Israel, or as testimonies of deportation to the Soviet Gulag have become foundations for the Baltic nations (Skultans 1997)).

Reconstruction includes reviving the record of what had been suppressed or silenced in the conditions before and giving rise to the cataclysm as well as during it. The revitalisation of pasts which had been silenced is not only the story of the birth of all nations (civil war and revolution, mobilising class, religious, and ethnic identities). It is their continuing story and a hostage to further dangers of silence, exclusion and explosive focal events, as well as the prehistories of what might just be a new politics of inclusion and reconciliation.

Erased and New Memory — Rumour, Terror, Demonisation

Let me start with demonisation, because it is so obvious an element of the sacred language of group memory formation. Demonisation will have its roots in established practices of accusation and accountability which can range from rituals of exorcism to feuds, raids, and wars, from religious cosmologies to ideological dogmas defining a centred world and its outer margins. Demonisation of people who can be distanced, and have a history of having been distanced, is frequently given a racial or ethnic character which fixes and licenses their victimisation adding to and prolonging a political or economic crisis.

Victims of the Cultural Revolution movements in China were often labelled 'ghosts' and 'demons'. 'Haunting' and 'demonisation' travel across all reference points, European and non-European. Ghosts and demons are objects of rites of exorcism and of sorcery, which in an Enlightenment tradition we exoticise. There are good reasons for bringing them home. Two elaborations of what they convey have, I think, gone further than any others. Both make excessive violence intelligible as an effect of a blurring of testable truth in which paranoid fantasies are transmitted and become images of hate and fascination.

Michael Taussig (1987: 134), referring to the colonisation of Amazonian countries, describes the reports by colonial investigators of the extremes of violence perpetrated on 'Indians' by colonists and their militia, and how the reports themselves transmitted the same fantasies which the perpetrators knew as reality. In summary, 'the savagery attributed to the Indians by the colonists' was perpetrated by the colonists in the name of civilisation. Demonisation occurs in what he calls 'epistemic and onto-logical murk', namely in cultures of rumour, fantasy and terror:

> All societies live by fiction taken as real. What distinguishes cultures of terror is that the epistemological, ontological, and otherwise philosophical problem of representation – reality and illusion, certainty and doubt – becomes infinitely more than a 'merely' philosophical problem of epistemology, hermeneutics, and deconstruction. It becomes a high-powered medium of domination, and during the Putumayo rubber boom this medium of epistemic and ontological murk was most keenly figured into consciousness as the space of death . . . Tenaciously embedded in this artful practice [of storytelling by the colonists] is a vast and vastly mysterious Western history and iconography of evil exemplified by the imagery of the inferno and the savage, which in turn is indissolubly wedded to images of paradise and good (134).

Such storytelling has more recently been linked to social memory of events which is an unfinished understanding. Veena Das (1998) notes that slaughters of Sikhs after the assassination of Indira Ghandi in 1984 were linked to stories of Operation Blue Star, the Indian army's forcible entry into the holiest Sikh place, the Golden Temple of Amritsar, earlier that year, and to images of communal slaughter at the time of partition in 1947. The past event is described in entirely different ways by distinct agencies and understood in opposing ways by different audiences: 'For each element of the story, there were allegations and counter-allegations. The narrative's unfinished character meant that the event lived on in different versions in the social memory of different social groups' (Das 1998: 118). This splitting of a past event into selected and opposed memories is more than commonplace indeterminacy. When rumours begin to spread of a crisis of state or a collapse of order, present suspicion and circulation of stories

> suddenly become the site in which elements of the past that were rejected, in the sense that they were not integrated into a stable understanding of the past, can press upon the world with the same insistence and obstinacy with which the real creates holes in the symbolic (ibid: 126).

This is a remarkably similar analysis to the crisis of representation which Michael Taussig calls murk, in which fantasy and reality are blurred and fears of the fantastic are acted upon, by defensive killing and exorcistic torture and dismemberment of the threatening victim. Stories without

authorship circulate as expectations of the worst. They have a perlocu-
tionary force, which is a voyeuristic pleasure in hearing them and a compulsion to pass them on, constructing panic and a hardening of empathy:

> Doubts and uncertainties exist in everyday life, but the worst is not what one
> expects to happen every time. In contrast, the zones of emergency are marked
> by diffused images of an unfinished past, efforts to void the other of all
> subjectivity, and a world increasingly peopled with a phantasmagoria of
> shadows (Das 1998: 126).

Instead of an individuation of people threatening violence, rumours
totalise them into a named aggregate with the characters of madness,
insensate capacity to withstand pain, and conspiracy to kill and take over.
They gain veracity from militants' own defensive calls for readiness to
strike (martyrdom), themselves produced by acts of wilful forgetting (in
this case of the closeness of Sikhs and Hindus and of joint wrongdoing
at the time of partition). '[T]he militant discourse travelled to the Hindu
constructions in giving form to rumours which in turn made brutal
violence against the Sikhs a "thinkable" response, even for those who
did not directly participate in the violence' (ibid: 124).

Crises of representation and reality create a difficulty and a responsibility for the empathetic third person who is historian and anthropologist.
For Taussig both difficulty and responsibility are the unfinished business
of de-mythification and re-enchantment of our (Western) selves and
otherness, and of accommodating the 'voice' which we record and represent. The second part of his book recounts meetings with Indian shamans
who are healers, including colonists among their patients. These healers
exorcise phantoms in a perspective where the mysterious and the terrible
is everyday – with expectations of violence and its inclusion in healing,
unacceptable and inexplicable in the terms by which we must seek to
represent them. Taussig seeks in various European sources (Kant, Benjamin,
Barthes, Bakhtin) ways to account for the improvisatory dialogue between
patient and shamanic healer and for his own account which he calls 'the
articulation of implicit social knowledge' (Taussig 1987: 460–7). It is
wrong to represent the shaman's knowledge as a system; it is a performance and an improvisation between a healer who stands for certainty and
a patient voicing confusion. So is his own account a dialogue and an
improvisation. Taussig leaves to a reader his encounter with obtuse meaning. At the same time, however, he escapes epistemological murk to say
what was the dominion enabled by murk and he conveys a strong sense
of what he understands the reality of the occurrence of violence and death
to have been.

Das (1998) has to deal with the same difficulty of representation. In a footnote she comments:

> I am tempted to say that the 'objective' conditions did not warrant this fear of a plot against the whole of society being hatched by Sikhs. But the problem in this essay is precisely to see a crisis by placing oneself within it and to explain how categories of people who are themselves vulnerable come to be attributed with such evil powers (ibid:128).

On the other hand she too can write with utter certainty that in this instance 'it was the Sikhs on whom the violence was being unleashed' (ibid: 125). This, it seems to me, is an inescapable responsibility. While it leaves articulation of the stories and the question of healing to a self-questioning dialogue, the third position at the same time listens and hears sides split from each other and hears and describes the split. Beyond that it tells its own story of events as far as they can be verified by the accounts and records which must be sought and checked assiduously.

It is also obvious that both Taussig and Das do more than retell stories. They contribute to understanding the processes which give rise to outbreaks of mass violence and so have a practical implication. They contribute to early warnings of such disasters in the future. Reconstructing what occurred and what went on in the preceding months and years leading up to victimisation, they focus on the way ritualised memories perform acts of healing or, on the contrary, harbour hostages to further violence.

The main insight I will add to this from my Chinese studies is that the heroes of popular cults in China have as an essential component the fact that they have died what are normally, that is by the norms of a complete life, conceived to be bad deaths. The cults that surround such heroes stand alongside other ways of ritually coping with bad deaths, which include massacres in rebellion or its suppression, communal warfare, or the deaths of the childless. Though they are unremembered, such deaths are located and imbued with an amoral or malignant power that needs to be exorcised or propitiated. The gods of popular cults are those who are named and remembered for having used this amoral, possibly malignant power for good, particularly for the righteous protection of a locality. They are commemorated in exorcistic festivals.

Such traditions will always contain conventions and ideas of what a good death is and of how a bad death should therefore be treated. But cataclysmic events test such ideas and conventions beyond endurance. Recovery from them and commemoration of them are likely to be improvised, and to run the danger of denial and of unfinished or unassimilable grief and shame.

Such events are points of reference for the telling and retelling of personal involvement or of witness from sidelines. Either acknowledged or ignored in larger histories and commemorations, they retell the larger versions and alter them in different genres and intimacies of transmission. They enter the present and its issues, defining criteria of conduct which bind and distance: criteria of honour, shame, accountability, trust and truth (good examples are to be found in Tonkin 1990 and Werbner 1995). Cataclysmic events are points of engagement between different authorities of inscription – state, local, and cross-border identifications. Focal events for a locality may be compatible with or crucially incompatible and excluded from focal, cataclysmic events of a greater totality whose commemoration purports to include them or is simply indifferent to them.

In sum, the project will focus on transmissions, and on the incompatibilities and potential conflicts of authority which their transmission involves.

Memory and Transmission: Archive

A key problem to be addressed is the recognition of inter-personal memory transmission by more powerful social commemoration and historiography, and of local by national memory, and therefore of course by the converse, denial or miscognition and exclusion which can silence and annihilate memories.

'Archive' is a term for the authoritative storing and inscription of memory. Writing of archive as a process and an act, and their symbioses with never-to-be-captured live memory in its own moment, Jacques Derrida's small book, *Archive Fever* (1996), provides an appropriate epigraph to this project. It is appropriate specifically through its linking of the external with the internal, the performative with the psychic, of authority with agency, without reducing them to each other. Archive, as Derrida says, is a prosthesis of memory, that which is already there as its inscription and as its residue. It is also memory's externality and its appropriation, the destruction of memory at the same time as the preservation of memory as record. Authorised from outside it can spell death and chaos. Yet at the same time the act of archival registration is at the origin of memory, just as the death drive is as originary as the pleasure principle. Archive is at once an order – a consignment – a commemoration and a collection; it is a power to establish the authority of foundation, which is destructive of a previous order, as in canon, or school, or religion, or nation. Psychically, the archive is a reworking and an impression on previous memory, yet it is that by which memory is lived; censoring, repressing, but also directing and sorting lived memory.

The social act of historiography, or of memoir and biography, or simply of marking a grave, inscribes and by the same act leaves out personal memory. Beside such inscription there is also the inter-personal transmission of memories. They too are transmitted situationally, and in genres ranging from those established in a family mythology to the standard repertoires of recording and transmitting events, remembering what to respect and what to deplore. However formulaic, each inscription varies what it re-inscribes. In all cases there is a destruction or obliteration of personal memory, parallel to the destruction and obliteration which occurs in the course of a person's living experience even as they name it (let alone recall it later).

Inscription and transmission are necessarily destructive as well as creative transformations of personal memory into history and monument. Conversely, biography, memorial and other kinds of social memory are emblems, models and genres for personal history. Occasions for telling and hearing the tale of a memory cross intervals between more than one lived memory which share a point of reference, a point which acts as a solicitation of a past. But another moment goes beyond such shared memory. Between generations, lived memories are transmitted from beyond the grave. Intergenerational transmission of memories is intimate yet parental and like memorial and history or tradition bears the authority of a life-giver and of fate – a haunting carried in the formation of habits and anxieties. This familial process of recognition and omission is likely to be gendered, a different transmission by men and women, by mothers and fathers, to daughters and to sons. Female transmission is likely to be less accommodated to or acknowledged by public commemoration except in the treasuring of the Family and its female progenitor, themselves. But this too will vary between commemorative traditions and the ways they are stretched to cope with unprecedented events in which the female as victim and agent is involved.

Learning a history is to learn a sense of the past and how it maps onto a graded sense of belonging and of separateness. Children learn from several sources, home, school, peers, how to live in an environment of historical references and so to associate themselves with certain time-frames. Taken together with time-focused cyclical events and processes of daily and seasonal life these references teach a sense of personal-self and associated-self made by or making history in some spatial scope and to some limited degree.

Maurice Bloch (1998: Chapter 7) makes two points which help in the avoidance of cultural wholism and relativism. With the help of vivid examples, Bloch argues that for any one subject there are several registers of transmission which may represent the same event, from the repetition of myth, through the formulaic telling of key events, to the detailed and anecdotal, and much else. Memory is a faculty, cognitive and emotional, common to them all and confined to no single one of them. With each of our subjects we will be dealing with several registers of the archiving and transmission of memory. Such registers may or may not be compatible with each other. We should not assume that incompatibility is a source of conflict or tension, of denial or exclusion. That will have to be detected empirically.

My guiding thought, however, is that these registers of memory will be affected by nation-formation and its stimulus of demands for recognition. In other words the transmissions of our subjects interact with another kind of authority. This authority, which is often narrative but which is also that of town planning, architecture, commercial image-making and art, is often called 'official'. Nations forge their political and cultural identities as well as the personal identities of their populations through the accumulation of immense archives of record and conservation and by the activation of those archives in academic and popular historical and biographical writing, heritage tourism, commemoration, and the forging of traditions. Both the accumulation of archives and their activation continue indefinitely. The material substrata and the stories of heritage and event are constantly under reconstruction. Collective and personal identities are reworked in the same processes. They are formed by exclusion as well as by inclusion.

Running between all is the work of historians, politicians, and humanitarian and other pressure groups. The work of the proposed project is a further inscription, tracing a new route between them. 'Herodotus thought of historians as the guardians of memory, the memory of glorious deeds. I prefer to see historians as the guardians of awkward facts, the skeletons in the cupboard of the social memory' Peter Burke (1989: 110). Two issues for enquiry arise here. The first concerns how focal events are recorded, commemorated and told and by what institutions. The second concerns the flexibility, tolerance of ambiguity and capacity for variation and inclusion which such institutions of commemoration and transmission allow.

Method: Comparative Case Studies

Turning now to the way to pursue such an enquiry, I will start with a simple statement of the research tasks involved in this project. Next I will discuss problems of comparison and selection. Beyond these practical considerations, I shall address some of the more profound problems of methodology which this project entails. Since my proposal is not just for myself but also for others, I will from here onwards use the plural of the first and second persons, inviting critical participation.

Note that this is a project for revisits to research sites with which you are already acquainted, or it is a project which would come at the end of another field study in a place in whose recent past there was a focal, cataclysmic event.

Research Tasks

1. From previous research, but also continuing throughout the new period of research by observation of shrines, monuments, and rites and by conversation and interview, determine (a) formal distinctions and (b) personal views of what constitutes a good death, what constitutes a bad death and how each are marked. Pay particular attention to mass graves and monuments, and to any changes in the rites and commemorations in the period before and after the cataclysmic event.

2. Again from previous research, record as much as possible the times and manner in which the cataclysmic event was ever mentioned by selected households (see sub-section below on Subject Selection) and by others.

3. In renewing acquaintance with the selected households, return to previous topics but not the specific event, in order to provide a fresh context in which any further mention of the event might take place and be noted.

4. Engage the household members if possible one by one, in remembering the cataclysmic event, noting reactions and how it is remembered. Ask each how they know about it. Ask each of the youngest generation how, if they know anything, they were told about it. Ask each of the older generations whether they have told the younger about it; if they have, ask them when and how this was done.

5. Start the process proper of engaging the subjects of research in the new inscription instigated by this research project, i.e. in what Alessandro Portelli has called the genre specific to oral history, a consecutive and sustained inscription, and thus not a spontaneous fragment but a 'history-telling' (1998: 25): (a) bring together the subjects' own archive of documents, photos, and other materials of the event, (b) ask them each to tell

it, in their own terms even though they are unlikely to have done so in a concerted way and with this particular audience.

As far as possible each member of the household should be asked to give their own account. If some are not willing or show no interest, probe their indifference by asking them to compare their attitude with others' overt interest. If some are interested but only together with another, take the joint story noting the contributions of each to it.

It is important to take every opportunity to note (a) how the audience for the retelling is perceived, and (b) what mythic or other rhetorical and genre models might be at the disposal of the tellers and used in the narration. But our responsibility goes further. We must check the story against the archive of the household and against other archives and narratives. It will be impossible to do this in every detail, but we will be responsible for constructing our own narrative of cross-checked veracity among conflicting accounts. The focal points of the project for comparing domestic archives and narratives with more general and collective ones (see 7. below) are events which have caused great harm, so we bear a responsibility to establish as well-grounded an account of these as we can. This will include weighing up the responsibility of various agencies and persons for the conditions and processes which gave rise to the event. Blame will certainly be assigned in the accounts we are given by our subjects and by the more collective inscriptions with which we compare them. We bear the responsibility of weighing them up, and going some way towards an account of the conditions, processes and agencies which brought about great harm (Feuchtwang 1998).

6. Of those known to household members as relatives, friends or acquaintances who died or disappeared in the event, ask how they were first commemorated and with what rites, and how their memories were subsequently marked and kept if at all. If rites occur during the period of research, observe and record them. In any case visit graves and shrines, both on your own to note the setting and details and also with the subjects of research, noting their responses. Ask them if (and if so how) the memorial and rites differ from those for deaths before and after the event.

There may be other restorations of what had been destroyed such as visits to sites of key events, which are themselves prompts for re-inscription, or the physical embodiment of a social memory such as domestic treasures or the very structure of a house (Bloch 1998: Chapter 6).

7. After 2–5 there will have been ample opportunity for any references which could have been made by the subjects to archives, narratives,

memorials, rites, anniversaries or fictional and documentary reconstructions which are not their own. All these should be noted carefully.

It is important to add to them any others which we can find or already know about, but note carefully which of these could have been known to our subjects but were not mentioned. The point here is to include what our subjects ignored or avoided.

It will not be possible to copy or fully describe each and every one. Make copies or give full descriptions only of the ones most frequently or emphatically mentioned, and those most obviously ignored by our subjects.

8. From each household select the most articulate and forthcoming, history-tellers in chief, and at least one from a younger or an older generation to re- or for the first time read, visit, or see the selected inscriptions and commemorations. How do they compare their own accounts and commemorations with each of the more general and collective examples?

9. Follow links of further reference from these selected inscriptions and commemorations to state-level, national and possibly inter- or cross-national ones, for further comparison and response by subjects and by ourselves. In particular, the most prevalent media of transmission should be selected: schooling, mass media, and centres of pilgrimage.

Conduct of Oral Historical Interviews

We are necessarily engaged in acts of conversion between genres – our's being those of oral history, life story, and ethnography. We set the terms and topics of interviews by our purpose and presence, but at the same time we are there to learn about the conventions and ways of talking and the transmission of memory which our subjects use. We negotiate with the genres and conventions of telling and of ordering the tale which our subjects find natural. Their choice will to some extent be affected by their having slotted us into expected roles. Recording the difficulties experienced by our subjects, the awkwardness and pauses in their responses is as important as recording their words. Pauses, hesitations, slowing, speeding and emphases should be registered because they indicate feelings, embarrassments. We must make educated guesses at all of these.

Comparison

Two major problems of method for this programme are how to establish a basis for comparing case studies and within each case study how to select from the stock of social memory what will be compared with the more intimate transmissions which the research itself will inscribe. Here is how I propose to deal with the first of these problems. The next section will indicate how I propose to deal with selection.

Comparison rests on a working hypothesis. It is that commemoration and transmission of cataclysmic events will challenge and transform the narrative conventions of nation-formation and local traditions of dealing with bad deaths.

1. Possibly the most authoritative registers of recognition and denial are those authorised by state institutions and by rival media of nation-formation. If religious institutions produce distinct registers, then they are likely to be equally authoritative, and the relations between state and religious registers is an extremely important topic in this research. Beside school curriculi, museums, histories, and memorials, other genres to take into account include memoir, fiction, biography and historiography whose narrative conventions are similar to or take as their points of departure those of nation-formation. That is to say they start out from the convention and assumption of a relativity of languages and their speakers and of histories and their subjects, as if they were communities of a mass population with a collective biography. At the same time, as Snead (1990) and Wollen (1994) have remarked, that very relativity also brings about a cosmopolitan, trans-national mode of inscription, disrupting and infecting narrative convention. From the earliest to the latest days of modernism, an eclectic or cosmopolitan mixing has developed alongside conventions of historical tradition, monument, vernacular realist narrative and the clichés of ethnic and national stereotyping in news media and tourism. But this only indicates the counterpoint of modernism and of nation-formation, rather than two separate processes. That counterpoint is the common basis of comparison between any two parts of the globe. Above all, the peculiar character of nation-formation is not just a relativity of centrisms. Whereas in the pre-national past it was more usual for contiguous histories and religions to be simply strangers to each other (e.g. Jewish and Catholic in Poland), nation-formation represents the demand for recognition by the other and by more authoritative, usually state but also international organisations.

Conventions of nation-formation as demonstrated by textual analysis must inform our comparison. But our studies will be enquiries into another kind of disruption or silence than those sought by critical analysis of literary and other media products. We will be studying narratives, rites and monuments which, by the convention of a mass subject, purport to include and provide recognition. Our question is whether they indeed deny, silence or are indifferent to inscriptions and memories within that mass subject. In the other direction, our question is whether the recognition, indifference or inconsistency between transmissions is a matter of concern or simply of different registers and genres of transmission. We will find that there are different traditions, including traditions of fiction and historiography, but mainly those of eulogy, obituary, and death rites incorporated into the conventions of nation-formation authorised in the settings of our case studies. This brings us to the second basis of comparison which is our main basis of differentiation.

2. Our comparisons will dwell on the tradition of death ritual, and in particular *the commemoration and means of exorcising bad deaths, and of turning them to good*. Traditions of death ritual and exorcism or healing – removal of evil or laying of ghosts, absorption of grief and grievance – are universal but they differ by locality within any one country and even more by country, where 'country' simply means a geographical space in which orthodoxies can be and have been set apart and reproduced. Accompanying death ritual are the ways nation founders and re-founders celebrate their heroes, martyrs and soldiers and the events (marches, parades, bonfire nights, etc.) which honour and shame them, themselves innovations built upon dynastic, princely or other pre-national state traditions of commemorating ancestors, triumphs and demons.

Selection

Selection of materials will be done by the links of reference stemming from the field sites and households selected.

Field Site Selection

Each site should present a definable location, by which I mean a theatre for landmarks of a shared past. Selection of a field site will depend on an established familiarity with it by researchers involved in this programme. We will select sites which have already been studied, and in which the customary death rituals are already recorded knowledge. Selection will necessarily also be determined by involvement of the field site in a cataclysmic event with clear human agency.

Subject Selection

Within each field site, choose four households with which you or a close intermediary has already established a relationship of trust. The household should contain three or more generations or be in close contact with a third generation of the family.

The definition of a household is deliberately loose. It is a domestic unit in which co-residents meet frequently in their everyday life: neighbouring households who do not share cooking facilities but frequently meet or eat together can be included. The point is to be able to observe the odd occasion in everyday life when past events are recalled by those who live with each other or are on terms of intimate contact.

Where those involved in the event can easily be distinguished into perpetrators and victims or into participants and victims, or into bystanders and victims, two households from each side should be chosen. Each pair should be from contrasting statuses of wealth, honour or education, however that was distinguished in the context of the site at the time of the event. It may be impossible to find descendants of victims at the site of their residence at the time of the event. In that case, households as near as possible should be found, where 'near' means in closest possible communication with the original site and with local inscriptions and commemorations of the event. Their distance, the silences or blanks in their memories, may in addition be compared with others who have moved or been removed even further. But this is optional.

Distances near or far question the limits of location, assumed in the idea of a field site. I retain the idea because some territorial mapping and point of reference is always drawn in memories of 'home' and 'grave'. They may, however, be several and separate, more than one home for one person's memories. A grave or memorial may not be in the same place as the home of the commemorated. Nevertheless, any one 'home', grave or monument will be in a mappable place of shared memory whose foci are familiar landmarks.

Drawing Boundaries

Since the topic includes the way boundaries and categorisations are drawn, it is important that we neither draw them in from our own assumptions nor simply confirm the preconceptions made in the stories we hear. The stories will probably refer to times long past and a common sense of identity and difference as if it had always been there, but this should be understood as a trope which fixes and hallows identification, not as an historical fact.

It is particularly important not to assume the definition of social boundaries, neither those of nations which states engender or which have been realised as states, nor those which could be described by the term ethnicity. Too often we all (psychologists, social scientists, advisers, journalists, parents, friends) resort to an assumed group solidarity as if it were always there (by kinship, ethnicity, religious community, shared history or genetic similarity). The assumption hinders, even blocks out any understanding of the processes of identification and intransigence which are involved. It seems to, but it does not explain the violence of emotion and the act of belonging or of hatred. Situations of crisis and disaster make use of social memory, which includes memories of community, institutions and associations to maintain it, and memories of its invasion or its being threatened by traditional enemies. But the lines drawn and the content of distinctiveness change, are adapted to new circumstances.

Transcripts

I turn now to an intriguing theme which is likely to arise in such a project: what James Scott (1990) calls 'transcripts'. I prefer the more active terms, re-inscription and transmission, emphasising a process and the need to include more gradations of inscription than Scott's dramatic opposition of official inscription and hidden transcription.

Humphrey (1994) has added to Scott's 'public' and 'hidden' transcripts another kind of transcript which she calls 'evocative', thereby initiating further distinctions between different kinds of hegemony and their ambiguities within which memories are inscribed and transmitted. She makes the necessary distinction between hidden transcripts closed off from public transcripts and evocative transcripts in which all members and subjects of a regime are at once dominators and dominated. Stories of dexterity in the use of official discourse (public transcripts) with other than official meanings are retold at every level of domination. Hidden, evocative, and other kinds of transcript yet to be distinguished will exist in various balances within any one hegemony, from the sharp lines of colonialism with which Scott deals and the tightly controlled ones of state socialism about which Humphrey writes, to fascist and other terrorist authorities, to the looser but powerful hegemonies of corporate consumer capitalism.

Within a state, local inclusion is ambiguous. Herzfeld notes the play between the fixity of national stereotypes and the ironies of situational and ambiguous identifications using the same terms 'civilised' and 'barbarian', 'Greek' and 'Turkish' (Herzfeld 1997: 47–9). These ambiguities are a kind of evocative transcription. Herzfeld has coined the term 'cultural intimacy' for the way social actors reformulate and recast official idioms in the familiarity of their encounters with outsiders and functionaries, using self-stereotypes of national character to exploit to the full their ambiguity and potential for irony and the failures of their own and official ideals (ibid: 2–4). Cultural intimacy, like evocative transcripts of various kinds is a mode of inclusion in all regimes, not necessarily a resistance nor an exclusion. We will need to examine when they are exclusive and incompatible.

The figures and stories we see and hear will convey standards and characteristics of honour and shame. They will transmit criteria of judging what is good and what is condemned. They will tell what can be expected (and what is conventionally established as realism) and what is therefore to be gained, what to be feared. All these are judgments by which domestic relationships and associations of friendship and the institutions of affiliation and alliance work. At the same time they are the intimate means of holding state institutions accountable. The frequently invoked analogy of home and parent with the supraordinate collectivity of a nation and its constituent localities (home town, mother country, fatherland) is not simply metaphoric. The greater community is represented in as well as by the smaller. But it is interpretable in several ways. The lesser is contrasted with as well as included in the greater.

Apart from ambiguity, evocative transcripts are, as Humphrey points out, ritualised and snapshot, out of the time of the consecutive histories which offer a past and a future for a political project and its subjects. 'Evocative' characterises all the very different genres of myth and of joke, or of the figure of a monster or a hero which encapsulates more than one story. It disrupts biography, history and narrative fiction more than it does ritual or theatre. Yet it is the quality that makes them vivid and memorable. Evocative transcription has its genres, themselves transmitted in cultural traditions within the different kinds of hegemony; it attaches itself to, subverts and occasionally recomposes public transcripts.

Our interviews will induce consecutive stories and we will have to tell our own reconstructions of events. But we will also be engaged in an articulation with mythic imagery and its performative effects, making improvisatory demands on whatever resources of representation we bring in.

Conclusion

Primo Levi (1988: 13) recalls a recurring dream which most survivors of the Shoah had, of returning home and with passion and relief describing their suffering, only to find they were not believed. In the cruellest and most typical ending, the loved interlocutor turns and leaves in silence. The holocaust was itself an archival act, with monuments and rituals of heroic national-racial pride and the demonisation of its enemies. The companionship of those who have similarly suffered a uniquely incommunicable or unhearable cruelty is forgotten in the glorified commemoration of justified violence. There is always an interplay between justification of violence and the cruelty of its infliction on the powerless. The heroic is disturbed by the incommunicability of cruelty.

Cruelty is incommunicable for different reasons by perpetrators and victims. Perpetrators are unable to acknowledge it, but quite possibly resent the shame or have no way to mourn the loss of a previous identity with the images of pride since repudiated by defeat and international opprobrium, shared by subsequent generations. Victims defend against the devastating feelings engendered by violation of the boundaries of their senses and the abjection of their selves. How this works itself out will differ according to the inscriptions of memory which preceded the violence and the invention of new forms of commemoration and new ways of telling the story after it.

The silence of the unspeakable and the unhearable can be commemorated. Designers of Holocaust memorials have tried to build the space of that silence and for that silence (e.g. Liebeskind in Berlin and Whiteread in Vienna). They are a healing – or a saving – acknowledgment of silence and cruelty, a retrieval with regret. The most common such retrieval is a simple listing of names whose personal memories cannot be known, any more than can those in a graveyard, but which thus massed together indicate the scale of the atrocious loss. The effort of naming them is a defiance of the attempted obliteration. How to finish the past without evasion, how to tell your story across the terrible disjuncture is as much a problem of an unmourned, unfinished past for a German or a Pole as it is for a German or a Polish Jew. Attempts to integrate the past without splitting it, to be able to absorb each other's accounts, to remember the wilfully forgotten are still being attempted against the odds (e.g. Hoffman 1998). Registering the splits, the silences and what has been forgotten by each in the story of the other or in the recorded evidence, as we will do in this project, is itself a contribution to reaching a more stable and a less haunting past.

Notes

1. I can be contacted at the Department of Anthropology, London School of Economics, Houghton Street, London WC2A 2AE, UK, or e-mail S.Feuchtwang@lse.ac.uk. Harriet Evans, Charles Stafford and Amal Treacher have given me great encouragement and useful suggestions in the design of this project, and I am most grateful for their friendship.

Bibliography

Bloch, M. (1998), *How We Think We Think: Anthropological Approaches to Cognition, Memory and Literacy*, Boulder: Westview.

Burke, P. (1989), 'History as social memory', in T. Butler (ed.), *Memory: History, Culture and the Mind*, Oxford: Basil Blackwell, pp. 97–114.

Das, V. (1998), 'Official narratives, rumour, and the social production of hate', *Social Identities* Vol 4 No 1, pp. 109–30.

Derrida, J. (1996), *Archive Fever*, Chicago and London: Chicago University Press.

Feuchtwang, S. (1998), 'Political judgment and academic freedom', *Identities: Global Studies in Culture and Power*, vol. 33, pp. 1–9.

Herzfeld, M. (1997), *Cultural Intimacy: Social Poetics in the Nation-State*, London and New York: Routledge.

Hoffman, E. (1998), *Shtetl: The Life and Death of a Small Town and the World of Polish Jews*, London: Secker and Warburg.

Humphrey, C. (1994), 'Remembering an "enemy": the Bogd Khaan in twentieth-century Mongolia', in R. Watson (ed.), *Memory, History, and Opposition under State Socialism*, Santa Fe: School of American Research Press.

Levi, P. (1988), *The Drowned and the Saved*, London: Michael Joseph.

Portelli, A. (1998), 'Oral history as genre', in M. Chamberlain and P. Thompson (eds), *Routledge Studies in Memory and Narrative* volume 1, *Narrative and Genre*, London and New York: Routledge, pp. 23–45.

Scott, J. (1990), *Domination and the Arts of Resistance: Hidden Transcripts*, New Haven and London: Yale University Press.

Silverman, M. and Gulliver, P.H. (1992) (eds), *Approaching the Past. Historical Anthropology through Irish Case Studies*, New York and London: Columbia University Press.

Skultans,V. (1997), 'Theorising Latvian lives: the quest for identity', *The Journal of the Royal Anthropological Institute* 3:4, pp. 761–80.

Snead, J. (1990), 'European pedigrees/African contagions: nationality, narrative, and communality in Tutuola, Achebe, and Reed', in H. Bhabha (ed), *Nation and Narration*, London and New York: Routledge, pp. 231–49.

Taussig, M. (1987), *Shamanism, Colonialism, and the Wild Man; A Study in Terror and Healing*, Chicago and London: University of Chicago Press.

Tonkin, E. (1990), 'History and the myth of realism', in R. Samuel and P. Thompson, *The Myths We Live By*, London and New York: Routledge, pp. 25–35.

Werbner, R. (1995), 'Human rights and moral knowledge: arguments of accountability in Zimbabwe', in M. Strathern (ed.), *Shifting Contexts: Transformations in Anthropological Knowledge*, London and New York: Routledge, pp. 99–116.

Wollen, P. (1994), 'The cosmopolitan ideal in the arts', in G. Robertson et al. (eds), *Travellers' Tales; Narratives of Home and Displacement*, London and New York: Routledge, pp. 187–96.

4

Screening Trauma: *Forrest Gump*, Film and Memory

Susannah Radstone

'So people are shown not what they were, but what they must remember having been' (Foucault 1989: 92).

'He described the moment when he saw his wife being taken away on a truck
– to the gas chambers, although he "didn't know that then". This phrase –
"but we didn't know that then" – haunted his narrative . . .' (King 1997: 50).

Like many recent US mainstream releases, *Forrest Gump* (Robert Zemeckis, US, 1994) concerns itself with the last three turbulent decades of US history. Focalised through the memories of the film's eponymous hero, Tom Hanks' 'intellectually-challenged' but undaunted Forrest is present at – and active within – those decades' defining moments: desegregation; Vietnam; Watergate. Forrest's virtual presence in history is achieved through the deployment of the very latest in computer-generated image technology, for while many of the recent 'contemporary history films' emanating from the US have spliced archive footage into their diegeses, *Forrest Gump* goes one step further by morphing the fictional Forrest into that archive footage so that he shakes hands with Kennedy and Johnson and stands by the university steps as Governor Wallace defies desegregation. With his scrubbed, boyish face and his crisp gingham shirts, the anodyne and impassive Hanks/Forrest responds to history's defining moments with homilies learnt from his mother, for instance: 'life is like a box of chocolates . . . you never know what you're going to get'. Though he comprehends little of the history he is moving through, Forrest's life turns out better than the lives of those to whom he is closest, towards whom history deals crushing and sometimes mortal blows. His Vietnam buddy dies in action; his superior, whom he saves in battle, loses his legs and Jenny, Forrest's childhood sweetheart, is abused by her father and later by her counter-culture lover, wrecked by drugs and finally, after giving Forrest a son, dies of an Aids-like virus. But the film invites identification not with these lives – permeated, as they are, with history and with suffering – but with the strangely impervious Forrest.

Much has already been written about contemporary Western culture's fascination – some would say obsession – with history and memory and with their simultaneous atrophy and virtual vivification through the manipulations of technology (Huyssen 1995; Jameson 1984; Sobchack 1996). Yet *Forrest Gump*'s seemingly unfathomable placing of a 'dim-wit' (Barnes 1994) at history's heart presents a paradox of presence and absence that arguably invites a modulation of emphasis and method, if not a paradigm shift. For questions concerning the appeal of a film in which the audience 'get(s) to see the images that shaped a nation's consciousness' (Zetlin 1994: 69) accompanied by the 'glazed look' (Hoberman 1994: 41) and 'utter vacancy' (Romney 1994: 41) of its central protagonist invite the deployment of theories and methods that might explain the hold exerted by that central protagonist, in the context of debates about experience, history, memory and the cinema. The difficulty presented by this task, however, is that its execution requires the reconciliation of apparently incompatible theories and methods developed within different disciplines.

For at least the last twenty-five years, film studies has variously deployed a range of psychoanalytic theories and methods in its analyses of the fascinations and meanings of the cinema and of specific films. Psychoanalysis has been called upon both to explain how the cinema may function as a machine to stabilise (ideologically complicit) subject positions (Metz 1975) and to illuminate the fascinations exerted by the spectacle of film, as well as film narratives and their protagonists. Like psychoanalysis itself, within which 'identification comes . . . to have the central importance which makes it, not simply one psychical mechanism among others, but the operation itself whereby the human subject is constituted' (Laplanche and Pontalis 1988: 206), psychoanalytic film theory places great emphasis upon processes of identification proposed by film. Unsurprisingly, perhaps, given the permeation through the wider culture of Freudian thought, the flood of newsprint prompted by *Forrest Gump*'s unexpected and spectacular success implicitly mobilises the concept of identification, too, in explanations linking the film's popularity to the traits of its eponymous 'hero'. *Time* Magazine pointed out, for instance, that until the release of *Forrest Gump*, only three movies in the past two decades had topped at the box office and won the Oscar for best picture: *Rocky* (John G. Avildsen, US, 1976), *Kramer versus Kramer* (Robert Benton, US, 1979) and *Rain Man* (Barry Levinson, US, 1988) – all 'canny, poignant fables of men in domestic crisis' (Corliss 1994: 41–2). Following on in this compromised tradition, *Forrest Gump* prompted the press to query the phenomenal appeal of this 'doe-eyed man-cub' into whose figure the film 'conflates some thirty years of recent US history' (Romney 1994: 41). As indicated by the two headlines 'Transatlantic Gumption' (ibid), and 'The Gumping of America' (Barnes 1994), much of this critical engagement with the enigma of Forrest's undoubted popularity invoked a conspiracy to avoid facing up to history through the deployment of Forrest as decoy. But if psychoanalytic concepts and theories differentially pervade cinepsychoanalysis and film journalism, that same journalism's recourse to conspiracy theory arguably links the reviews to the film *Forrest Gump*, for, as this essay will go on to argue, both the film and its discussion in academia and reviews are arguably marked by symptoms that have been associated with traumatic memory. Analyses, that is, turn out to repeat, rather than to illuminate, aspects of the film. Two inter-woven determinants play their part in shaping these analyses: firstly, a theoretical and methodological tension around memory that produces its own blind spots, and secondly, a more general cultural context that shapes not only films, but also criticism. Both these determinants need further elaboration, before *Forrest Gump*'s phenomenal appeal can better be understood.

The theoretical and methodological tension around memory in film studies arises from cinepsychoanalysis' difficulty in addressing memory – a paradoxical difficulty, given the cinema's inextricable connections *with* memory. Similarities between memory and the cinema have often been remarked upon. In form, the visuality of cinema shares much with memory's images of the past. For example, mainstream cinema's editing strategies – such as the fade-in and the fade-out – are often motivated from the narrative point of view of a protagonist's acts of memory. In art cinema, on the other hand, non-linear narratives themselves may know-ingly evoke the visual (and aural) associations of memory's tropes. This linking of the cinema's formal strategies with memory's vicissitudes is best exemplified by the term 'flash-back' which designates both a cine-matic edit that links the present with the past *and* the involuntary and spontaneous recall of (usually traumatic) events (Turim 1989: 5). In content, too, the cinema has been inextricably linked with memory. Like the family album, home movies and videos become repositories for the memories of real-life families, groups and individuals. Meanwhile avant-garde and art cinema, as well as mainstream fiction films, have regularly concerned themselves with the remembered lives of their fictional protago-nists. More recently, the cinema's over-arching concern with memory has arguably intensified and developed new registers. In art cinema and the avant-garde, this concern continues, or is even, perhaps, intensifying (in the films of Andrei Tarkovsky or Chris Marker, for instance). This intensification of interest in memory has played a part in generating, indeed, a spate of 'new' autobiographical films which deploy purposeful self-reflexivity in relation to memory's instability. A concern with memory has been evident, too, in recent – particularly US – mainstream entertainment cinema. In science fiction cinema, for instance, the subject of memory has become a recurrent narrative theme. In *Blade Runner* (Ridley Scott, US, 1982) and *Total Recall* (Paul Verhoeven, US, 1990), for example, science's potential challenge to memory's place in the constitution of identity's essence has been raised.[1] Meanwhile, in the increasingly popular 'contemporary history film' – in *Born on the Fourth of July* (Oliver Stone, US, 1989), for instance – as well as in *Forrest Gump* – memory bridges the domains of fiction and history; of the personal and the public; of the past and the present.

Memory's historical and contemporary association with the cinema must be set beside, however, cinepsychoanalysis' paradoxically difficult relation *to* memory – a difficulty that stems, in part, from a continuingly contentious theoretical move made early in the history of psychoanalysis concerning its understanding of the role of memory in the aetiology of (particularly hysterical) neuroses. For although Freud's understanding of hysteria originally linked its emergence to the repressed *memory* of unacknowledgeable, traumatic events – childhood seduction or abuse (Freud and Breuer [1893–5] 1974) – Freud later and famously abandoned this 'seduction theory' for an understanding of hysteria that connected its symptoms, rather, to unacknowledgeable *fantasies* of a sexual nature (Freud [1905] 1977), leading his later critics to accuse him of slighting the outer world in favour of the inner one (Masson 1984), by emphasising the psychical role of fantasy at the expense of memory.[2] Though this critique caricatures, somewhat, the effects of Freud's retreat from the 'seduction theory', in psychoanalysis and, by extension, in cinepsychoanalysis, something of an opposition, rather than a more nuanced differentiation between memory and fantasy has arguably remained in place. In psychoanalysis, this has led to what one analyst and commentator has described as a regrettable 'insistence on the priority of the imagined – juxtaposed, if necessary, to the happened' (Bollas 1995: 103). In cinepsychoanalysis, too, a similar trend can be discerned. On the one hand, cinepsychoanalysis simply shares with all semiotically-inclined analytic methods a refusal of reflectionist models of culture. Yet an emphasis upon the mediated nature of all cultural representations and a refusal of reflectionism need not necessarily prioritise fantasy over memory – itself a highly mediated form of representation. However, cinepsychoanalysis' indebtedness to Marx, Althusser, Freud and Lacan, as well as to Saussurian semiotics, has resulted in an approach that emphasises the 'imaginary' in relation to ideology, subjectivity and spectatorship. Not only films, but the cinematic apparatus itself is likened to an imaginary machine (Metz 1982), wherein images marked by a paradoxically absent presence lead to analogies between the cinema and a Lacanian formulation of language (Lapsley and Westlake 1988). Initially, this approach emphasised the cinema's role in the maintenance of ideologically-complicit subject positions.

Later, however, cinepsychoanalysis sought a more nuanced and less deterministic understanding of the psychical work performed by film. Fantasy was then deployed to stress the potential for ideological *resistance* residing in the multiple and fragmentary identifications offered by film – a move which made explicit that active agency of the unconscious in the negotiation of culture which is implicit in all mobilisations of the concept of fantasy. Be that as it may, whether fantasy is deployed in analyses that stress ideological complicity or dissent, the organising opposition that implicitly underpins all such approaches is that between memory and fantasy, and it is the cinema's relation to the 'imaginary' which has – following psychoanalysis itself – remained dominant in film analysis. Thus cinepsychoanalytic analyses of mainstream, art, or avant-garde 'memory films' may have difficulty reaching for analyses which can critically address both the associations these texts propose between fictional or actual happenings and their remembrance and the relation between such texts and historical audiences. Instead, cinepsychoanalytic readings find themselves locked into perspectives that routinely interpret texts and text/spectator relations in relation to either the rehearsal or subversion of psychoanalysis' fantasmatic ur-narratives.[3] The extent to which this approach – with its foregrounding of imaginary relations and, not least, the imagined 'presence' of an 'absent' Phallus – can aid in the analysis either of Forrest Gump's paradoxically 'absent' presence on history's stage or of the *appeal* of that 'blank page' (Barnes 1994) at the heart of *Forrest Gump*'s memories is arguably limited, then, by the incommensurable relations between memory and fantasy perpetuated in cinepsychoanalysis. Obstructed in the quest for adequate, psychoanalytically informed approaches to memory films, the would-be analyst is encouraged to look elsewhere for appropriate theories and methods.

Other disciplines do, indeed, offer approaches to the study and analysis of memory that may be called upon by film studies. In cultural studies and in history, indeed, an attention to and prioritisation of memory has marked much recent and innovative research.[4] In these less psychoanalytically oriented fields, however, memory is construed in opposition to history, rather than to fantasy. Thus, while in cultural studies, as well as in 'new' history,[5] history becomes negatively associated with the authority of master narratives, with the 'public' and with 'objectivity', memory has become positively associated with the embedded, the local, the personal and the subjective. Memory becomes a rich source, then, for those seeking alternatives to dominant versions of the past. In the work of the Birmingham Centre for Contemporary Cultural Studies, for instance, analyses of autobiographical memories revealed both how public history shaped identity and, conversely, how marginal memories could overturn established histories.[6]

During the 1980s and under the influence of theorists including Antonio Gramsci and Michel Foucault, much of this research productively explored relations and tensions between official history and its contestation by 'popular' or unofficial memory. Gramscian-influenced research analysed the power relations at stake in history's relation to memory's sedimentations of common-sense and folklore (Centre for Contemporary Cultural Studies 1982). Foucauldian research, too, mobilised the concept of popular memory in relation to an analysis of the micro-politics of power (Foucault 1989).

The turn to memory represented by such work formed part of a broader movement, however. Postmodernism's problematisation of grand narratives, objectivity, universality and totality invited the substitution of memory's partial, local and subjective narratives for those of an authoritative 'H'istory. A key aim of memory research has been to explore, then, the subjectivity of memory, opening a door to the examination of *lived*, historical experience and its complex relation to 'H'istory. Moreover, postmodernism's questioning of 'H'istory arose, in part, under the impact of the Holocaust, which led theorists to question not only the 'progress' of modernity, but also the capacity of history and literature to represent the enormity and, some would say, the uniqueness of that event (Maier 1988; Friedlander 1992). In the consequent theoretical revisions that brought insights from memory studies closer to the theorisation of history, history began to be read as the symptom of the past, rather than simply as its triumphant record.

Moreover, much of this memory work has been marked by an acute awareness of memory's status as *representation*. Thus, for instance, oral historians have analysed the emplotments, genres and tropes of particular memories (Passerini 1987; Chamberlain and Thompson 1998), producing analyses that contest the notion that either history or memory can deliver 'truth', but foregrounding, rather, analytic methods that focus on how memory produces its representations of the past (Carter and Hirshkop 1997: vi). In cultural history, too, the formation of nations and ethnicities has been viewed in relation to memory formation – as has the formation of national and ethnic identities.

Though memory research within cultural studies and history is not untouched by psychoanalytic ideas (Kuhn 1995; King 1997; Vidali 1997), and though these fields do commonly understand memory as mediated representation, what can fall out of the picture in the disciplinary shift that pits memory against history, rather than against fantasy, are those understandings of memory formation and mediation specific to psychoanalysis. Thus, while, for instance, oral history's understandings of memory formation might place stress upon those popular or folk genres through which memories may be formed, psychoanalysis would stress, rather, the determining force of unconscious processes upon the production of memory. The psychoanalytic understanding of memory encompasses two related fields: those of temporality and symbolisation. Each of these aspects of the psychoanalytic understanding of memory plays its part in producing a particular problematisation of understandings of memory dominant within cultural studies and history. If psychoanalysis merely contributed its understanding of unconscious processes of symbolisation to the analysis of memory, its insights would be more readily assimilable within history and cultural studies. Like dreams (Freud 1900), memories' condensations and displacements might then be interpreted to uncover what has been repressed in the experience of an event. Such an approach would introduce psychoanalytic insights concerning the marks left by repression into the study of cultural memory. Yet though such an approach would be assimilable into history or cultural studies, its assimilability would reside in its remaining tied to history's model of narrative, which posits a chain of events occurring in linear time and linked by cause and effect – a model that is put in question by the psychoanalytic understanding of the temporality of the unconscious, and, more particularly, of memory. This understanding of psychical temporality hinges on the concept of *Nachträglichkeit*, or 'afterwardsness' (Laplanche 1992).[7]

This concept refers to a process of deferred revision, where 'experiences, impressions and memory-traces may be revised at a later date to fit in with fresh experiences or with the attainment of a new stage of development' (Laplanche and Pontalis 1988: 111). Such a conception sits most uneasily with analytic theories and methods shaped by history's conception of linear narrative and cause and effect. The proposal that 'memories' of the past are shaped by more recent experiences reverses history's model of cause and effect, by making the present, to some extent, the 'cause' of memory's representations of the past. *Nachträglichkeit*'s ruling out of 'the summary interpretation which reduces the psychoanalytic view of the subject's history to a linear determinism envisaging nothing but the action of the past upon the present' (Laplanche and Pontalis 1988: 111–12), thus produces an irreconcilability between psychoanalysis and theories and methods grounded in historical time, narrative and causation. In place of the quest for the truth of an event, and the history of its causes, *Nachträglichkeit* proposes, rather, that the analysis of memory's tropes can reveal not the truth of the past, but a particular revision prompted by later events, thus pitting psychical contingency against historical truth.

Moreover, for Freud, at least, the psychical 'reality' revealed in memories was understood to be more closely associated with primal *fantasies* than with historical reality. As one authoritative commentary usefully points out, Freud's growing awareness of the tenuousness with which reconstructions related to historical reality led him to introduce 'a new idea – that of the *primal phantasies*: the idea of a substrate, a structure which is the phantasy's ultimate foundation, and which transcends both the individual's lived experience and his imaginings' (Laplanche and Pontalis 1988: 113–14). Embedded in the idea of the primal fantasy are certain notions of inner reality that may sit uncomfortably with those views of identity dominant within history and cultural studies. Firstly, it suggests that inner reality is shaped by certain unchanging, universal and ahistorical fantasies related to human sexuality. Secondly, it suggests a view of inner reality within which desires and fantasies that run counter to conscious control hold sway – a view of inner reality that many, and not only academics, may have difficulty accepting. Finally, though psychoanalysis posits a relation between events and memory, the introduction of the concept of the 'primal fantasy' further complicates any attempt to map memory straightforwardly onto events, since it adds to the view of memory as the later revision of events, the proposal that those revisions are inextricably woven together with fantasy. As I have already argued, cinepsychoanalysis has tended to emphasise fantasy at the expense of history and memory. Yet it is incorrect to suggest that Freud's revised accounts of hysteria's aetiology – his abandonment of the 'seduction theory' – substituted fantasy for the memory of traumatic events. Rather, in Freud's later writings on trauma, fantasy and memory come to be conceived of not as binary opposites, but as complexly related terms. On this view, traumatic symptoms emerge where a seemingly innocuous event prompts *memories* of an earlier event that now becomes associated with inadmissable *fantasies*.[8] Thus while, as Laplanche and Pontalis usefully point out, 'it is only *as a memory* that the first scene becomes pathogenic by deferred action' (Laplanche and Pontalis 1988: 467–8), that pathogeny derives not from the remembered event itself but from the attempt to defend against the fantasies that now emerge in association with such memories.

Memory's non-linear temporality and its indivisibility from fantasy that emerge here, in Freud's revised understanding of traumatic memory, pose difficulties for cultural studies and history. It is therefore unsurprising that, with some notable exceptions,[9] humanities research has played upon and elaborated memory's relation to history, rather than to the complex relation psychoanalysis proposes between memory and fantasy. Yet, as I have already stated, the centrality, in memory studies, of questions concerning *lived* experience and subjectivity differentiate this field from history's earlier concerns with objectivity.

One consequence, however, of history's incompatibility with psycho-analysis, and of the arguably related dominance of the memory/history paradigm within the humanities has been the sheer difficulty of addressing the question of how memory is shaped not just by the external, but also by the *inner* world. In the attempt to resolve this difficulty and under the influence of postmodernism's post-Holocaust concerns, disciplines operat-ing a memory/history opposition have drawn not from Freud's writings on traumatic memory, but from non- or, indeed, anti-Freudian, rather than psychoanalytic theories of trauma.

These theories of trauma have been drawn upon to elaborate the relation between the 'outer'and the 'inner', the event and its registration or recording. The increasing prominence of such theories within academic discourse can be accounted for, in part, by their apparent capacity to elaborate those relations in terms that are both less antipathetic to the temporality of history and less troublingly interwoven with the concept of fantasy than what I'll call a more properly psychoanalytic under-standing of traumatic memory. Though hardly unified, the body of ideas concerning trauma thus drawn upon by academic disciplines, or 'trauma theories' as they will henceforth be termed, do share certain common features. These increasingly influential theories of trauma posit, in the words of one commentator, 'the existence of a dissociated mental realm that contains and to an extent seals off recollections of things too painful to bear . . .' (Kenny 1996: 153). In the most recent fourth edition of the highly influential US psychiatric nosology, *The Diagnostic and Statistical Manual (DSM IV)* of the American Psychiatric Association (1994) this dissociative trauma is linked to an increasing number and variety of mental disorders. At the same time, a similar understanding of the traumatic effects of 'forgotten' events has come to inform wider popular cultural movements and a 'politics' of memory characterised by victimization and blame (Antze and Lambek 1996: vii–xxix), represented most notoriously, perhaps, by the 'recovered memory movement'. Spearheaded by Jeffrey Masson's *Assault on Truth* (1984) which called for a return to the Freud of the 'seduction theory', the recovered memory movement stresses the traumatic effects of childhood sexual abuse and rejects absolutely Freud's revised understanding of the role of the repression of *fantasy* in the formation of neurotic symptoms.

These understandings of trauma currently informing and being deployed by psychiatry, academic discourse and cultural movements places immense stress, then, upon the effects upon the inner world of unassimilable external events, describing the effects of such trauma in terms of dissociation. On this understanding, the term trauma refers to an event which, due to its shocking and possibly incomprehensible nature, prompts a shutdown in normal processes of assimilating or 'digesting' experience. In such cases, this undigested experience is understood to come to occupy a walled-off area of the memory, giving rise to symptoms commonly referred to as post-traumatic shock disorder (PTSD). Though a very wide variety of symptoms are now attributed to PTSD, its aetiology is inextricably tied to the 'toxicity' of the *event,* and the difficulties and costs of the struggle to confine this event within a separated-off part of the memory. It is the centrality accorded to the event by this theory of traumatic memory which provokes its proponents to 'hate Freud' (Hacking 1996: 76), for his abandoning of the seduction theory. Yet though Freud's distinction between event and trauma *is* a crucial one (Laplanche and Pontalis 1968), it was Freud who was originally responsible for 'the importation of repressed memory into the Western mind' (Hacking 1996: 77). Thus while there *are* differences between psychoanalytic understandings of traumatic memory and understandings disseminated by US psychiatry and the 'memory politics' movements, these differences ought not to be exaggerated.

Nevertheless, two crucial differences between the trauma theory of *DSM IV* and those psychoanalytic understandings of memory initiated by the post-seduction theory Freud and his later followers secure the appropriateness of the former for academic disciplines operating an opposition between memory and history: its models of temporality and of the relation between an external event and its registration within the inner world of psychical reality. Theories of traumatic memory and PTSD remain wedded to a linear (historical) model of temporality and a reflectionist understanding of the mind's relation to external events. At stake across both these differences is the issue of the inner world's *mediation* of the external world, a mediation which is foregrounded by psychoanalytic theory and minimised by trauma theory. Where temporality is at issue, the psychoanalytic concept of 'afterwardsness' posits traumatic memory not as the registration of an event, but as the outcome of a complex process of revision shaped by promptings from the present. Trauma theory, on the other hand, posits the linear registration of events as they happen, albeit that such registrations may be secreted away through dissociation. Where the relation between an event and 'psychical reality' is at issue, psychoanalytic theory suggests that what is at stake in the formation of traumatic memory is the relation between the triggering second events and '*the phantasies they activate*' (Laplanche and Pontalis 1988: 468, emphasis mine). Conversely trauma theories associate trauma not with the effects of triggered associations but with the ontologically unbearable nature of the event itself.

Trauma theories appear to offer to disciplines operating a memory/history opposition, a conceptual model of the relation between the inner world of memory and the external world of (historical) events. What emerges in this comparison of a psychoanalytic theory of traumatic memory and 'trauma theories', however, is the extent to which trauma theories' return to the Freud of the 'seduction theory' abandon psychoanalytic theory's later insights concerning the role of unconscious processes – processes that my allusions to 'afterwardsness' and memory's relation to fantasy have attempted to summarise – in the production of memory. In short, what trauma theory excises in its return to the early Freud is psychoanalysis' later insistence on the agency of the unconscious in the formation of memories. As Ann Scott has pointed out, in the specific context of a discussion of sexual abuse, this excision of unconscious agency has even led exponents of trauma theory to reject the term 'seduction' in favour of 'rape' or 'assault', since the former term implies a degree of suggestibility, at the very least (Scott 1996: 15). This example is a telling one, for it reveals the links between trauma theory's rejection of unconscious agency and its broader vision of a Manichean universe peopled by good, passive, innocent victims and bad, active, guilty perpetrators.

As I have already argued, trauma theories' appeal for historically-oriented humanities disciplines resides, in part, in those theories' consonance with a linear, historical model of temporality and in part, in trauma theories' prioritisation of the event in their understandings of memory formation. Yet trauma theories have become central within *both* the humanities *and* a popular social movement of memory politics, or 'victim culture' characterised, as has already been stated ,[10] by accusations linked to memories of damaging past abuse. Analyses of the emergence and proliferation of victim culture might also contribute, therefore, to an understanding of the take-up of trauma theories within the humanities.

Victim culture has been linked both with millennial hysteria (Showalter 1997) and with the fragmentation and ungraspability of authority and power in contemporary Western society (Craib 1994). Accounts concur, however, that the accusatory scenarios and the emphasis upon external phenomena shared by, for instance, the recovered memory movement and sufferers from chronic fatigue syndrome result from an inability to acknowledge inner conflict. In place of the acknowledgement of the part played by an inevitably refractory internal world in the shaping of lives, victim culture seeks cause and cure for disappointment, shortcomings, or even 'simple unhappiness . . . firmly . . . outside the self' (Showalter 1997: 4). This linking of problems with external causes can substitute conspiracy fantasies for the acknowledgement of the mind's own agency in their production – fantasies which together constitute what Elaine Showalter has somewhat hysterically termed (Radstone 1999) an advancing 'hysterical plague' (Showalter 207).[11]

Showalter's thesis might be extended to suggest that the academic dissemination of trauma theories, with their relentless emphasis upon external events and their impact upon the inner world may form part of a broader psycho-social conjuncture that has also given rise to victim culture. The dominance of trauma theories within the humanities might arguably represent, in other words, one aspect of a contemporary cultural malaise, rather than a form of analysis. This cultural malaise is supported, according to Ian Craib, by forms of psychotherapy that collude in the promulgation of fantasies of the achievability of a self at total peace with itself. For Craib, the emphasis such therapies place on management and control contributes to rather than militates against the adoption of 'false selves' (Craib 1994: 162). What is dangerously different about the false self of late modernity, argues Craib, is that whereas previously, commitment to such a false self was critical,[12] 'late modernity seems to encourage the adoption of a false self' (ibid). Trauma theories lie at the heart of the psychotherapies and approaches which, with their emphasis upon the role of external causes or even 'villains' in the sufferings of 'victims', foster fantasies of control and omnipotence which shore up rather than dismantle modernity's false selves. In contradistinction to the emphases upon the role of others, or of external agents common to such psychotherapies, Craib offers an alternative psychoanalytic approach to suffering: '(I)t is part of the disappointment that psychoanalysis has to offer,' he suggests, 'there is no simple world of villains and victims . . . there are no such things as undifferentiated and pure traumas; and there is no straight-forward way of dealing with what has become known as . . . post-traumatic stress disorder' (ibid: 188).

Craib's thesis does associate the adoption of false selves with the increasingly fragmented and ungraspable nature of external reality. How-ever, unlike the therapies against which his book is partly directed, *The Importance of Disappointment* avoids placing exclusive emphasis upon *external* determinants in the formation of victim culture – an approach central, as I've already suggested, to trauma theories themselves. His concluding refutation of 'undifferentiated trauma' insists both that the impact of the *external* world will always be met by the determining agency of the *inner* world and that memory, therefore, cannot be conclusively differentiated from fantasy.

Taken together, Craib's and Showalter's theses suggest that the central-ity of trauma theories within victim culture can best be understood in relation to a defensive and fragmented psycho-social culture that lacks adequate containment and within which authority, responsibility and agency have become increasingly complex and diffuse. In this context, the inevitably conflictual nature of the inner world has become hard to bear, leading to paranoid conspiracy *fantasies* peopled by innocent victims and wicked perpetrators. Though trauma theories' emphases on external events and their compatibility with linear narrative structures certainly contribute to their appeal within the humanities, the centrality of trauma theories within victim culture *and* the humanities testifies to the suffusion of contemporary 'common sense', including 'academic' common sense, by those theories' underlying fantasies.

On its surface, the film *Forrest Gump*, too, appears to have been formed by the fantasies and 'common sense' that run through victim culture. The childhoods of both Forrest and Jenny, for instance, are marked by 'traumatic' experiences of physical disablement and sexual abuse which Forrest, at least, learns to 'put behind him', while the film's moral universe conforms to the Manichean values typical of victim culture's fantasies. Though, as this article will go on to argue, *Gump* only *appears* to have been shaped by victim culture, it clearly and indelibly marks reviews of the film. Though responses to *Forrest Gump* present themselves, then, as *analyses* of its 'gumption'(Romney 1994), or 'common sense', it is that same 'common sense', I'm suggesting, which has shaped both victim culture *and* film reviews and academic responses to *Forrest Gump*. Like the conspiracy theories identified by Showalter, reviews of *Forrest Gump* described it 'Gumping' (Barnes 1994) America. In descriptions reminiscent of 'alien abduction' narratives, reviews suggested that audiences have been 'taken over' or even brainwashed by the film's deceit (Joseph 1994) and 'dishonesty'. In identifying *Forrest Gump* as 'a hideous and hollow Hollywood pretence' (Hibbert 1994) and, most typically a 'rewrite (of) history' (Parisi 1994) reviewers construct the film's audiences as passively and helplessly falling under the 'evil' spell of *Forrest Gump*. These paranoid readings of *Forrest Gump* arguably constitute a popular echo of Michel Foucault's academic theorisations of French contemporary history films, to which I will return. Like Foucault, these film reviewers accuse *Forrest Gump* of playing a part in the reprogramming of 'popular memory' (Foucault 1989: 102), and in both cases – in the case of Foucault, and of these film reviews, audiences emerge as either innocent victims or hopeless suckers.

Reviews of *Forrest Gump* are shaped by conspiracy fantasies supported by victim culture. Such reviews emphasise the film's capacity to overwhelm its audiences, but, like the trauma theories that underpin victim culture, they oversimplify the relation between the external and the inner world by stressing the film's impact upon a passive audience. As one review stated, however, *Forrest Gump* 'hit a nerve that is vibrating all over America' (Barnes 1994). The metaphor deployed here has associations with early understandings of the parallels between physiological and psychical trauma. Nevertheless, it shifts attention from the power of the film to the inner constitution and processes of its audience and raises questions, therefore, about the relation between *Forrest Gump*'s popularity and active *processes* of spectatorship – understandings hindered by trauma theories and facilitated, I now want to argue, by a *psychoanalytic* understanding of trauma that links suffering not only to external agents but also to the impact of fantasies and the active mediation of the unconscious.

Ian Craib's contention that there can be no 'undifferentiated trauma' need not imply that the concept of trauma must be abandoned. This insistence on the inevitable 'differentiation' of trauma returns us, however, to the distinction between *psychoanalytic* understandings of trauma, and those 'unpsychoanalytic' understandings of trauma circulated within victim culture. For psychoanalysis, memory – and, most particularly, traumatic memory – is inevitably interweaved with the determining agency of the inner world and its fantasies. One particular fantasy – the conspiracy fantasy, or the fantasy of an overwhelming external influence or agent – has been linked, indeed, with traumatic memory (Bollas 1995). The paranoid conspiracy theories and fantasies of passivity that I have identified in reviews of *Forrest Gump*, and which Ian Craib and Elaine Showalter have linked with victim culture can be understood psychoanalytically, therefore, as symptoms *associated with* trauma. What this suggests, in other words, is that the humanities' and victim culture's supposed *explorations* of trauma might actually be shaped, themselves, by the distortions of traumatic fantasy.

This possibility is supported by Christopher Bollas, who, in his 'The Functions of History' (ibid), forcefully makes the case for a psychoanalysis that can attend to both memory and fantasy as they emerge in the consulting room. In an evocative and Winnicottian[13] description of the impact of 'things done', Bollas points to their initially 'unthinkable' nature: 'As I imagine it, when the real is presented – as a thing done to us, or as a narrated thing done – we do not as yet know how to think it. There is something unthinkable about such facts of life' (ibid: 112). Bollas continues by describing the 'blank nothing' (ibid: 114) created by trauma, or the '*hit* of the fact' (ibid: 113): a space, or gap which 'interrupts the fecund exploration of unconscious processes' (ibid: 114). Referring to Winnicott's experiments with small infants, Bollas suggests that faced with new facts, an initial looking away, or loss of thought may be psychically necessary (ibid: 112). Most significantly, for my present purposes, Bollas goes on to distinguish between the ordinary or healthy sense 'of one's development inside a structure . . . derived from (the self)' and the traumatic sense of 'one's development inside a structure *imposed on the self*' (ibid: 114, emphasis mine). This traumatic sense of inhabiting a structure imposed on the self reveals the links between trauma and paranoid fantasies and conspiracy theories which, as fantasies, testify, in distorted ways, to the arrest of unconscious dissemination by the hit of an 'unthinkable' thing done. Bollas associates this conspiratorial fantasy structure with a sense of temporal suspension and the arrestment of psychical dissemination. In contrast to trauma theory's concept of dissociation, however, which stresses only the impact of an event, Bollas's understanding of traumatic temporality describes a *remembered* gap, or '*looking* away', a psychic *act* that leaves its trace, and that *can* (depending upon the quality of the containing environment) be followed by *Nachträglichkeit* – by those enlivening acts of revision which begin to transform that inert past (ibid: 143), and release its subject from its unthought burden. For psychoanalysis the preconditions for moving from 'unthinkability' to unconscious elaboration (or 'play') depend upon both the extent of the initial 'arrestment' and the quality of either infancy's caring environment, or, in adulthood, the quality of the analytic environment.

Ian Craib's thesis moves us, however, from a consideration of the environments of infancy or clinical psychoanalysis to a consideration of the quality of environment produced by contemporary society, politics and culture. The quality of the environment Craib describes, I want now to suggest, is anything but conducive to the capacity to return to and begin to elaborate the 'unthinkable' past. Instead, as Craib eloquently points out, in the fragmented, uncontaining, and confusing contemporary environment, there arises a culture which *fosters* conspiracy, 'victim culture' and, as I've suggested, the academic appeal of 'trauma theory'. As Christopher Bollas' work shows, this is a culture marked not by an *understanding* of trauma, but by the temporality and fantasies that are characteristic of traumatic memory, as it is described by psychoanalysis. Victim culture, that is, as well as the academic appeal of trauma theory might better be understood as *symptoms* of, rather than an as *analyses* of traumatic memory.

The reviews of *Forrest Gump* that I referred to earlier trade in paranoia and conspiracy theory, and have been formed in a culture within which fantasies of innocent victims, and an incapacity to acknowledge psychic agency holds sway. Culture, however, is neither uniform nor undifferentiated, and a change of perspective can reveal a different landscape. By way of conclusion, I want to return to the question of cinepsychoanalysis, memory and fantasy via a critical reading of an 'unpsychoanalytic' and implicitly Foucauldian analysis of *Forrest Gump* – an essay which forms a chapter in Robert Burgoyne's study of Hollywood's representations of contemporary US history (Burgoyne 1997). Though other chapters in this study *are* informed by psychoanalytic theory, the absence of psychoanalysis from the chapter which concerns itself with *memory* is particularly telling, as is this chapter's recourse to Foucauldian theory which, as I pointed out earlier, has been much drawn from by humanities research operating a memory/history opposition.[14] In the following rereading of *Forrest Gump*, I will therefore endeavour to show how the application of a psychoanalytically informed understanding of traumatic memory – an understanding that is, that attends to memory's temporality and to its relation with, rather than its opposition to fantasy[15] – can produce a different reading of *Forrest Gump*, and a less damning analysis of that film's popular appeal.

As I argued above, notwithstanding the cinema's multiple relations with memory, film studies has, since its beginnings, routinely associated the cinema with fantasy and with dreams. With the impact of 'post-seduction theory' psychoanalysis upon film studies, the rift *between* memory and fantasy widened. With the rise of 'memory studies' within the humanities, film studies, with its central concern with fantasy, offered a potential site for the articulation of memory *with* fantasy. Unfortunately, however, this potential has not, on the whole, been realised. Instead, the study of memory within film studies has, like memory studies within the humanities more generally, tended to operate an opposition between memory and history. In so doing, film studies' potential cinepsychoanalytic insights concerning memory's mediation by the unconscious have been overlooked.

Very much in keeping with this general tendency, Robert Burgoyne's recent essay argues that *Forrest Gump* emphasises memory 'to construct an image of nation that can . . . float free of the historical traumas of the 1960's and 1970's' (ibid: 107). Burgoyne's 'Prosthetic Memory/Prosthetic Nation' forms part of a collection addressing the construction of nation in selected US contemporary history films, and constitutes a critical response to Alison Landsberg's optimistic appraisal of 'prosthetic memory' (Landsberg 1995), glossed by Burgoyne as 'mass cultural technologies of memory [that] enable individuals to experience, as if they were memories, events through which they themselves did not live . . .' (Burgoyne 1997: 105). While Landsberg looks to the politically progressive potential of mass-mediated technologies of memory to offer sites for 'mediated collective identification' (ibid), Burgoyne deploys the term in the service of a darker vision: '*Forrest Gump* revises existing cultural memory . . . Organic memory is refunctioned and redefined . . . to produce an improved image of nation . . .' (ibid: 108). Though their critical evaluations of 'prosthetic memory' diverge, both Landsberg and Burgoyne produce analyses of films which emphasise the overwhelming power of the media (and, particularly, of new electronic technologies) to implant (Landsberg 1995: 175) or refunction (Burgoyne: op.cit.) memory.

This vision's consonance with victim culture's sense of overwhelming and yet diffuse structures of power (Craib 1994), 'conspiracy theories' peopled by passive and helpless 'victims' (Craib 1994; Antze and Lambek 1996; Showalter 1997) and a sense of a structure imposed on the self (Bollas 1995) is striking. The concept of 'prosthetic memory' evokes, indeed, the claims and counter-claims concerning the eliciting of 'false memories' in the now infamous struggles over memories of sexual abuse, otherwise known as the 'memory wars' (Crews 1995) – an association which underlines the links between this approach to cinema and Showalter's 'hystories' or narratives of victimhood, amongst which she includes the recovered memory movement and *its* 'perpetrator-victims' (Showalter 1997: 144–58). More striking still is the *passivity* implied by the concept of prosthetic memory, in the context of film theory's multiple recent theorisations of the *active* as well as passive aspects of spectatorship (Mayne 1993). But most striking of all, in this context, is Burgoyne's conclusion. Like Foucault, whose analysis of the theme of French history films was 'that there's been no popular struggle in the 20th century' (Foucault 1989: 92), Burgoyne decries *Forrest Gump*'s forgetting of 'the most significant memory of all, the memory of historical *agency* that is the most enduring legacy of the sixties' (ibid: 119, emphasis mine). It is ironic, though utterly understandable, that in this Foucauldian analysis whose framework is the opposition between memory and history, what comes into view is the film's 'forgetting' of potentially resistant memories of historical agency. Rendered inaccessible, or 'forgotten', within this framework, however, are cinepsychoanalytic insights concerning fantasy and the *agency* of spectators – insights whose inaccessibility is related to that splitting-off of memory from fantasy, which, as I have been arguing, is itself symptomatic of contemporary culture's imbrication with traumatic memory. In short, what gets forgotten, here, are psychoanalytic insights concerning the mediation – the shaping *power* – of the unconscious in the production of memory. As I argued earlier, psychoanalytic approaches to memory focus on both temporality and symbolisation.[16] The reading of *Forrest Gump* that emerges from such an analysis differs in significant ways from a reading that focuses soley on the relation the film constructs between memory and history.

Burgoyne's analysis of *Forrest Gump* understands its foregrounding of memory in relation to the production of an image of nation that can 'float free of the historical traumas of the 1960's and 1970's' (ibid: 107). Though this analysis is implicitly Foucauldian, its stress on the separation between (historical) traumas and (national) memories appears to be informed also by trauma theory's concept of dissociation. Burgoyne's central critique of *Forrest Gump* concerns its splitting of memory from history which he links to the film's attempt to construct prosthetic, or, more baldly, 'false' memories that forget a recent history scored both by violence and by radical challenge. To this end, Burgoyne emphasises throughout both the dissociation between Gump's memories and that history of violence which is 'in effect noted but bracketed in the film' (ibid: 112), and Forrest's incapacity to understand that same history which he is, unbeknownst to himself, shaping: 'Only Gump's ignorance protects him from the scarifications of history and the resulting distortions of character that plague most of the other figures who populate the film' (ibid: 109).

Burgoyne's 'Prosthetic Memory/National Memory' responds critically to Vivian Sobchack's appreciative reading of the film (Sobchack 1996), which responds, itself, to yet another reading of *Forrest Gump* informed by weak conspiracy theory and accusations of 'false memory'. Robert Angell's *New Yorker* piece (Angell 1995) viewed the film as 'a "moony" and "fantastic" dream in which ignorance and niceness win out over historical consciousness' (Angell, quoted in Sobchack 1996: 1). According to Angell, *Forrest Gump* presents 'the shambles and the horror of our recent American past made harmless and sweet because the protagonist doesn't understand a moment of any of it' (ibid). Sobchack counters this view of the film by pointing to its knowing subversion of the boundary between both the significant and the trivial and the personal and the historical, concluding that *Forrest Gump* forms part of a new historical consciousness which erodes the boundaries between the significant and the trivial while producing 'a sense in which we believe we can go right out and "be" in history' (Sobchack 1996: 5). While Burgoyne's reading clearly seeks to counter Sobchack's emphasis upon *Forrest Gump*'s revised vision of *agency*, he omits to consider the centrality of questions of temporality to Sobchack's analysis. For Sobchack, it is the impact of new technologies of representation on previously dominant notions of historical *temporality* that are responsible for the new consciousness represented in *Forrest Gump* (ibid: 4–5). Sobchack's analysis of the form of agency inherent within *Forrest Gump*'s revised historical temporality might be supplemented, moreover, by a psychoanalytically informed analysis of the film's complex temporality. For many commentators, the conjunction of Forrest's blankness with the film's address to a more knowing audience is deemed merely self-contradictory. As one reviewer puts this, '(i)t's one of the movie's paradoxes that such knowing, audience flattering jokes are so at odds with the protagonist's supposed "innocence"' (Charity 1994: 67). But *Forrest Gump*'s morphing of the fictional Forrest into archive footage of recent US history invites the spectator to identify with his uncomprehending witnessing of a series of painful and traumatic historical events: Vietnam, Kennedy's assassination, Watergate. As Burgoyne himself puts it: Forrest appears 'impervious to the historical events that erupt in his immediate proximity' (Burgoyne 1997: 108). At the same time, and as many commentaries have pointed out, this incomprehension gains its dramatic force, whether understood in relation to irony or poignant humour, or both, from the audience's greater understanding and knowledge. In short, the film's overall legibility depends upon its juxtaposition of memory prompts – its address, that is, to a relatively knowing audience – with the identification it invites with the less knowing, or even 'ignorant' Forrest. This ambiguous identification which weaves together understanding and incomprehension contributes to what so many reviews have seen as *Forrest Gump*'s unaccountable capacity to move. While so many critics jumped to the conclusion that the film's affect was linked only to Forrest's ignorance, and that the film was therefore trading in a historical common sense, or 'gump' that might be likened to 'false memory', psychoanalysis provides another view of the force of this affective identification.

Forrest Gump's 'memories' of recent US history are constructed by means of the insertion of its 1990's 'hero' into archive footage of earlier decades. The 'doe-eyed' (Romney 1994: 41) Forrest looks on vacantly as history unfolds. Through its morphing of Forrest into the archive, *Forrest Gump* constructs a visual 'literalisation' of *Nachträglichkeit* – of that complex 'afterwardsness' of remembrance represented by the phrase 'but we didn't know that then' (King 1997: 50). This psychoanalytic reading of *Forrest Gump*'s temporality reverses that of Burgoyne, whose suggestion that the film 'wip(es) the slate clean . . . in an effort to disengage cultural memory from public history' (Burgoyne 1997: 14) assumes that this engagement had already been made – an assumption that overlooks psychoanalysis' understanding of the inherent latency of the (traumatic) event. While identification with Forrest encompasses an acknowledge-ment, then, of the 'gap' or 'blankness' created by traumatic events, the film's comprehension depends upon its successful address to the audience's capacity to remember. The literality with which Forrest responds to events around him lends greater weight to this reading, given the evidence concerning trauma's association with literality (Caruth 1991: 3). On this reading, then, *Forrest Gump* emerges not as prosthetic or 'false' memory, but as a point of affective identification through which traumatic memory begins to be worked through. If, on Burgoyne's Foucauldian reading, *Forrest Gump* implants 'what they *must* remember having been' (Foucault 1989: 92, emphasis mine), a reading informed by psychoanalytic under-standings of memory's temporality suggests, rather that the film begins to acknowledge what they *couldn't* have known then.[17] On this reading, moreover, new technology, which constitutes an aspect of that ungraspable environment which Ian Craib believes to be inhibiting reality-testing and promoting false selves, emerges here in relation not only to pathology, but also to the struggle towards understanding. Though for the reviewers, as well as for Burgoyne, then, *Forrest Gump* is viewed as a film that 'doesn't wake people up to their times' (Walker 1994: 32), this psycho-analytically informed reading of the film's temporality of *Nachträglichkeit* suggests, rather, that the film remembers both an initial 'looking away' as well as the beginnings of remembrance – a reading that suggests an analogy with 'waking' rather than with 'dreaming', or, by extension, fantasy.

So far, this reading of *Forrest Gump* has suggested that Burgoyne's view of the film's 'implantation' of memory is influenced by victim culture, which is, itself, a symptom of a traumatised society's inability to acknowedge the activities and conflicts of the inner world. In opposition to this view, a reading informed by psychoanalytic understandings of memory's temporality has been proposed. On this reading, what comes into view is *Forrest Gump*'s address to a spectator moving between an initial 'looking away' and the beginnings of revision – a spectator, that is, caught up in the movement, affect and activity of *Nachträglichkeit*. This rereading pits Burgoyne's emphasis upon the film's excision of memories of *historical* agency against its engagement with *psychical* acts of revision. Yet, as has already been argued, while trauma theories oppose memory to fantasy, psychoanalytic understandings of memory point to its imbrication *with* fantasy.

So far, this reading has emphasised the contribution psychoanalysis can make to an analysis of memory's temporality. But psychoanalyis can also illuminate the symbolic and imaginary aspects of *Forrest Gump*'s affective appeal. *Forrest Gump*'s form, address, narrative and characterisations conform to those of film melodrama. By way of conclusion, this reading will therefore explore the affective fantasies engaged by the film's melodramatic strategies.

Burgoyne's analysis assumes that *Forrest Gump*'s apparent failure to represent memories of historical resistance to acts of national violence such as Vietnam, (or, I might add, memories of *perpetration*) signals the film's attempt to excise such memories from national identity. This fundamentally reflectionist stance ignores, however, the question of genre and generic strategies; it ignores, that is, 'the relation between representation and affect, and affect as representation . . .' (Elsaesser 1996: 149). Melodrama criticism's insights concerning the meaning of the powerful affects and fantasies triggered by the genre's narration, *mise-en-scène*, and so on can, however, shed light on *Forrest Gump*'s affective appeal. If *Forrest Gump*'s temporality arguably reveals an address to an active spectator caught between an initial 'looking away' and the beginnings of remembrance, the film's melodramatic strategies, too, address specific spectatorial fantasies and affects, that might be analysed to reveal an understanding of the politics of contemporary US memory divergent from that revealed by Burgoyne.

Forrest Gump's pejorative critical reception may have been due, in part, to the 'pejorative terms' in which melodrama tends to be received (Gledhill 1987: 5). Yet melodrama's classical features – its Manichean universe peopled by the all-innocent or the utterly villainous, its tear-jerking narration, and its musical and visual expressivity – have been associated with the displaced expression of that which has been repressed, or is unrepresentable by history (ibid). The appeal of Forrest's 'blankness' can certainly be associated with an identification suspended between an initial ignorance and the later 'impact' of remembrance: 'what we remember', as Nicola King has put it, 'are events which took place in a kind of *innocence*' (King 1997: 51, emphasis mine). But the appeal of this innocence, so ubiquitous in melodrama, can be linked also with fantasy structures familiar to psychoanalysis. If *Forrest Gump*'s interweaving of Forrest's ignorance with the audience's knowledge initially appears paradoxical, so too does the film's representation of historical agency. While Forrest is clearly present and active in the making of major historical events, the film likens this presence to that of the feather tracked at the film's opening and ending – a feather bobbing on the random or fateful whim of history's breeze. Forrest emerges as both omnipotent and utterly passive. According to psychoanalysis, however, this convergence of passivity and omnipotence is anything but paradoxical, but constitutes, rather, two sides of narcissism's coin. Infantile narcissism is understood by psychoanalysis as a necessary developmental stage in which the child experiences itself as part of the parent, who is fantasised as all-powerful. This fantasy of omnipotence can then be drawn on to counter a growing awarenesss of insufficiency, incompleteness and dependency. In adulthood and at times of stress, such fantasies may be re-evoked. According to one commentator on melodrama's characteristic affects and fantasies, the confluence of feelings of powerlessness with fantasies of omnipotence is inextricably linked with melodrama's characteristic orchestrations of temporality and point of view. Steve Neale's 'Melodrama and Tears' (Neale 1986) takes issue with Franco Moretti's analysis of the relation between tears and agnition (the retraction and re-establishment of point of view). For Moretti, tears are linked with feelings of *powerlessness* that accompany a recognition that comes too late. Steve Neale counters Moretti by pointing out that his argument cannot explain why such tears are mingled with pleasure. Neale adds to Moretti's analysis of agnition, temporality and affect, an argument concerning the fantasy that underpins melodramatic tears. Tears, argues Neale, testify to the acknowledgement of powerlessness in the face of the irreversibility of time. But those same tears are linked to the fantasy that the demand that they represent might be met. When the small child cries, its tears testify to a fantasy of omnipotence: the mother will respond (ibid: 22). The general question of melodrama's relation to traumatic memory's temporality and associated fantasies cannot be addressed here. Nevertheless, though neither Neale nor Moretti associate the temporal and fantasy structures they analyse with the structure of *Nachträglichkeit*, the delayed agnition and affects identified by Neale certainly appear in keeping with my analysis of *Forrest Gump*'s marking by traumatic memory, and with what is most significant about that analysis: that *Forrest Gump*'s spectator is not the passive recipient of 'implanted memories' but is caught, rather in the affects and *activities* of *Nachträglichkeit*, which include fantasies of omnipotence and powerlessness.

As we have already seen, Ian Craib points to the convergence in contemporary Western culture of fantasies of innocent victimhood with fantasies of omnipotence. The convergence, indeed, of this classically narcissistic pairing arguably typifies what I have described as the defensive fantasy structure mobilised by victim culture to defend against a more complex vision of the relation between an unacknowedgeably complex inner world and its relation with the complexities of historical agency and responsibility. I have already referred to Ian Craib's eloquent description of the social conditions which are currently fostering these defensive fantasies of omnipotent passivity in a culture rendered incapable of grasping the power and limits of both unconscious fantasy and conscious will. If melodrama criticism has classically associated the genre's displaced expressivity with its capacity to side 'with the powerless' (Vicinus 1981: 130), my own reading of *Forrest Gump* has suggested that its address to an audience imbued with both absolute power and powerlessness speaks to that audience's ongoing struggle with the past.

Burgoyne's analysis stresses *Forrest Gump*'s purposeful forgetting of that 1960s countercultural agency unassimilable to the 'consensual' politics of national memory it is the film's project to implant, while leaving aside questions of memories of national predation. If a psychoanalytic analysis of *Forrest Gump*'s temporality suggests that victim culture may be beginning to give way to a capacity for revision, an analysis informed by psychoanalytic understandings of memory, rather than *by* the trauma theories of victim culture, has suggested, too, that the hold of victim culture may be being worked through in a cultural space – the cinema – deploying new forms of electronic technology that, for Craib, arguably foster that very culture. But this analysis' focus on two aspects of psychoanalysis' understanding of memory: temporality and symbolisation, or fantasy, suggests that this process is a halting one. For if *Forrest Gump*'s temporality suggests an address to a spectator acknowedging the 'pastness' of victim culture's fixation with 'innocence' (we didn't know that then), the insistence with which the film continually plays upon passive omnipotence suggests the continuing strength of victim culture's defences. Nevertheless, what emerges in this reading of *Forrest Gump* is a film which addresses itself to an audience caught in an *active* and ongoing struggle to remember – a struggle whose outcome remains uncertain, but which a psychoanalytic understanding of memory can reveal.

Notes

1. For a fascinating elaboration of the concept of 'prosthetic memory' in relation to *Blade Runner* and *Total Recall*, see Landsberg (1995).
2. Throughout this essay, I refer to Freud's, or, 'the psychoanalytic' understanding of memory. My point throughout, is to emphasise the interweaving of fantasy with memory in the psychoanalytic understanding of the latter. This is, of course, a major over-simplification of Freud and of psychoanalysis, since Freud's understanding of memory and of traumatic memory underwent continual revision throughout his writings, particularly regarding the question of the relation *between* memories of traumatic events and psychical predisposition. It remains, however, that psychical predisposition entails dominant *fantasy* scenarios.
3. This lack has, in part, begun to be made good by recent research into the historical reception of film by specific audiences. Such research has begun to ask how memory shapes the responses audiences give to interviews or questionnaires (see Stacey (1993); Stacey (1994); Kuhn (1996)).
4. See the introduction to this volume for a discussion of the recent prioritisation of memory within the humanities.
5. Here, I am referring to contemporary debates about the status of historical knowledge. For pithy summaries of and selections from these debates, see Jenkins (1991) and Jenkins (1997).
6. For one account of a particular memory project at the Birmingham Centre for Contemporary Cultural Studies, see Clare and Johnson in this volume.
7. This abbreviated account of a psychoanalytic understanding of psychical temporality is informed by Jean Laplanche's writings on the topic, which, as he points out, differ considerably from Freud's views (Laplanche 1992: 220). John Fletcher and Martin Stanton's dossier of Laplanche's writings includes, also, some very useful commentaries on this topic (ibid).
8. This summary obviously vastly oversimplifies Freud's constantly evolving understandings of memory, trauma and fantasy. For longer and far more helpful summaries see Laplanche and Pontalis (1988), 465–73.
9. I refer here, to the often inspiring research which has been presented, over the last several years, at the London 'Psychoanalysis and History' seminars organised by Sally Alexander (Goldsmiths College) and Barbara Taylor (University of East London).

10. See page 12 above.
11. Here, Elaine Showalter's thesis concerning 'hystories' follows Freud's revision of the 'seduction theory' in suggesting that the 'memories' that underpin hystories might better be understood as fantasies linked to unacknowledgeable feelings and desires. For a longer discussion of Showalter's *Hystories* see Radstone (1999).
12. By 'critical' I take Craib to mean knowing and consistent with reflective distanciation.
13. Bollas derives his understanding of the initial effects of 'things done' from Donald Winnicott's (Winnicott 1971) analysis of young children's play. The example he quotes describes an experiment in which Winnicott presented a young child with a new plaything, which could only be interesting to the child after an initial gap, or pause, in which the child recovers from its 'unthinkability' (Bollas 1995: 112).
14. Burgoyne's essay shares with Foucault's 'Film and Popular Memory' (Foucault 1989) an emphasis upon film's capacity to 'refunction' or 'reprogramme' memory: '(t)oday, cheap books aren't enough. There are much more effective means like television and the cinema. And I believe this was one way of reprogramming popular memory, which existed but had no way of expressing itself. So people are shown not what they were, but what they must remember having been' (ibid: 92).
15. I am certainly not the first to call for the integration of cinepsychoanalysis' foregrounding of the cinema's relation to fantasy, with an approach which foregrounds the cinema's place in the constitution of history and memory. (See, for instance, Geoffrey Nowell-Smith (1990)).
16. Here, I am using the term 'symbolisation' in its broadest sense to refer to any 'mode of indirect and figurative representation of an unconscious idea, conflict or wish' (Laplanche and Pontalis 1988: 442).
17. This clearly begs the question of the relationship between an abstract 'spectator' and real, historical audiences. Here, I suggest a reading that prompts remembrance after an earlier turning away. But while older audiences will have lived through the represented events, for younger audiences the film will prompt, or 'implant', as Burgoyne would have it, memories of unexperienced (though not unknown) events. My analysis assumes both a time lag between 'facts' and remembrance, and a particular historical psycho-social context that impacts upon the capacity to remember.

Bibliography

American Psychiatric Association (1994), *Diagnostic and Statistical Manual of Mental Disorders*, 4th Edition, Washington D.C.: American Psychiatric Association.

Angell, Roger (1995), 'Two Dreams', *The New Yorker*, 13 March, 7.

Antze, Paul and Lambek, Michael, (1996), 'Introduction: Forecasting Memory', in Paul Antze and Michael Lambek, (eds), *Tense Past: Cultural Essays in Trauma and Memory*, New York and London: Routledge.

Barnes, Clive (1994), 'The Gumping of America', *Evening Standard*, 17 August, 13.

Bollas, Christopher (1995), *Cracking Up: The Work of Unconscious Experience*, London: Routledge.

Burgoyne, Robert (1997), *Film Nation: Hollywood Looks at U.S. History*, Minneapolis and London: University of Minnesota Press.

Carter, Erica and Hirschkop, Ken (1997), 'Editorial', in *Cultural Memory, New Formations* 30, Winter, v-vii.

Caruth, Cathy (1991), Introduction to 'Psychoanalysis, Culture and Trauma', *American Imago*, vol 48, no 1, 1–12.

Centre for Contemporary Cultural Studies (1982), *Making Histories: Studies in History Writing and Politics*, London: Hutchinson.

Chamberlain, Mary and Thompson, Paul (1998), *Narrative and Genre, Routledge Studies in Memory and Narrative*, volume 1, London: Routledge.

Charity, Tom (1994), review of *Forrest Gump*, *Time Out*, 5–12 October, 67.

Corliss, Richard (1994), review of *Forrest Gump*, *Time*, 1 August, 41–2.

Craib, Ian (1994), *The Importance of Disappointment*, London: Routledge.

Crews, Frederick (1995), *The Memory Wars: Freud's Legacy in Dispute*, New York: New York Review of Books.

Elsaesser, Thomas (1996), 'Subject positions, speaking positions: from *Holocaust, Our Hitler,* and *Heimat* to *Shoah* and *Schindler's List*', in Vivian Sobchack (ed.), *The Persistence of History*, (op.cit.), 145–83.

Foucault, Michel (1989), 'Film and Popular Memory', in *Foucault Live (Interviews 1966–1984)*, New York: Semiotext(e), 89–106.

Freud, Sigmund and Breuer, Joseph, ([1893–95] 1974), *Studies on Hysteria*, Penguin Freud Library, volume 3, Harmonsdsworth: Penguin.

Freud, Sigmund ([1900] 1976), *The Interpretation of Dreams*, Penguin Freud Library, volume 4, Harmondsworth: Penguin.

Freud, Sigmund ([1905] 1977), 'Fragment of an analysis of a case of hysteria ("Dora")', Penguin Freud Library, volume 8, Harmonsdsworth: Penguin.

Friedlander, Saul (1992) (ed.), *Probing the Limits of Representation: Nazism and the 'Final Solution'*, Cambridge (Mass.): Harvard University Press.

Gledhill, Christine (1987), 'The Melodramatic Field: An Investigation', in Christine Gledhill, (ed.) *Home is where the Heart is: Studies in Melodrama and the Woman's Film*, London: British Film Institute, 5–39.

Hacking, Ian (1996), 'Memory Sciences, Memory Politics', in Paul Antze, and Michael Lambek, (eds), *Tense Past*, (op. cit.).

Hibbert, Tom (1994), review of *Forrest Gump*, *Premiere*, vol 2, no 10, November, 78–9.

Hoberman, J (1994), review of *Forrest Gump*, *Village Voice*, 12 July, 41.

Huyssen, Andreas (1995), *Twilight Memories: Marking Time in a Culture of Amnesia*, New York and London: Routledge.

Jameson, Fredric (1984), 'Postmodernism, or the Cultural Logic of Late Capitalism', *New Left Review* 146, 53-92.

Jenkins, Keith (1991), *Re-Thinking History*, London: Routledge.

Jenkins, Keith (1997), *The Postmodern History Reader*, London: Routledge.

Joseph, Bobby (1994), review of *Forrest Gump*, *Morning Star,* 8 October, 7.

Kenny, Michael (1996), 'Trauma, Time, Illness and Culture: An Anthropological Approach to Traumatic Memory', in Paul Antze and Michael Lambek (eds), *Tense Past: Cultural Essays in Trauma and Memory,* New York and London: Routledge.

King, Nicola (1997), 'Autobiography as Cultural Memory: Three Case Studies', in *Cultural Memory, New Formations* 30, 50–62.

Kuhn, Annette (1995), *Family Secrets: Acts of Memory and Imagination,* London: Verso.

Kuhn, Annette (1996), Spoken paper on current research given in 'Historiographies and National Cinema Cultures: A Methodological Debate' workshop, Society for Cinema Studies conference, Dallas, Texas.

Landsberg, Alison (1995), 'Prosthetic Memory: *Total Recall and Blade Runner'*, in Mike Featherstone and Roger Burrows (eds), *Cyberspace/Cyberbodies/Cyberpunk: Cultures of Technological Embodiment*, London: Sage, 175–89.

Laplanche, Jean (1992), 'Notes on Afterwardsness', in John Fletcher and Martin Stanton (eds), *Jean Laplanche: Seduction, Translation, Drives,* London: Institute of Contemporary Arts, 217–23.

Laplanche, Jean and Pontalis, J. B (1968), 'Fantasy and the Origins of Sexuality', *International Journal of Psychoanalysis,* 49, 1–18.

Laplanche, J. and Pontalis, J. B (1988), *The Language of Psychoanalysis,* London: Karnac Books.

Lapsley, Robert and Westlake, Michael (1988), *Film Theory: An Introduction,* Manchester: Manchester University Press.

Maier, Charles (1988), *The Unmasterable Past: History, Holocaust and German National Identity,* Cambridge (Mass.) and London: Harvard University Press.

Mayne, Judith (1993), *Cinema and Specatorship,* London and New York: Routledge.

Masson, Jeffrey (1984), *The Assault on Truth: Freud's Suppression of the Seduction Theory,* New York: Farrar Straus Giroux.

Metz, Christian (1975), 'The imaginary signifier', *Screen* 16, 2 Summer, 14–76.

Metz, Christian (1982), *Psychoanalysis and the Cinema: The Imaginary Signifier,* London: Macmillan.

Moretti, Franco (1983), *Signs Taken for Wonders,* London: Verso.

Neale, Steve (1986), 'Melodrama and Tears', *Screen,* vol 27, no 6, pp 6–22.

Nowell-Smith, Geoffrey (1990), 'On History and the Cinema', *Screen,* vol 31, no 2, 160–71.

Passerini, Luisa (1987), *Fascism in Popular Memory: The Cultural Experience of the Turin Working Class,* trans. Robert Lumley and Jude Bloomfield, Cambridge: Cambridge University Press.

Parisi, Paula (1994), 'Forrest Gump Gallops Through Time', *American Cinematographer,* vol 75, no 10, October, 38–40.

Radstone, Susannah (1999), review article of Elaine Showalter, *Hystories,* Kim Lacy Rogers and Selma Leydesdorff with Graham Dawson (eds), *Trauma and Life Stories, Routledge Studies in Memory and Narrative,* London: Routledge.

Romney, Jonathan (1994), 'Transatlantic Gumption', *New Statesman and Society* 14 October, 41.

Scott, Ann (1996), *Real Events Revisited: Fantasy, Memory and Psychoanalysis,* London: Virago.

Showalter, Elaine (1997), *Hystories: Hysterical Epidemics and Modern Media,* New York: Columbia University Press.

Sobchack, Vivian (1996), *The Persistence of History: Cinema, Television and the Modern Event,* New York and London: Routledge.

Stacey, Jackie (1993), 'Textual Obsessions: Method, Memory and Researching Female Spectatorship', *Screen,* vol 34, no 3, 260–74.

Stacey, Jackie (1994), 'Hollywood Memories', *Screen*, vol 35, no 4, 317–35.

Turim, Maureen (1989), *Flashbacks in Film: Memory and History,* New York and London: Routledge.

Vicinus, Martha (1981), 'Helpless and Unfriended: Nineteenth Century Domestic Melodrama', *New Literary History*, vol 13, no 1, Autumn.

Vidali, Anna (1996), 'Political Identity and the Transmission of Trauma', in *Cultural Memory, New Formations 30,* 33–45.

Walker, Alexander (1994), review of *Forrest Gump, Evening Standard,* 6 October, 32.

Winnicott, Donald (1971), *Playing and Reality,* London, Tavistock Publications Ltd.

Zetlin, Monica (1994), review of *Forrest Gump,* in *Cinema Papers* 102, December, 68–9.

Part II
Memory/Subjectivity/Culture

5

'Memory, Subjectivity and Intimacy: the Historical Formation of the Modern Self and the Writing of Female Autobiography'

Gillian Swanson

This chapter is about the relationship between the historical formation of modern subjectivity and the place we give to memory in the intersection between the individual and culture. One of the premises of my approach will be to suggest that memory does not exist as a separate realm from authorised domains of knowledge, but is itself constituted through historically specific cultural knowledges. At the centre of our understanding of memory is a concept of the subject which, from the late eighteenth century, comes to be constituted as a perceptual, emotional and intellectual centre from which the particularities of an individual's character and life are expressed. This 'subject' is a very particular construction, a modern Western subject which embodies a particular, modern way of understanding the world based on its registration on individual consciousness. Such a recognition points us to the conclusion that imagining a 'self' – and writing autobiography from this perspective – is an historically specific gesture, a result of seeing subjectivity as a valid centre of meaning and knowledge. As a result of the perspectival nature of subjective perception, though, memory is rendered problematic as an authoritative form of knowledge about 'the world' rather than 'the self'.

Sexual subjectivity – the framing of characteristics and attributes, ways of feeling and behaving, according to a system of sexual differences – is also a historical, rather than solely a personal, achievement. In particular, those cultural motifs of the private self which are denoted by 'the individual' – as opposed to the public persona of the citizen – are more firmly associated with femininity and lead them to become more easily aligned with the female subject. The major part of this essay therefore charts the historical formation of a way of thinking that prioritises individuality and the 'inner self', and shows how this is linked to the sexual subject by situating the feminine in relation to privacy, intimacy and the subjective. The final section looks at how this understanding of the co-ordinates of subjectivity allows us to navigate the space of subjectivity – of experience and circumstance – and examines the ways in which memory becomes located in the space of privacy and intimacy, and the movement of bodies in space.

One dimension of this tracing of sexually specific concepts of subjectivity leads us to examine the fragility of a claim to coherent subjectivity: the individual as a centre registering impressions and generating expressions of a unified character; an individual with a unique identity; an imagined continuous, unified and interiorised self. For the concept of 'the subject' has, built into it – even at the moment of its consolidation during the nineteenth century – a form of instability. Its constitutive features – the intensification of the private and intimate self, the self as fundamentally relational – act against the imagined unified persona of public masculinity, the citizen-subject. As the cultural motifs of the 'individual' act to align the subjective self with the feminine, so too those disunifying elements that characterise the concept of subjectivity *per se* become inscribed onto that of femininity. The question that this research raises, for those who may wish to write female autobiography, is to what extent these motifs – and their capacity to disturb a chimerical wholeness – still haunt our conceptions of female subjectivity and our ability to trace its processes of becoming.

The Modern Subject: Memory, Intimacy and 'Becoming'

In his consideration of the development of the modern novel, Mikhail Bakhtin (1981) argues that the development of novelistic form is linked to the introduction of new ways of conceiving of time and space, history, memory and the present. In his account, the epic is the world of a heroic past, a valorised and inaccessible world of origin and unity, national beginnings. The world of the epic is the world of 'fathers' – ancestors and founders – separated from contemporary reality and distanced from the time of the author and audience, whose only perspective can be that of reverent descendants. The epic is a pre-modern form, then, in which memory acts to sacralise an 'absolute' past. This past, which lacks the relativity of a relation to the present, is postulated according to an unchangeable tradition: absolute and conclusive, complete and closed. The epic's claim to an authentic essence 'beyond the realm of human activity' precludes openendedness, indeterminacy, continuation, and thus is constructed in the absence of relativity, of human perspective (ibid: 11–17).

> The epic world is constructed in the zone of an absolute distanced image, beyond the sphere of possible contact with the developing, incomplete and therefore re-thinking and re-evaluating present . . . a zone outside any possible contact with the present in all its openendedness (ibid: 17–19).

One of the defining characteristics of the modern novel, in contrast, is its operation on the same 'time-and-value plane' as that of contemporary reality: 'the zone of "my time", from the zone of familiar contact with me' (ibid: 14). It can thus build in temporal continuation, with all the openendedness, lack of fixed value and meaning, and perspectival relativity that this brings with it. The form of the modern novel, therefore, builds in the contemporary viewpoint, 'the realm of human activity', rather than presenting its narrative, through epic memory, as unquestionable and absolute – valorised, impersonal, immutable.

Bakhtin's reading of the modern novel constitutes an account of the introduction of the subject into representation and simultaneously demonstrates the conditions of possibility for subjective knowledge. As if by chance, it simultaneously provides an account of the formation of modern subjectivity – modern ways of conceiving the world with a subjective consciousness at its centre. The presubjective fails to accord individual consciousness a status of centrality – 'subjects' took on their meaning from those places they occupied within the life of the polis, or the nation state. In the pre-subjective period of the novel national designations are absolute. As hero, author and audience are fused in the distanced zone of epic memory – as functions of an event, a time, the inherited positioning of tradition – a hierarchy of authority is embodied in the symbols and gestures of epic representation.

> In the world of (epic) memory, a phenomenon exists in its own particular context, with its own special rules, subject to conditions quite different from those we meet in the world we see with our own eyes, the world of practice and familiar contact (ibid: 18).

While memory, in the epic, ossifies the past into a world of hierarchical meaning outside human intervention or familiarity, the novel is distinguished as a genre whose epistemological parallel is no longer epic memory but knowledge, as narrative and meaning is formed through human intervention in the contemporary field, or the 'zone of contact' and recognition. Knowledge lacks the distance and the unified quality of the absolute which is to be found in epic memory: it develops within the contemporary field of human activity and intelligence, is thus open to evaluation and is compromised by relativity. The achievement of the novel, then, is the achievement of the introduction of subjectivity into representation, a subjectivity that is itself the product of this new ascendance of a relative and evolving field of knowledge over the absolute and final view of epic memory, as the co-ordinates of representation and the anchors of the articulation of selfhood become established in contemporary time and space. In Bakhtin's argument, it is the introduction of the author into novelistic representation that marks this literary and epistemological shift. For with a relative realm of knowledge, the novelist may write in ways which acknowledge that incomplete contemporary world which forms (his) own landscape, may enter into 'dialogic relations' with that which (he) represents, including (his) own narration and the language of the hero (ibid: 28). For Bakhtin this has two main effects: the first is that the novelistic image becomes one which is integrated into the realm of contemporary existence and reality; the second is that this new time/space relation leaves the novelistic image – and that 'contemporary reality' which now forms part of the novelistic field – open to a new kind of 'problematicalness . . . an eternal rethinking and re-evaluating' deriving from the (multiple) perspective of the subject (ibid: 31), in short a field we are more familiar with describing in terms of our modern concept of 'memory'.

But a third effect, with which Bakhtin is less concerned, is that the subjective, which now forms part of this process of integration between representation and reality, itself becomes formed in the image of the inconclusiveness and relativity which perspective and recognition brings to the novel and its conception of space and time, both of history and of the contemporary present. What Bakhtin describes when he notes the incorporation of perspective and human interjection into the novelistic field of representation, is in fact a new way of thinking of the subject: it is, in fact, the beginning of the formation of the concept of the 'subjective' in all its relativity and openendedness, in all its indeterminacy and its intimacy.

This is implicit in his argument that both reality and the depiction of the individual in the novel lack 'essence'. This he sees as following from the disintegration of the integrity of the single and unified world view in favour of 'varying "truths"', and the introduction of viewpoint in the construction of the individual character, a 'tension between the external and the internal man' which prevents him being 'completely incarnated into the flesh of existing sociohistorical categories', into the flow of tradition as fate or destiny ibid: 357). With the introduction of the 'spontaneity of the inconclusive present' (ibid: 27) both reality and the individual are given a new sense of continuation and future. They are thereby character-ised by a lack of wholeness and completedness, and thus a new *instability,* which renders them historical. This is what allows Bakhtin to make his claim that the novel 'is the genre of becoming':

> when the present becomes the center of human orientation in time and in the world, time and the world lose their completedness . . . (they) become historical: they unfold . . . as becoming, as an uninterrupted movement into a real future. as a unified, all-embracing and unconcluded process (ibid: 30).

Bakhtin also notes that '(e)pic disintegrates when the search begins for a new point of view on one's own self' and remarks 'how important it is for subjectivity' but this is as far as his observation on subjectivity *per se is* taken (ibid: 34). Nevertheless, it is possible to see in his analysis the absolutely constitutive link between a new historical consciousness and a new conception of subjectivity, not as essence, but *as itself historical,* caught up in the process of 'becoming'.

In another of Bakhtin's unelaborated notes, he indicates the different way in which 'memory' might be conceived when situated in the exchange between the historical and the subjective. Discussing the Socratic dialogues as a precedent for the modern novel, he states:

> 'Memory' in memoirs and autobiographies is of a special sort: it is memory of one's own contemporaneity and of one's own self. It is . . . personal memory without pre-existing chronological pattern, bounded only by the termini of a single personal life (ibid: 24).

Again, the contemporary viewpoint allows a 'new orientation in the world and in time', and thus a 'diversity' within contemporary reality (ibid: 25): subjectivity therefore allows memory to be understood, now, in the light of what Bakhtin has referred to as that relative field of 'knowledge', incorporating difference and familiarity, as well as all the other correlates of an ongoing, inconclusive and processual, historical subjectivity. The novel therefore reconfigures memory in this light, and now has to be seen in terms of shifts towards a new 'temporal orientation and . . . zone of contact' (ibid: 33). In other words it needs to be seen in terms of the new historical attitude towards time and the introduction of the personal vantage point through the proximity of the image to the familiar 'my time' of the flow of life.

The novel's field of memory is therefore comprised of 'unofficial' language and thought, which embrace the 'living forms' of familiar speech and profanation (ibid: 20), as well as those extraliterary genres such as letters, diaries, political manifestos, philosophical tracts, moral confessions and forms of rhetoric (ibid: 33). It is this material everydayness of the novel's formal components and referents which most assure its relationship to a historicised subjective consciousness, and which create a field of convergence in the notion of memory as it becomes redefined by the ascendancy of the novel. For modern memory is thus constructed on a plane of intimacy, a plane on which history and subjectivity are now able to meet, but one which is inflected by the cultural meaning of the particular rituals and interactions of private life.

In nineteenth century life, the recording of memories became an essential gesture with which individuals could claim a place in the world and in time, converting the 'trivial moments' of banal quotidian life into 'fruitful duration' as they became saturated with the sentimental meaning of the souvenir (Martin-Fugier, 1990: 262–3). Diaries, passbooks, photographs, relics, all became associated with the documentation of familial bonds, identity and futures and the recording of secrets and confidences: a relational zone of the personal and private, of intimacy and emotion (ibid: 263-5). As such, these rituals transferred the realm of memory into the space of private life, and it became fundamentally connected to the making of individual identity, with both temporal and spatial connections to the domestic and the feminine.[1]

While the modern subject may have become consolidated over the course of the nineteenth century and the subjective may have been formed as a key dimension of individual experience and functioning, it was accompanied by a keen anxiety over the appropriate domains for its expression. There was an ambivalence concerning the representation of the subjective and especially of those dimensions of human experience which were not fully disciplined according to moral imperatives concerning restraint and self-control: the sexual, sensory experience and excitation, the instincts, and the nerves. These were the features of instability which drove the controversies and moral approbations which surrounded the appearance of the sensation novel in the last quarter of the century, a genre whose narratives and character types were based on exactly those sexual and psychological maladies of the 'dangerously subjective'. The popularity of the sensation novel, its public vilification, and the commentary on its function as a symptom of modern moral disease in medico-psychological texts, all indicate a widespread attentiveness to the constitutive risks associated with the delineation of a personal and intimate emotional economy as part of modern subjectivity (Bourne Taylor, 1988: 4–6, 27–39). The proposition that there were specific dangers accruing to an individuated and psychologised subjectivity show how far pre-subjective conceptions of (fundamentally masculine) personhood persist, recycling a claim to those archaic models of origin and tradition, complete-ness and hierarchy, which is now made by reference to a new standard of coherence and identity. Against this background, the incursion of the subjective, as a constitutive element in the functioning of the modern subject, can only put the disciplined, attentive, impersonal functioning of moral consciousness, triumphing over the limits and wilful temptations of the senses, at risk. Hence it becomes segregated to a place outside the everyday functioning of modern public life. Its frailties – the disorders of the senses, nerves and sexuality – are thus connected to a 'feminine sensibility' that is managed by its spatial and psychological removal from public life and masculine character. By its association with the feminine, then, the subjective, the individual and the private came to be seen as antipathetic to the domains which constitute 'history', eventually being fundamentally defined by this opposition.

This is the constitutive instability at the heart of notions of modern subjectivity, one which elicits a disciplined attention to the delineation of appropriate forms of subjective expression and the manifestation of subjectivity in representation. This does not simply *limit* the articulation of the subjective, as is so often claimed, but, more accurately, it operates to draw the contours of subjectivity and its function in representation. For it is in the exchange between those new forms of representation – of the intimate, the personal, of the materialised forms of individual memory and its claim to a *historical* consciousness – and those proscriptions upon their public circulation and the representation of the subjective, that the co-ordinates of how we understand and articulate the relationship between subjectivity, memory and history are formed. This is an ongoing and uneven process which is not fully resolved at any moment. Perhaps it is enough to note the historical co-existence of contradictory attitudes to subjectivity, their contesting of an essentially speculative postulation of the individual, the personal and the subjective, in order to find the practical means of revising those notions of subjectivity in ways that give them historical force – a way of 'becoming'.

Mobile Subjectivity: City, Home, Body as the Space of Exile

The foregrounding of perspective, towards the end of the nineteenth century, brings the relation of the self and the social world to the centre of subjectivity, marking it with an unresolved and fluid status. Its insertion into a newly defined field of historical memory, its relegation to a domain of private life 'outside' history all create an ambivalence, an uncertainty of relations between public and private, masculine and feminine, particularly within masculinity. For it is masculinity which bears this divide within itself, in its claim to a part in history, to a unified and coherent public self which can transcend the disturbances created by the unruly incursions of the subjective. As the constitution of effective masculinity rests upon the management of the delicate relations between subjectivity and public character, the presence of the subjective produces a realm of instability within the category of masculinity itself: an historical divide, or a 'foreignness to itself', which arises through the abolition of unitary meaning in relation to character, and the incorporation of viewpoint into subjectivity. The very formation of the modern subject puts at risk its claim to an archaic story of individual essence, a narrative consistency between origin and realisation, and perspectival stability.

It is the instability in the modern concept of subjectivity that was highlighted in those new ways of describing subjective experience, which is why such disciplines as psychoanalysis develop challenges to the proponents of mechanical objectivity in the same period. In other words, psychoanalysis' account of the fundamental instability of the subject – through which it postulates a realm of the unconscious continually threatening to disrupt the imagined integrity of unified subjectivity – is a product of the history of the concept of the subject, and its emergence in association with the new recognition accorded to the *relative* realm of the subjective. Psychoanalysis – and its origins in alienism – therefore functions partly as a critique of previous organicist concepts of mental life, dependent upon a unified biological system whose disruption could only be defined in terms of pathology. It can therefore be taken as symptomatic of those new ways of conceiving of the exchanges between different dimensions of experience and their traces in an individual's psychological formation and interaction. The inherent instability which psychoanalysis proposes is referred to by Julia Kristeva as the experience of the 'foreigner' or 'stranger', as the self becomes seen as 'divided' and fragmented by the flow of interaction, experience, memory:

> With Freud indeed, foreignness, an uncanny one, creeps into the tranquillity of reason itself, and, without being restricted to madness, beauty, or faith anymore than to ethnicity or race, irrigates our very speaking-being, estranged by other logics, including the heterogeneity of biology . . . Henceforth, we know that we are foreigners to ourselves, and it is with the help of that sole support that we can attempt to live with others (Kristeva, 1991: 170).

Kristeva's argument that Freudian psychoanalysis brings into knowledges of the self an acknowledgment of estrangement, of the constitutional divide in subjectivity that is so damaging to conceptions of public masculinity, is set beside a recognition of the alternative 'pull' of nationalism towards a unified masculine embodiment, in the figure of the citizen:

> nationalism has become a symptom . . . of the nineteenth and twentieth centuries. Now, while it does go against universalist tendencies . . . nationalism nevertheless ends up . . . with the particularistic, demanding, individualism of contemporary man. But it is perhaps on the basis of that contemporary individualism's subversion, beginning with the moment when the citizen-individual ceases to consider himself as unitary and glorious but discovers his incoherences and abysses . . . that the question [of the foreigner] arises again . . . (Kristeva: 1991: 2).

A new kind of unity, then, is claimed in the figure of the citizen-individual, that public masculine being. But it is one shot through with the acknowledgment of gaps and incoherences, the failure of an essential, inviolable unity that is brought about by the fragmentation and relationality of a culturally specific subjectivity which is produced historically through those divisions accorded to public/private, exterior/interior, the real/the imagined, the world/the individual, in a particular period. This is the 'exile' of a subjectivity which can only lay claim to a fractured history of mobile attachments, momentary illuminations, and incomplete identifications:

> We live by a series of encounters – with friends, lovers, books, places – but every encounter, as Jacques Derrida says, is 'separation', a 'contradiction of logic' in that it signals an encounter with something other than ourselves, a long-felt absence, that element of difference that breaks the illusory unity of the self. For the story . . . is always already about the foreigner in ourselves (Kamboureli, 1993: 143).

What is the space of this foreigner, of this experience of exile, within a masculine, public, economy of the self? Just as nations developed in parallel with the creation of the modern city, so these cities became places of exile: of migration and dislocation and the loss of the moorings of continuity. As the exile world in the city becomes frozen by 'generations clinging to the past . . . divided in their memories between the horrors or deprivations that had impelled them to move and longing for a vanished home', the exile nevertheless 'must travel beyond the realities summoned through memory in terror and regret; an exile must go forward in time'

(Sennett, 1990: 135–6). The exile therefore can only retrieve a space within which to mobilise the imagined wholeness and stability of viewpoint embodied in a concept of the self in an acceptance of the recognition of difference instigated by the encounter. The challenge is to perform an *embodiment* of home, as the mobile body becomes the space of the self, the site of a new form of memory which brings the remembrance of the past into the corporeal tracings of the present.

This is itself a point of tension in the retrieval of a newly adjusted masculine historical present. For spatially, inhabitation of the city cannot offer the intimacy that subjectivity requires. Its logic would lead it to a further retraction, into the private space of the home, into an intersubjective, unresolved and relational space of perpetual becoming: into, in fact, the dissolution of its own premise. What is so threatening to 'the self' of masculinity are the dimensions of subjectivity that undermine a unified, historically achieved, public character situated in epic time. The intensification of the private and intimate self, life oriented around the intimacy of the familial and the sexual, the relationality of a subjectivity composed from the imprint of 'the encounter', and the pressing *presence* of corporeal being, all imply a series of displacements which prevent the integration of being and action which epic memory allowed.[2] It is these dimensions, as they constitute the foreignness of a subjectivity operating within the historical present, that become marked with the cultural meanings of femininity: the very motifs by which the contemporaneity of the subject can be marked become associated with 'the feminine'.

Perhaps this is one reason that 'urban life' becomes understood as constituting a *feminised* public space, associated with the escalation of the consumption and entertainment industries and their facilitation of women's public presence (Wilson, 1995; Swanson, 1995). These commercial exchanges are most pressingly evident in the modern city's public manifestation of prostitution, as the prostitute becomes a symbol of the negative outcomes of the city's blurring of boundaries between public and private spaces and activities (Petro, 1987). In more general terms, the activities of commerce afford a new orientation of public life towards the encounter in the second half of the nineteenth and the beginning of the twentieth centuries. As the 'cultural reagent' of commerce remakes civic life in its own image, and public subjects – or 'the public' – become addressed as aggregates of consumers, so private life erupts into public space through the newly developing media, *or publicity* (Taylor, 1992: xvi–xvii, Colomina, 1994: 6). As Beatriz Colomina argues, publicity dissolves the boundaries between public and private, so that individuals are addressed not as part of a unified body, of 'the public', but as members of the audiences that each medium of publication reaches, independent of the place this audience might actually be occupying. But of course, the fact that (for the most part) this audience is indeed at home is not without consequence. The private is, in this sense, now more public than the public. . . . As Nietzsche saw it: '. . . Individuality has withdrawn within . . .' (Colomina 1994, 7–8).

The concerns expressed about this new relation were a feature of late modernity, and are evident in writings appearing at the turn of the century which imbue new technologies of travel, information, entertainment etc. with a potential to destroy the traditional sense of privacy, as a segregated dimension of experience operating at a remove from the public sphere, by allowing it to become orchestrated in the public spaces of new urban environments. As a result of these spatial and experiential reorganisations, we can also see the challenges that the incursion of the private – now seen as an ever-extending private – into public life, brings to the concept of the public subject around which masculinity takes on its meaning. If 'individuality has withdrawn within', the 'feminisation' of city space, in comparison to the abstract space of nation, of citizenship, of the 'longue duree' of stilled epic time, represents in material terms the problematic of exile: a state of fragmented being, a dividedness, that is seen as foreignness only in a comparison to epic being. It is this sense of dividedness which haunts those negative assessments of the effect of urban life on the subject, a mourning of the loss of a fantasy of perfect wholeness, a fantasy itself based on an imputed divide between whole subjects founded in sexually differentiated terms and anchoring the polarities around which public and private may be stabilised. The sense of dividedness which is brought about by the collapse of such distinctions – which women's involvement in the public business of urban life makes visible – is made sense of in terms of feminine displacements, as women become seen as alien to city life, polluting its orderliness. The result for masculine subjectivity is a sense of exile, as it flees those spaces which act as imaginary guarantors of its stable and uncontaminated vision, or 'truth'. The result for the meanings accorded to femininity is its distillation of the motif of displacement, as it is seen as finally incapable of occupying a secure space of unified meaning.

How, then, can feminine subjectivity embody a 'dividedness' that can be understood as imbued with the instability and lack of unity inherent in modern concepts of subjectivity *per se*? Those concepts of exiledom and foreignness inform the notion of femininity as 'lacking' completion, meanings which we inherit as the co-ordinates of female subjectivity. Yet while a 'lack' of completion at the heart of subjectivity may be displaced onto femininity, and feminine corporeality, they also distract us from the burden of that fantasy of unity which encumbers masculinity. While the introduction of the concept of the exile renders masculine subjectivity a fraught construction, in its constitution through the matrix of a modern 'self', that same matrix offers femininity a dividedness that can be embraced. Without the need to adhere to such fantasies of wholeness, we encounter a greater fluidity in the enactment of the feminine as an aspect of embodied subjectivity, the 'becoming' self of corporeal being. To take advantage of the legacy of femininity's displacement from the narratives of subjective unity – to rewrite the cultural history of feminine subjectivity as one which makes possible a mobile and embodied subjectivity – we need first to relativise the sense of loss that the concept of the exile assumes in its reference to the dividedness and fragmentation of modern being, to the dissolution of epic memory and time. As Richard Sennett points out:

> It is a modern habit to think of social instability and personal insufficiency as pure negatives. The formation of modern individualism has in general aimed at making individuals self-sufficient, that is to say, complete rather than incomplete (Sennett, 1990: 371).

This 'modern habit' is thus based on an imagined unity from which fragmentation can be seen as a negative, a negative which is only meaningful from a perspective which continues to situate subjectivity according to a divide between the intimate realms of the self and those of 'history', the formation of the disinterested public self in flagrant disregard of the incompleteness at the heart of the subject's experience of modern 'civilisation'. This divide replicates and reinforces the opposition established within sexual classifications, and so assumes a position *outside* the feminine, one that can only see those attributes of the feminine as antipathetic to the transcendent historical subject of that archaic story of masculine unity and epic achievement, and its correlate, the 'modern master image of the individual, detached body' (Sennett, 1990: 374). For the spaces of corporeality, relationality and private life do not constitute a 'foreignness' to the cultural constitution of feminine subjectivity or its claim to a historical situatedness: it is precisely those intimate inscriptions of memory which offer it a materialised being.

Where, then, do we find the traces of another sort of memory, as constitutive of a subjectivity whose meanings are founded upon corporeal materiality, the relation of the encounter, the dimensions of intimate being which can only exist in the incomplete spaces of the intersubjective? It is no coincidence that Gaston Bachelard (1969) sees the 'house' as the site of these traces, in his formulation of a spatialised subjectivity torn between immobility and becoming. Although he does not postulate this subjectivity as feminine, his model offers an alternative to that predicated on an elusive completeness which can only be fulfilled within an epic frame, and which consistently haunts the masculine subject. Bachelard, instead, argues that being is formed by our inhabitation of intimate space, the space in which 'we take root, day after day, in a "corner of the world"' . . . our house is our corner of the world' (Bachelard, 1969: 4). Located in intimate space, being is as fragmented as the intimate space of home, a space not of (self-) *realisation* but of (intersubjective) *encounter*. The subject is thus dispersed across the minutae of the topography of home, connected to the mass of detail and event, without a central orienting motif, such as that which nation or polis performs for the citizen-subject. 'Home' is essentially mobile, unfixed, harnessed to the narrative movement of memory-formation, yet stilled in the memorial gesture of attaching meaning to objects, to material space, of investing the meaning of self in the relation of bodies and spaces.

It is its connection to corporeal being, the inhabitation of space, and the absorption into the 'immensity' of memory – or as Bachelard describes it, the daydream – which gives the house its metaphorical charge: '(t)he word habit is too worn a word to express this passionate liaison of our bodies, which do not forget, with an unforgettable house' (ibid: 15). The ability to remember, to daydream, investing the spaces of the present with memories, collapses time, renders it immobile and finally disposes of the fantasy of operating in the epic time of historical achievement. In this memorial space, time is stilled around the present:

> Memories are motionless, and the more securely they are fixed in space, the sounder they are. To localize a memory in time is merely a matter for the biographer and only corresponds to a sort of external history . . . For a knowledge of intimacy, localization in the spaces of our intimacy is more urgent than determination of dates (ibid: 9).

By locating memory in the spaces of intimacy, Bachelard allows us to conceive of subjectivity as formed around the coincidence, not the polarisation, of being and becoming. For the daydream offers both a connection to the ordinary intimate spaces of the present, and the ability to exist in the 'spaces of elsewhere', of displacement, outside the constraints of temporal locatedness: 'the daydream transports the dreamer outside the immediate world to a world that bears the mark of infinity . . . a limitless world' (ibid: 183–5). Far from propelling us towards that stilled time of epic memory and the achievement of unified subjectivity, however, this form of temporal infinity is based around the endless possibilities for subjective becoming that the intensification of the intimate environment can provide, 'the intensity of a being evolving in a vast perspective of intimate immensity' (ibid: 193). Here, then, in the space of intimate memory, we can find a connection between the intensity of the familiar, the personal, the subjective – of corporeal and fragmented being – and the immensity of becoming. This is a different sort of relationality, borne from the intensity of domestic space, and forming the subjective from the connection to environment, a relation only gesture can perform, the 'passionate liaison of our bodies . . . with an unforgettable house'.

Modern subjectivity is therefore based on a gestural relation to environment, uncomfortable only to models of detached, masculine public subjectivity to which relationality is antipathetic. For gesture both contains and relates, attaches, and in its attachment changes the nature of the original being, in the 'shocks' that the environment can exert on the individual's subjective composition. The argument that 'shocks' were exerted on the individual by the unfamiliar stimuli and new demands of modern life – notably the urban experience of the crowd, and the jarring physical action and speed of railway travel – was common in nineteenth century Western nations. The Freudian concepts of the 'stimulus shield', the reciprocal concepts of the pleasure principle and the reality principle, and to a lesser extent his concept of neurosis, were devised in complement to such a model of the formation of the subject in response to the sensual stimuli deriving from its environment (see Shivelbusch, 1979: 152–60; Sennett, 1994: 372). Walter Benjamin, using Freud's concept of the stimulus shield, sees the 'shocks' of urban life as making 'true' remembrance – that which is only possible from the perspective of a stable and enduring subjectivity characteristic of the pre-modern historical consciousness – impossible (Benjamin 1970: 87–91). His essay on the decline of storytelling, the rise of the novel and the introduction of a new culture of 'information', mourns the demise of a confidence in modernity's ability to mobilise a masterful subjectivity, and as such it can be seen as symptomatic of the crisis of subjectivity developing in the era of late modernity, which he characterises in terms of a lowering in value of 'the experience' which should be 'viewed from a certain . . . proper distance and angle of vision' (ibid: 83). As storytelling, which performs this manouevre, declines, so the novel rises in its place, a form in which 'no event any longer comes to us without already being shot through with explanation' (ibid: 89). Benjamin's reading of this process is itself shot through with a very different pessimism from Bakhtin's account of the same process. As, in his view, the 'amplitude' of the narratives of storytelling is destroyed by the subject pressing (him)self into the frame in which the event becomes represented to us, so it is potentially eternally modified – and modifiable. This is the quality Benjamin refers to as standing 'in direct opposition to reality'; the 'new form of communication' which is 'information' (ibid: 88). In contrast to epic memory, which is based on 'the possibility of reproducing a story' (ibid: 97), modern memory is – in Bakhtin's terms – dialogic, bringing about an encounter between subjectivity and environment that Benjamin sees as translated in a central novelistic preoccupation: 'the "meaning of life"' (ibid: 99). The novel for Benjamin is, as it is expressed by Lukacs, a process of overcoming the divide between subjectivity and environment, 'inwardness and outside world', the unity of 'insight' into 'the meaning of life' as the 'centre around which the novel moves' (Lukacs, cited Benjamin, 1970: 99). But this can be grasped only in a vision made possible when the subject steps outside of his own particular and relative subjective perception, when he sees – in his insight – the 'unity of his entire life . . . out of the past life-stream which is compressed in memory' (Lukacs, cited Benjamin, 1970: 99). Lukacs' approach to the novel is thus a programmatic one symptomatic of the elements he (and Benjamin) fear will destroy that which is made possible by epic memory, the evasion of a purely subjective view in a transcendent vision of authoritative (epic) 'truth' and the evasion of the 'solitude' of the novelist in his harnessing of his own subjective vision to a communal humanity of readers inspired to a 'divinatory realisation of the meaning of life' (Benjamin, 1970: 100–1). To evade the disintegrating effects of a modern culture created from new technologies of 'information' on the integrity of the subject, and to restore those dimensions of 'truth' which have been lost in the prioritisation of individual perception (or the modern concept of subjectivity) Benjamin suggests, some element of storytelling needs to be restored to modern practices of writing: 'the storyteller is the figure in which the righteous man encounters himself' (ibid : 109). It is this which will prevent 'reality' from giving way to a 'remembrance', derogated by virtue of its harnessing of memory to individual perspective, or 'point of view' (ibid: 100).

The essentially gestural relationship to environment characteristic of modern subjectivity, according to which subjectivity is perpetually modified in the dialogue between pyche and environment, brings the subjective into an encounter with the particularistic, finally locating it in the domain of the corporeal, with the sensual as its major mediating mechanism. But in this relation between the intimate, the corporeal and the particularistic, and the immensity of becoming, is formed the tension, the difficulty implied in a perspective framed according to 'intimate immensity'. For while being in the 'space of elsewhere' offers a recognition of the difference of encounter, of being in the space of encounter, the *intersubjective* (ibid: 125–32), it also implies a lack of immersion, of situatedness and of impermeability, those very traits which so threaten the dream of unified being. The lack of immersion inherent to the intersubjective carries within it the melancholy of leaving aside the attachment to a prior state in which the lack of wholeness, the need 'to go on', did not press so heavily. This is the tension between immobility and becoming, that dividedness, that Sennett describes above in the paradox of the exile: frozen in their mourning of a past and the melancholy of longing for a vanished home, the migrant of the modern city must leave this seductive attachment to memory in order to become, to take memory into new forms of inhabitation, those new forms of corporealized encounter which exist in the present. For Bachelard, this is the dilemma of intimacy and memory, that one may become 'shut up in his weight, the prisoner of his own being' (Bachelard, 1969: 194): immensity, the daydream detached from temporal locatedness, carries a voluptuousness which allows being to ally itself to *becoming*:

> it opens up unlimited space. It . . . teaches us to breathe with the air that rests on the horizon, far from the walls of the chimerical prisons that are the cause of our anguish (ibid: 197).

This is a different conception of dividedness from that of the 'foreignness' of exile, a concept of dividedness that allows for an expansive approach to subjectivity not through the frame of the epic, but through that of intimacy and attachment, spatial locatedness and corporeal memory. While Bachelard still attempts to reconcile this into a 'unity', it may better be conceived as a perpetual tension, allowing a movement and historicity that takes it beyond any notion of transcendental integration. Located between the immediacy of intimate inhabited space and the spaces of 'elsewhere', between here and there, we incorporate difference and loss into a contingent self, formed in the movement of gesture but taking us into the world of reverie, a dislocated space of distractedness – not the abstract space of dreamscape but instead a known and specific space of everyday intimacy, the 'zone of "my time" . . . the zone of familiar contact with me' (Bakhtin, 1981: 14). The space of reverie therefore takes over the articulation of immediate space, redescribing it outside of bodily coherence and containment, allowing both an extension and dispersal of the self, a becoming wrought at the cost of fragmentation.

This is a subjectivity formed according to the co-ordinates of the feminine. Lacking wholeness, and the authority of epic being, it therefore reforms through other processes. Rather than eternally bound to the loss of wholeness, the failure of the coherence of an integrated and unified self, it is formed through the logic of the encounter, of the fragmented spaces of intimacy and private life, of the present of corporeality – the zone of 'my time' as a route to immensity, the zone of becoming.

Tracing Subjectivity: Migrancy and Corporeal Memory

The concern of this essay has been to examine how it is possible to develop a historical approach to the cultural co-ordinates of conceptions of subjectivity: in the transition to a new field of historical memory that materializes the inscriptions of the self and thereby situates it within an ongoing, relational and inconclusive field of knowledge; in the debates surrounding the nature of the self in modern urban life and in representations; in the rituals and gestures of sentimental attachment and emotional connection formed in the space of private, familial, life; in the 'incursion' of the private into the space of public life; in the threat to unified masculinity that the dividedness of segregated realms of experience entails. Responses to these changes are manifested in debates surrounding the epistemological value of objective knowledge as it transcends the dangers and temptations of the subjective viewpoint and its sensual contaminations of moral discipline and restraint, and in concerns over the 'foreignness' of the fragmentation and incompleteness of modern being as embodied in the figure of the exile. These are the ways in which a modern notion of the subjective has inflected the way we understand memory: not the fixed historical achievement of epic memory, but a fragmented field of perspectival knowledge, based on the intimate tracings of corporeal inhabitation, the alliance of gesture and encounter, and the expansiveness of reverie into that realm of intimate immensity, the possibility of becoming.

The recognition of the particularity of the sense of possibility and anxiety which accompanied the development of the subjective as the centrepiece of the modern individual is a part of both the work of the cultural historian and the work of the writer. For this acknowledgement of the contingency of our notions of self, our sense of the ways in which knowledge and experience work, can also help us explore the relationship between subjectivity, history and memory in representation, particularly, for my purposes, in autobiography.

We can see the concerns expressed in response to the developing visibility of a partial subjectivity – dislocated and wandering inside the secure spaces of that dualistic world view upon which a new middle-class conceptualisation of sexual difference was based – as symptomatic of an adherence to the imaginary wholeness of masculine transcendence and the unified view of 'history' in contrast to 'remembrance'. If we do adopt such a perspective, though, it does not suggest that feminine subject-ivity as it is thus defined – as lack of wholeness, dislocation, 'exile' and fragmentation, associated with the private or intimate spaces of personal life and the rituals of domestic detail and particularity, the processes whereby memory is inscribed in those spaces of encounter, the space of 'home' – is simply a ruse, falsely representing women according to negative traits. For what this history has shown is that it is in the *exchange* between masculinity and femininity that sexual difference is made, rather than simply in the image of masculinity. The motifs of femininity that we inherit from such a history inhabit our cultural imaginary in a more pervasive way than a simple ruse could do, imbuing the domain of personal relations and memorialised space and being with a subjectivity which makes the intimate imaginable and offers a set of co-ordinates for the perspective from which memory can be articulated. But just as we accept the historical weight of the feminine subjective, so we need to understand those ways in which we may engage with it in order to make it our own; to move towards a dialogic version of femininity arising from the specifi-cities of narratives that do not claim the spurious authority of transcendent subjectivity. How is it possible to write female autobiography in ways which acknowledge the contingency and cultural relativity of our notions of feminine subjectivity, in ways which connect up the stories of female experience with the historically formed motifs of their conception *as* feminine? How do we evade the privileging of the subjective, and memory, as truth – as giving a now untenable narrational authority – while retaining it as an object of attention and analysis. And how do we do this while also retaining those forms of recognition it may inspire in the reader, a familiarity with its parallel in the connection between other bodies and other homes, the relationality specific to the intimate performance of those 'passionate liaisons', those corporeal memories we invest in the spaces of our daily inhabitation.

There are no absolute answers to these questions, of course, except insofar as they depend upon the delicate prising apart of those historical strands by which our fragmented experience of self is formed. The result of this critical activity is to see fragmentation of self as a positive quality, and to chart it through the dimensions of female subjectivity that delineate our own autobiographical narratives, to restore those lost dimensions to domestic detail in a way which refuses the literality of secure meaning and fixed location. For modern memory is constructed on this plane of *intimacy*, a plane on which history and subjectivity converge, and whose inscriptions of memory can be investigated as the material articulations of historically situated subjective narratives.

It is for this reason that the autobiographical project appears to me as one in which we are compelled to explore the radical homelessness that immensity brings to the process of becoming, a process in which we can only situate ourselves as migrants, losing the fantasy of perspectival wholeness and being perpetually caught in the tension of movement and irresolution. But unlike the figure of the nomad – characterised according to a wanderingness, a space of perpetual departures – the figure of the migrant, formed also by displacement and dislocation, offers autobiographical writing a different option, a movement towards a new space of arrival. It is not only my own experience as a migrant – and that need to create again the dimensions of intimacy that sustain a sense of subjective cohesion and continuity – that leads me to find in the concept of migrancy a convincing metaphor for the process of forming new narratives, woven from the fleeting moments of corporeal inhabitation. It is also that these are the narratives which – like those rituals which memorialise subjective life by saturating domestic trinkets with the sentimental meaning of the souvenir – press themselves into intimate spaces imbued with the meanings which nostalgic recollection imparts. While a melancholic attachment to longing and loss may provide the destabilised perspective that memory rushes to fill, the migrant is able to move forward, impelled to create the components of a new intimacy: to move around new spaces with different contours, to orient the body towards new landmarks, to allow memory to emerge in the crevices of unfamiliar anecdotes, to attach a timeless significance to everyday objects. It is thus that we come to find ourselves at home in a changing landscape comprised of the banal moments of everyday life, poised at the edge of new forms of becoming, inhabiting the space between origin and destiny.

I left the places of my memories for a homelessness I thought would allow me to remake their stories into a different self, a self of dreams and possibilities. But how could I have anticipated the other side of those futures, that I would become engulfed by a mourning for objects I had never held, which I could neither give up nor properly keep with me except as the evidence of my departure?

. . . In remembrance, I became immobilised, a motionlessness of nostalgic recollection. Lost in the memory of previous times, revisiting the places of my other stories, my former selves, I was suffocated by the weight of their

positioning. I stayed in limbo, found no place to move forward from, no route that could be made between origin and aim, no direction from which to become . . . Without the attachment of my histories to the contours of these foreign spaces, without being able to read myself into their crevices, I could not escape the fantasies of solidity that remembrance held.

The horizon falls away and becomes soft. I can't make out the place where the sky meets the land, neither the place of my departure nor that of my arrival.

I find myself in a house with strange shapes and too many doors, unable to imagine arrangements of objects and things that would fit, unable to make passages between them, to recognise myself in my journeys around these determined spaces . . .The humid air clings to my face, in the heat I can't feel my skin. The edges of my body are lost to me . . .

I rail against the place of my abandonment . . .

As, slowly, my memory relocates itself, I trace myself into this landscape, find a synchrony with the space that surrounds me. In the movement of ordinary living and banal enactments, I invent a place. The voice of remote recollection reverberates across new horizons . . .

As I disperse myself across new and illegible deserts, you are multiplied, transformed. In the movement between, I escape the immobility of remembrance. And I lose its ecstasy. Passing between the history of my becoming and my hope, my anticipation and my possibility, I find only a fluid body, the site of a new enactment and an endless repetition.

The ground moves out from under my feet.

I invest other bodies with the pattern of our separation. I move towards their forms, take on their skin, and I read my connection in other landscapes, in the smoke as it trails across the empty sky in the dying light.

Your likeness burns its traces in my flesh, till I can see you no more . . . but only a shadow cast . . . of a loved object already lost.[3]

Notes

1. 'Home and the hours of darkness: these defined the spatial and temporal limits of privacy around the individual . . .' (Perrot 1990b: 453).
2. Explaining the importance of a shifting sense of place to the representation of 'personal displacements' as a motif of modernity in urban fiction, in a discussion of E.M. Forster's work, Richard Sennett notes, '. . . even as the people in *Howard's End* lose certainty about themselves, they become physically aroused by the world in which they live and they gain more awareness of one another. Forster conceived of displacement somewhat as Milton thought of exile from the Garden in *Paradise Lost*. In Forster's novel, personal displacements have a specific social dimension' (1994: 351).
3. Extract from Swanson, unpublished mss, with reference to Bachelard (1969) and Kristeva (1987).

Bibliography

Bachelard, Gaston (1969), *The Poetics of Space,* Boston: Beacon Press.

Bakhtin, M.M. (1981), *The Dialogic Imagination: Four Essays by M.M. Bakhtin,* Edited by Michael Holquist, Austin, Texas: University of Texas Press.

Benjamin, Jessica (1990), *The Bonds of Love: Psychoanalysis, Feminism and the Problem of Domination,* London: Virago.

Benjamin, Walter (1970), 'The Storyteller', *Illuminations,* London: Jonathan Cape.

Bourne Taylor, Jenny (1988), *In the Secret Theatre of Home: Wilkie Collin, Sensation Narrative and Nineteenth-Century Psychology,* London: Routledge.

Colomina, Beatriz (1994), *Privacy and Publicity: Modern Architecture as Mass Media,* Cambridge, Mass. and London, England: The MIT Press.

Corbin, Alain (1990), 'The Secret of the Individual' in Michelle Perrot (ed.), A *History of Private Life: From the Fires of Revolution to the Great War,* Cambridge, Mass and London, England: The Belknap Press of Harvard University Press.

Daston, Lorraine and Galison, Peter (1992), 'The Image of Objectivity', *Representations,* 40, Fall.

Davidoff, Leonore and Hall, Catherine (1987), *Family Fortunes: Men and Women of the English Middle Class 1780–1850*, London: Hutchinson.

Kamboureli, Smaro (1993), 'Of black angels and melancholy lovers: Ethnicity and writing in Canada', in Sneja Gunew and Anna Yeatman, *Feminism and the Politics of Difference:* Allen and Unwin, Sydney.

Kristeva, Julia (1987), 'On the melancholic imaginary', *New Formations*, 3.

Kristeva, Julia (1991), *Strangers to Ourselves*, Hertfordshire: Harvester Wheatsheaf.

Martin-Fugier, Anne (1990), 'Bourgeois Rituals' in Michelle Perrot (ed.), A *History of Private Life: From the Fires of Revolution to the Great War*, Cambridge, Mass and London, England: The Belknap Press of Harvard University Press.

Perrot, Michelle (ed.) (1990a), A *History of Private Life: From the Fires of Revolution to the Great War*, Cambridge, Mass and London, England: The Belknap Press of Harvard University Press.

Perrot, Michelle (1990b), 'Introduction' to 'Backstage', in Michelle Perrot (ed.), A *History of Private Life: From the Fires of Revolution to the Great War*, Cambridge, Mass and London, England: The Belknap Press of Harvard University Press.

Petro, Patrice (1987), 'Modernity and Mass Culture in Weimar: Contours of a Discourse on Sexuality in Early Theories of Reception and Representation', *New German Critique*, 40: 115–46.

Sennett, Richard (1990), *The Conscience of the Eye: The Design and Social Life of Cities*, New York: Alfred A. Knopf.

Sennett, Richard (1994), *Flesh and Stone: The Body and the City in Western Civilisation*, London and Boston: Faber and Faber.

Shivelbusch, Wolfgang (1979), *The Railway Journey: Trains and Travel in the Nineteenth Century*, New York: Urizen Books.

Swanson, Gillian (1995), '"Drunk With The Glitter": Consuming Spaces and Sexual Geographies', Sophie Watson and Kathie Gibson (eds), *Postmodern Cities and Spaces*, Oxford and New York: Basil Blackwell.

Swanson, Gillian (unpublished manuscript), *Becoming.*

Taylor, William R. (1992), *In Pursuit of Gotham: Culture and Commerce in New York*, Cambridge, Mass and Oxford: Oxford University Press.

Wilson, Elizabeth (1995), 'The Invisible Flaneur', in Sophie Watson and Kathie Gibson (eds), *Postmodern Cities and Spaces*, Oxford and New York: Basil Blackwell.

−6−

Children: Memories, Fantasies and Narratives: From Dilemma to Complexity
Amal Treacher

The media devotes much space to heated discussions concerning children, child abuse, the neglect of children, and the 'drop' in childrens' educational standards. These discussions are frequently unsubstantiated, however, by knowledge of and debate about the nature of childhood and the specificity of child development. Childhood seems to be a space, and children objects, about which many people seem to feel entitled to hold strong opinions based on little knowledge. But while assumptions and opinions about it permeate the media and everyday conversation, childhood remains a marginalised topic within some theoretical frameworks. Cultural studies, social psychology and sociology for example, regard childhood as the raw material for later life rather than an aspect of life to be studied and understood in its own right.[1]

Brannen and O'Brien have recently argued that children and childhood have only ever been studied indirectly via areas such as the family, gender, health and education. Exploring issues of childhood and children, they say, is a new and vexed area, for 'whilst sociologists have rightly criticised the asocial nature in which psychologists in particular have often approached human development, sociologists have sometimes themselves fallen into traps, for example by assuming little differentiation between childhood and adulthood' (Brannen & O'Brien 1995: 737). For Brannen and O'Brien, children need to be addressed as *children* rather than as little adults, so that we can become fully cognisant of their abilities and capacities, and gain a greater knowledge of the developmental challenges they have to face. In other words, instead of treating childhood as time spent in a 'waiting room' before emerging into adulthood, we should rather attempt to conceptualise childhood in its full specificity. In short, Brannen and O'Brien put the case for 'a social science of childhood which gives central place to the construction of childhoods and their different structural conditions and inequalities whilst at the same time elucidating childrens' own experiences, definitions and constructions of their daily lives' (Brannen & O'Brien 1995: 737). However, as Pam Alldred has pointed out, political and social spaces for childrens' voices to be heard have opened up in the past 5–10 years as exemplified by the UK Children Act and the UN Convention on the Rights of the Child (Alldred 1998).

The call to listen to voices of children may assume either the similarity of children to adults or the essential differences of childhood from adulthood. Both positions produce their own difficulties. In particular, the complexities of the relationship between childhood and adulthood are elided in each. In approaches which argue that children are different from adults there are, as Alldred argues, 'risks of reifying children as Other, or reinforcing ideas of their specific weakness and neediness, and the corollary reinforcement of the superiority, centrality and dominance of adult culture' (ibid: 166). Further, conceptual risk lies in distancing children from adult life as if they have no viewpoints, perceptions or experiences of adult life, thereby constructing children as innocent and naive beings. Within this viewpoint childhood and adulthood are conceived of as so different from each other that they are seen to share no preoccupations or emotional challenges. Serious difficulties also arise, however, when children are conceptualised as the same as adults since the particularity of childhood with its specific cultural value and emotional and psychic challenges is missed entirely. Within this viewpoint children and adults exist in a timeless zone in which generation, experience and different social and emotional challenges do not occur.

For developmental psychology, cognition, language and perception unfold progressively from the immaturity of childhood to the maturity of adulthood. In psychoanalytic theory, however, there is no such smooth unfolding. From the beginning of life, fantasy, anxiety and relationships with others intervene to form subjectivity, and emotion, anxiety and fantasy determine perception, cognition and language development. These two main strands of thinking about children which can be gleaned in developmental psychology and psychoanalysis are the two theoretical frameworks most associated with conceptualising children and childhood. Conventionally, developmental psychology has centred on discovering how we learn through focusing on cognition, language development and perception – the mechanisms of human functioning. Within this account, fantasy and the emotions are marginalised, neglected or stitched on over mechanisms of functioning, without being fully taken into account. Psycho-analysis prioritises the conscious and unconscious structure of subjectivity and focuses on emotion, desire and fantasy life. These differences bear critically on theorisations of subjectivity. Frosh sums this up thus:

> Psychology takes as the object of its discourse the already constructed individual 'subject' and asks, 'How do her or his psychological parts work?' Psychoanalysis looks at the fragmented neonate and questions, 'How does this one become a "subject" at all?'. . . Different motivations, different directions. (Frosh 1989: 250).

For psychology, the continual assumption is that the subject is already formed and the human being is the originator of personal meanings and the passive receiver of social demands. For psychoanalysis the subject and the social are less discrete. It is not just that psychoanalysis pays attention to the unconscious, feeling and fantasy life, but that its stress on the unconscious processes that underpin psychic life in children and adults questions the notion of a unitary, coherent individual who develops smoothly from one stage to the next.

These issues of how to theorise and place childhood all bear considerably on how we understand and conceptualise childhood subjectivity. It has become commonplace to argue for the social construction of childhood and there is more than some truth in this assertion. The social constructionist position leaves aside, however, the question of how the impact of the various social, familial and emotional dynamics bear upon and form children's subjectivity. To put the difficulty differently, how can we theorise the interplay between unconscious forces, the particular interventions of a social and cultural formation, and the developmental challenges of cognition, language and perception on the formation of childrens' identities? This particular challenge is complicated by a theoretical imperative to place the formation of identity within a particular social context which intervenes to form both subjectivity and the conceptual questions that are asked of it. As Jordonova argues, it is only ever possible to write the most partial and localised history of children as they are the most temporary of social subjects, not just because they grow up, but also because ideas of childhood and children – developmental, historical, social and cultural – seem to be ever on the shift (quoted in Steedman 1995: 6).

Three particular dynamics need to be borne in mind when researching children and childhood. First, we have all been children and have experienced childhood with its particular joys, difficulties and challenges. We approach the research through having been there and one's own experiences, needs, memories and personal and social narratives intervene in a loaded and evocative manner. Second, as an adult thinking about childrens' experiences one can be involved in searching for one's own lost childhood. The research can become a nostalgic search for that which is lost and gone, or indeed, that which may not have been there at all. As Steedman points out, the desire to discover the childhood of another can be the desire to rediscover and possess one's own childhood – a search or want that is bound to lead to disappointment, loss and dissatisfaction (Steedman 1995: viii). These emotional needs may impact on the research, on what is discovered or not, on what can be perceived and thought through or what has to remain absent. The task is to listen and think as clearly as possible while carrying one's own emotional baggage and yet engaging in a creative act of projection and identification (ibid: ix). Third, adults are researching children from a different vantage point – that of adulthood. Adults are in a different place, bearing different pressures, and facing social and emotional challenges. From this place we can misunderstand, disavow or idealise childhood experiences. Jordonova puts the difficulties pithily: '(we) are the products of societies that currently hold complex, deeply contradictory, and largely unarticulated views about children. Our capacity to sentimentalise, identify with, project onto, and reify children is almost infinite' (ibid: 6).

Memory: Remembering and Forgetting

Memory's place and functioning within subjectivity can be used as a powerful example to draw out the different emphases of developmental psychology and psychoanalysis. Developmental psychology attends to memory as one aspect of child development while psychoanalysis has been preoccupied with memory's relation to fantasy life. Cognitive psychology theorises memory as expanding with age and with greater cognitive capacities. Childrens' memories and ability to recall improve with age for two reasons: first, the child's knowledge becomes both greater and better organised, and second s/he develops strategies or methods of remembering which improve with age. Memory is therefore conceptualised not as an isolated cognitive skill but rather as a term for a collection of cognitive processes. The arguments are that children develop greater capacity for memory due to an improvement in basic capacities such as memory size and/or speed of simple mental processes. There are changes in 'children's knowledge about their own memory such that they can regulate their remembering more appropriately' (Meadows 1993: 50); and, lastly, an increase in knowledge generally means that children are less likely to come across unfamiliar situations. Cognitive psychology shows no interest whatsoever in either the content of memory, or what is remembered and why. Memory is seen as developing unproblematically with age. While developmental psychology hints that memory is intimately involved in social endeavours, it has not engaged in research into why children remember what they do and the emotional conditions necessary for remembering and forgetting.

Within developmental psychology's framework, fantasy and the emotions are neglected entirely, while for psychoanalysis, fantasy, the emotions and memory are inextricably linked. Indeed, for psychoanalysis, memory can never be viewed as unproblematically unfolding, for remembrance and forgetting engage complex psychic processes and difficulties. The baby wakes hungry and longs for the breast to feed itself or maybe for comfort and cries to communicate its wish, but the breast takes its time and in the delay between demand and gratification the baby hallucinates the breast and gains a fantasy of satisfaction. In this example, need, fantasy, wish and memory are interrelated, but, critically, in order to satisfy its need, the baby draws upon a memory of sensations of being fed and satisfies itself momentarily through a fantasy of the breast. Within this framework, therefore, memory and fantasy work together to deal with loss, absence and frustration, a continual dynamic which persists from childhood to adulthood. For psychoanalysis, memory and fantasy are in play in relation to unacceptable wishes and desires, and the ego works to repress that which is unacceptable, so that it is out of sight, out of hearing and out of mind. Within the psychoanalytic framework, memory and forgetting are closely intertwined as the individual, overwhelmed by feelings, fantasies and memories, uses available defences in order to forget. The dynamics of repression, denial and splitting are continually in operation. There can never be remembering or forgetting without fantasy, emotionality and unconscious motivation. It is a curious feature of the human condition that, 'we are the creatures who refuse to remember who we are; and yet, from a psychoanalytic point of view, there can be nothing human without competent forgetting' (Phillips 1994: 29). It is around the issues of forgetting that cognitive psychology and psychoanalysis meet, for while cognitive psychology argues that the child can regulate its memories, psychoanalysis argues that the child has to repress difficult emotions and fantasies. For developmental psychology time is linear and unproblematic as development occurs in relationship with biological maturation. For psychoanalysis, however, the unconscious is timeless and the relationship between past and present is neither progressive nor linear. For Klein, indeed, the past and present are one – as indicated by her use of the term *states* rather than *stages*.

These different conceptualisations of memory foreground questions of time and timelessness which return us to the central and complex issue of the relationship between the experiences of childhood and adulthood.

Where time is understood to be linear, then the differences between adulthood and childhood come to the fore. If, on the other hand, the relationship between the past and present is understood to be more permeable, then so too is the relationship between childhood and adulthood. In my understanding, childhood subjectivity is both specific with its own dynamics while being also a preparation for, and a looking forward to, adulthood. Childhood is complex, involving aggression, sexuality and unconscious life. Embedded within this understanding of childhood is a view that children, like adults, are struggling to make sense of their own and others' worlds and attempting to locate themselves and others within the social and cultural spheres. In undertaking work on childhood subjectivity, my aim is neither to move the point of origin of fantasy and narratives further back and therefore nearer the 'truth', nor to compare adults with children, but to produce an engagement with children's subjectivity and its specific complexity.

Psychoanalysis prioritises the internal life of the child. Its engagement with social and cultural spheres focuses on the emotional and psychic processes involved in their perception and representation. Commenting on some children's pictures she had seen of a village that had been flooded but where no-one was hurt, Gianna Henry emphasises their variety. Henry welcomes this opportunity to see different responses to an external event and argues that:

> In terms of the internal world, I would like to suggest that at least one of the reasons why the same experience was portrayed in such different ways by the different children was the fact that it was filtered through an internal frame of reference: I would take the very varied representations of the flood to have derived from great differences in the children's inner reality (Henry 1986: 1).

Within this psychoanalytic and clinical viewpoint the unconscious and feeling are continually in operation effecting, producing, distorting, and informing action, representation, perception and communication. I am not suggesting, however, that emotions can merely be added into the developmental psychology equation to produce a more complex theory of identity. Rather, I am calling for the recognition that emotion effects profoundly what is thought and perceived. The role of emotion and fantasy in childhood impacts critically on method as well as upon theory. As Urwin demonstrates in a careful and exploratory article on developmental psychology and psychoanalysis, what is needed is a careful and complex method which attends both to the role of emotion per se, and to the workings of unconscious processes, particularly phantasy and mechanisms of defence (Urwin 1986).

For psychoanalysis, children's play involves unconscious processes, fantasies, anxiety, symbolisation and the achievement of a new relation to external reality. For developmental psychology, play enables the learning of adult roles and means of functioning. Psychoanalytically speaking, working-through[2] is also achieved through play: the destruction heaped upon dolls and toys can be seen as the workings of the super-ego and 'one might speculate that some release from self-judgement is achieved through the emotional dynamics of relationships with other family members, as the child meets actual consequences of acting out destructive impulses' (ibid: 281). Children play with various feelings ranging from destruction to tenderness. They thereby depict and work through their psychic conflicts, fears and actual events to move towards understanding and internalising social rules and power: as Urwin puts it: 'the workings of phantasy may be identified in relation to a social reality, defined in terms of specific social practices which are themselves regulated through systems of power' (ibid).

The Family Romance

In this chapter I wish to explore some aspects of childrens' narratives of themselves and the social world that they inhabit using examples from a pilot study. The pilot study was conducted by Phil Cohen[3] and myself in order to discover and elucidate children's fantasies, memories and narratives of family life, specifically concentrating on the 'Family Romance'. In Freud's account of the 'Family Romance' (1909) the child fantasises, and believes that s/he was adopted, kidnapped, or abandoned, due to extreme circumstances and through no fault of the 'original parents', and that one day these superior and original parents will return and restore the child to its rightful position. Many childhood narratives and fantasies centre on a belief that the child is really a prince or princess who is destined to rule, to be beautiful, and to possess riches, power and untold happiness. The child holds with verve to the unconscious belief that his or her 'real' but unknown parents are a 'better' class altogether than the 'boring' and 'inferior' couple with whom they have to live and who deliberately make the child's life a constant misery by depriving them of sweets, making them tidy up, bath and go to bed early. This fantasy has many nuances and variations but the basic scenario is this: the young child is disappointed that its real parents do not live up to their exalted expectations of them and their position in life, so they are replaced by a set of imaginary parents who are wonderful, understanding, powerful and extraordinary beings. Puzzled as to why this fantasy was so pervasive and why so many people were convinced that they had been adopted or kidnapped, Freud argued that this fantasy underpins much of the way children imagine their parents, their lives and their real status. The pilot study had three aims: first, to collect childrens' narratives of family life; second, to discover whether or not they had fantasies of the family and if so their content; third, to theorise the relationship between fantasy, narrative and memory. Through paying attention to the narratives children tell, a more complex view of childhood subjectivity will be drawn out in order to move towards a clearer understanding of narrative, memory and fantasy, and how this triad of elements constitutes and impacts on children's identity.

An Account of the Pilot Study

At a school in Brixton, South London, we talked to twelve children (an equal number of girls and boys) aged nine, from various ethnic groups: white, mixed-parentage, African-Caribbean and Chinese. The children's ability ranged from intelligent and articulate, to those having a degree of difficulty conveying meaning and formulating thoughts. We met with the children weekly for six afternoons. The children engaged in the pilot study with energy, commitment and generosity. The sessions were lively, difficult to control and disrupted by discipline issues. It became impossible for one of us to conduct the session and the other to take close notes as we had first intended, because it required two of us to keep the group to task. On reflection, twelve children in a group were simply too many. This meant that full observation could not take place and this has limited the findings, as a proper noting of the childrens' interactions, power issues and dynamics could not be adequately undertaken. The sessions were often extremely noisy, and we continually feared that the headmaster would arrive and put an end to the project. As would be expected, the boys dominated the sessions, leading one of us to note 'boys, boys, always the boys – where are the girls?' The dynamic seemed to be that the boys could leap in and take up the space while the girls were slower and required more of a build-up. The children ranged across the usual degrees of emotional strength and vulnerability. Some could hold their own and persist with their own preoccupations and thoughts, but others found this more difficult which led either to a wish to dominate and control the group, or to a more withdrawn stance. The children related to us in a variety of ways: some engaged with curiosity and liveliness, others were more needy, requiring reassurance and more emotional commitment.

We decided to use various activities as a route into collecting and discovering children's narratives of origins. We thought that storytelling by us and the children would enable a collection of their narratives. A range of activities took place: drawing, telling stories and being read to, making finger puppets and acting out a story. Finally the group modelled clay babies in order to narrate stories about birth and arrival. Ethnographic studies, while useful, tend to neglect the question of fantasy and narrative and assume tight fits between what is observed and what is felt or meant by the participants. We wanted to find a route into speaking with the children about their meanings, activities and fantasies. As the class was in a school which encouraged creative activity, the children's participation in making finger puppets and acting out their scenarios was on the whole unproblematic.

The children were often excited and involved but there was a continual feeling of chaos and a sense that boundaries were being pushed and tested. The experience and the observations that we made fitted in with the following understandings of children's perceptions and interactions at this developmental stage: having learnt the rules children are now beginning to question them and look for wider patterns. At this age, school has increasingly become a space in which children can explore where they and others fit in, and build up an awareness and knowledge of groups and how they function. Further, children will now talk at length with friends about other children, teachers and adults. Along with a growing awareness of the world in which they live, this age-group is also struggling with questions of difference. Their independence is growing and the child is better able to form and sustain friendships without the help of the family. Similarly, they can be concerned with their place in the social sphere and how this can be maintained with confidence. At this age, children's vulnerability in this area can be poignant, as is illustrated by an example from the pilot study: Mark centred a play each child was asked to construct around the mantra, 'have faith in yourself, Mark, have faith'.[4]

The school context affected the children and what they produced, for their play or their work concentrated on their teachers, who often figured as cruel, withholding and controlling figures, rather than on their parents. It was unclear quite who the children thought we were – other teachers? People sent to test them or their teachers? Strange outsiders? People who provided a relief from school tedium? Moreover, we do not know how their fantasies about us contributed to what they produced and what was withheld. Concentration on the school environment made it difficult to get at family dynamics. There was often much concern about getting the drawing or the telling of the story 'right', and the children expressed the fear that they would be told off if they got it 'wrong'. Although we tried to reassure them about this, it is unclear quite how much effect this had.

Throughout the sessions we attempted to do too much and we could not finish what we had intended to do, but it was also difficult for us to concentrate on one theme. A continual worry was that we were asking too much of the children, and that the play was too emotionally provocative. On reflection, we were demanding too much from them and from ourselves. The sessions became easier when we moved from a room adjacent to the classroom to a self-contained room. The boundary was clearer, the children became less distracted and we could focus more closely on the task in hand. Our use of technology was problematic; we tape-recorded all, and video-taped some of the sessions. Increasingly, and especially after the sessions, it became apparent that the technology was intrusive and unhelpful, for there was a continual fantasy that the video would capture it all – the image, the event, all the children – and that there was no need for human observation. Moreover, we became preoccupied with the aesthetics of the image. We realized too late that with a large group of children it is almost impossible to differentiate between the voices on a tape. Perhaps more problematically, there was a more unconscious fantasy that the video and audio tapes could 'think' for us so they became containers for our minds; not aids as such, but rather 'things' that would do the work for us – observing, relating and thinking on our behalf.

From Being at a Loss to Becoming Textured

In an evocative article entitled 'Why Oedipus' Christopher Bollas argues that children are engaged in understanding and knowing the complexity of living. In this article which focuses on the 'Oedipus complex' Bollas argues that during this phase the child discovers that it has a mind and that others have one too (Bollas,1993). Prior to this, the child imagines that its thoughts, feelings or perceptions have come to it from outside of itself, the dream has visited as opposed to recognising that it produces the feelings and perceptions, the dream itself. Within this framework the pain and difficulty centre on the recognition that life is complex. This increased awareness involves the realisation that the world is more complicated and uncomfortable than had previously been thought. For Bollas, the entry and passage through the Oedipus complex is a painful experience through which children learn about themselves. It is a complex of feelings, thoughts and experiences that are specific to childhood, and not just – as has been understood within some theoretical frameworks – the entry into adult sexuality. For Bollas, then, the child moves from being in a dilemma to being in a complex.

By way of illustration that children of this age group are involved in creating and understanding their complex social and cultural spheres, I will draw upon an example from the pilot study. We asked the children to make three puppets: one of a magical figure, one of someone who bullied them and the third of themselves. They were then to construct a play using these puppets. We wanted to discover more closely childrens' understandings and responses to situations of possible complexity. The children engaged with this with energy and imagination. Anne acted out a story in which she goes to the wizard and asks him to make her child-minder a nice person. The wizard does so and the childminder allows Anne to eat as much ice-cream, cake and sweets as she likes. Anne is then sick in the night and does not want a repeat of the situation, so she returns to the wizard and asks him to make the childminder a little bit nice and a little bit horrid. He refuses, saying he can only do magic that makes people one thing or the other and so Anne has to choose. She declares, 'I will have her as she is, then.' There are many ways that this story can be interpreted. It could be interpreted in terms of splitting, so that Anne cannot bear to see her child-minder as both nice and horrid;[5] or it could be that Anne is struggling to come to terms with her actual childminder with whom she did not get along (she continually spoke about this); or it could be a gentle protest to her parents for lumbering her with this woman. Perhaps, recognising her powerlessness to change things, Anne reconciles herself to the situation in a humorous and gentle fashion. This vignette illustrates that Anne and the other children were able to draw upon inner and outer resources in order to come to terms with the world as it is. They brought their capacities as thinking, perceptive and social beings to bear on their cultural and emotional worlds. As Winnicott has pointed out, children will make comments and part of the point of this is the wish to demonstrate that they have been thinking. Adults are often called to witness, simply no more than this, the child's capacity to think and make sense of their experiences (Winnicott 1996: 106).

The passage to emotional maturity involves many difficult aspects of reality. Within a psychoanalytical framework, especially as outlined by Bollas, an aspect of emotional growth is the acceptance that there is an inevitable gap between one's need and fantasy for adoration and the love that is actually given. One aspect of this that the 'Family Romance' expresses is the refusal to recognise that one is not loved unconditionally or adored for the sheer fact of one's existence. The impossibility of the demand to be adored unconditionally does not diminish the fantasy, need or demand for total adoration. And indeed, this demand can often be a defence against profound disappointment – a protection and protest that one is inevitably not loved enough. The 'Family Romance' is a poignant preservation in fantasy of ideal parents who do not disappoint or frustrate. In fantasy these are split off from the actual parents as the child gains more knowledge of parental failings and vulnerabilities. Freud stressed the nostalgic element in the construction of the 'Family Romance' and argued that the fantasy was '. . . only an expression of the child's longing for the happy, vanished days when his father seemed to him the noblest and strongest of men and his mother the dearest and loveliest of women . . . and his phantasy is no more than the expression of a regret that those happy days have gone' (Freud 1909: 224). Splitting the parents into the ideal and the real, preserves their special position *and* enables a coming to terms with the reality. Fantasy and memory come together to create a poignant narrative. The 'Family Romance' draws from a memory of a time when one was adored and relished and when parental love was total and combines this with the preservation, in fantasy, of the wish that someone, somewhere, will love unconditionally. This occurs alongside the growing knowledge that the child is painfully gaining of the impossibility of this demand. The narrative is over-determined as it brings together a memory and a fantasy which preserve a previous experience in which one's parents were idealised and perceived as without flaw or vulnerability, while stubbornly defending against parental failings and simultaneously acknowledging them.

As a psychic structure the 'Family Romance' is both a fantasy and a memory and a memory of a fantasy. By this I mean that the narrative preserves an experience from a time when the parents adored the baby and invested it with many hopes for the future. But in babyhood the baby appears flawless – it cries, demands food, requires enormous amounts of nurture and attention, but the parents are still getting to know the baby and the baby's flaws and more negative qualities can only be glimpsed. In this period both parents and children are getting to know one another and both can and do imagine highly idealised images of the other. There is, however, a difference between the baby and the parents: parents do this only in part. But the 'Family Romance' as a narrative preserves in memory this experience of acceptance and love as well as a memory of the time when the child thought and experiences its parents as the most wonderful beings. It preserves a time when the baby *and* the parents were perceived as perfect.

The 'Family Romance', therefore, is a hybrid structure constituted through both memory and fantasy which coexist and feed one another to produce a narrative of subjectivity. The 'Family Romance' is a powerful fantasy which contains many potent psychic processes and feelings.

Within a Kleinian framework phantasy accompanies all thought and feeling.[6] As Hinshelwood puts it: 'unconscious phantasies underlie every mental process, and accompany all mental activity' (Hinshelwood 1991: 32). For Klein even activity which seems free from any relationship to an object is accompanied by unconscious phantasy: either phantasies of doing something to objects or passively being acted upon by them. Hinshelwood sums it up thus: 'all through Klein's work, as well as that of her colleagues, the investigation has been into the way in which internal unconscious phantasy penetrates and gives meaning to "actual events" in the external world; and at the same time, the way the external world brings meaning in the form of unconscious phantasy' (ibid: 37).

The 'Family Romance' pulls in a number of different ways in terms of the narrative, fantasy and memory nexus. The 'Family Romance' is both an internal fantasy and is a response to the external world. The disappointment exists every which way: the child discovers its own and others' limits, that it does not get everything, does not have everything, and that, at some level, life is about struggle and enjoyment, pleasure and difficulty – a further move from the pleasure principle towards the reality principle. Bollas's enriching views on the Oedipal complex are enlightening, for childrens' narratives are often about their own worlds and they are often a means of coming to terms with their own fantasies, needs and emotions, their passions and the passions of their parents. This is illustrated in Carolyn Steedman's *The Tidy House* (1982). Steedman reproduces the narrative of three working-class girls, written at school. Steedman analyses this narrative in terms of the children's position as working-class *and* as girls. The narrative relayed in *The Tidy House* illustrates childrens' capacities to learn about and come to terms with the adult world and its relationships, their knowledge, acceptance and disavowal of sexual and emotional relationships between adults. For Steedman, the story reveals both the girls' perceptions and views of these relationships as well as their specific location as working-class girls. The children produced a narrative in which at points, pleasure and desire are explicit. In this narrative the children are clear that parents and adults have sex and that this is what you do if you want a baby. But there are narratives and fantasies in which parents' passions and longings are denied. When the children in our pilot were asked to make up a story about babies, using clay to construct the infants, the babies appeared as if by magic. Not one narrative introduced the possibility of the activity required to procreate. The 'Family Romance' allows the fantasy that the child begets itself. Indeed, this narrative can jettison the reality of the couple, for as Joyce McDougall has argued, a profound narcissistic wound for all arises through the realisation that one is not the whole, that for intercourse and a partnership to occur there has to be another (McDougall 1996). So the 'Family Romance' can, in part, get rid of parents' bodies, parents' passions and desires and in their place it produces an immaculate conception. Within this fantasy, reproduction occurs perfectly, an ideal body produces another ideal body. This fantasy is based on a contradictory acknowledgement and disavowal of parental sexual activity and desire by the child. The fantasy can be interpreted as a wish for that time when the child was innocent of such knowledge and unaware of his/her exclusion from the parental couple. In their struggle to accept and gain knowledge of the relationships, the family constellation and the particular feelings and fantasies that these evoke, children are contradictory and partial but they have to, and do, struggle to move to a different place. If healthy conditions pertain, the individual child can move from being in a quandary, perplexed and doubtful, to being able to perceive relationships in a more integrated, intricate and wholesome way.

Family Narratives and Children's Autobiography

This chapter then begins the theoretical task of edging towards an understanding of the complex of memory, narrative and fantasy. This task continually raises questions about the influences that come to bear on an autobiography – the development of subjectivity. Some aspects of contemporary cultural theory focus on biography and autobiography, through the analysis of oral histories and the production of life-stories. These tellings and theorisations of lives centre, however, on adulthood and its fantasies, memories and confessions, and focus the way *adults* make sense of their past and present. The common assumption is that childhood becomes the raw material for the adult's life – it becomes that which is reworked, understood and put into a narrative retrospectively. The assumption is that children do not develop an autobiography or a narrative which is culled and reworked from the fantasies and memories of their families, and their cultural and social circumstances.

There are four issues involved in children's narratives, memories and fantasies. First, what narratives do children tell about themselves, their family and their place in the social and cultural spheres? Second, which cultural sources, both from within and outside the family, do children draw upon for content and form? Third, what is the interplay of class, ethnicity and gender in the production of these narratives, and how do the family's social and economic location impact on the child's identity? And fourth, what is the interplay of the unconscious, fantasy, memory and emotionality?

As Steven Rose points out in *The Making of Memory* (1995), we need memories to define ourselves. Further, memories and the artefacts of memory, e.g. photos, function as proof that we are observing, feeling and thinking beings. In our pilot study the children were keen to prove both that they had a past which they remembered, and that there was a continuation between themselves and their family. It was at times difficult to know whose 'story' or 'memory' belonged to whom; there was often much confusion about the object or subject of the narrative. To state the obvious, we gain our narratives of self from a variety of sources – family, school, the media, peers and internal fantasy life. This complex of sources and points of contact is critical for the ongoing sense of self and reveals the impossibility of an isolated individual producing their own narrative.

John Byng-Hall's study of family myths and legends (1995) marries object relations with theorisations from family therapy. His central questions concern how such scripts and myths are used within the family to construct the identity of the family and its members, and how the myths and scripts determine the family's behaviour, feelings, attitudes and values. In short, Byng-Hall argues that family scripts give the family an identity. In our pilot study there were many examples of children recounting what may have been a story told by another member of the family when they had been asked to supply a memory of their own. For example, one child told of being lost in an art gallery. When she later repeated the story it was identical with no variation in tone, words or intonation. This child had so taken in this story that it was difficult to find a space in which she could negotiate it. While these stories were repeated with energy and liveliness, the childrens' faces – especially that of the child who was lost in the art gallery – took on a trance-like expression; it was as if they had entered another world. But was this a world of safety gained from the family story, or a world of repetition with little meaning? Were the stories important to the child because they had somehow become mythologised? It is unclear whether or not these stories function as a social screen (Freud, 1899), thereby allowing a whole set of other imaginings to occur. Certainly, these stories gave these children a status in the group and gave them an identity: for the girl who was lost in the art gallery, her story affirmed her competence aged two; for the boys with their stories of winning over older brothers, such stories enabled them to tell of rivalry and of course of winning, in order to prove their status and power and also as a challenge to their boy peers. These stories had become internalised and functioned to give a sense of coherence to the child and, more importantly, a sense of self. The pleasure they took in the stories came from knowing their histories, that they had pasts which the family could contain, retell and hold in mind. Further, the children constructed these stories actively, to negotiate and make sense of their childhoods and their social spheres. Such stories are not just constructed en route to adulthood. For the child, they are points of negotiation of their external and internal worlds. It is tempting to conceptualise children as only preparing themselves to be adults and to enter the social and cultural meanings of adulthood thereby missing the specificity of childhood and the active and intelligent sense that children have to understand and locate themselves within their own important arenas.

Memory, Fantasy and Place

Subjectivity is complex and contradictory. While there are aspects of psychic life which move to deny the parental relationship and the reality of one's own position of limitation and dependency, there are other pulls at play which move towards recognition, acceptance and richer relations with others. Most of the children in the pilot study struggled with locating themselves in their families and wider communities, with knowing and tolerating good and bad aspects of themselves and others – in short, with developing a solid sense of self and others. But as has been indicated above this does not take away other unconscious desires and fantasies to be transported to a better place altogether. For the family romance expresses a wish to be the prince or princess who is found and restored to his/her rightful place, and perhaps also to be the adult who does the rescuing and the abandoning. We still do not know quite which characters the children in our pilot study took up, consciously or unconsciously. They joined in with great energy and produced stories of travel and nail-biting adventures of abandonment which always included a rescue. Their versions of the 'Family Romance' were imaginative. One centred on a baby being kidnapped and left alone in a country mansion. The parents arrive but do not recognise their own child. When they finally do so, the child is now able to do anything it wants, and goes to San Francisco. Another story centred on a baby who is left outside a shop. It is then looked after by grandparents who are kind, but somehow the baby is put in a box and left at the airport. It goes to Scotland but is again rescued. Another concentrated on two babies who are swopped over and then the mistake is discovered when an adult realises that the boy is not a girl. After much activity involving planes, baggage and airports both children go to Spain. As can be seen, the stories are rich and brought forth much emotional material about confusion of identity, abandonment, and painful depictions of adults' misrecognition of children. The stories always ended with a rescue and finally arriving in a better place altogether. Tellingly, not one child chose for their 'baby' to live in England. In a delightful essay on *The Wizard of Oz,* (Victor Fleming, MGM, 1939) Salmon Rushdie wishes poignantly for a good pair of ruby slippers which can help one to reach a better place. Rushdie points to the yearning in Judy Garland's voice as she sings 'Over The Rainbow', and comments 'what she expresses here, what she embodies with the purity of an archetype, is the human dream of leaving, a dream at least as powerful as its countervailing dream of roots' (Rushdie 1992: 23). No matter what their family history of diaspora, the children we studied expressed these seemingly contradictory wishes and impulses: they longed at times to be elsewhere and also longed to be home.

This chapter has documented some narratives that children tell of themselves and their families and has moved towards analysing these stories in relation to the triad of narrative, fantasy and memory. In conclusion, I will contrast two quite different narratives from the pilot study. One boy in our pilot told of the journey his grandfather would have taken to arrive in Britain, and he told it as if he had taken the journey himself, using the present tense, with all the energy of first-hand experience. He had so internalised and lived this story that he had no sense that he could not have been there. When the other children pointed this out with much derision, he shrugged: it made no difference, he just did not care, for he *had* done this journey. I think it has to be understood that through the child's internalisation of his grandfather's story it had actually become his own. He had so introjected it that he had taken the journey in fantasy and it had become utterly real to him – in the retelling it became his journey, his life that was being told. This is probably a family story which has been told, retold, remembered and recollected over and over again. But in contradiction to this boy, one girl in the pilot study, whose family came from Guyana, became very animated because she had been to Spain. She knew Guyana was important to her family and was not neglectful or unmindful of this but her liveliness came from the fact that she had been to Spain. This may of course have been due to the fact that other children found it easier to relate to Spain rather than to Guyana, and therefore she avoided exclusion from the group or it could be that this is what was important to her. It is difficult to know quite what purpose these narratives served for either child or indeed where they gained their social, family and personal meanings that gave these narratives such matter. It is even more difficult to judge quite what status these narratives held in terms of these two children's fantasy lives. They were, however, telling them to audiences which seemed, on the surface, quite different. For the girl, her audience was her peer group and her story confirmed her own position within it. Her audience could share her story with her and we all took pleasure in her enjoyment and excitement. For the boy, the audience for his narrative of a journey seemed to be himself, or may have been his family even though they were absent.

Both children were attached to their narratives, the memories evoked and the internal place they provided. They used the narratives to link themselves to others – either their peer group or their families. The narratives provided poignant means of expressing attachment to people and places. Family narratives can concentrate on the family itself, but they can also look outwards to locate the teller in the wider spheres of community, centring on nation, people, town, race. Individuals and families have a wider relationship to the community in which they live and there is often a need and a wish to locate oneself in a wider historical field. These narratives can be put to various uses: they can make sense of a life and locate an individual within a wider sphere of influences and identity, not simply inter- and intra-family; but they are also, in part, the way in which historical subjectivity is gained and forged, for they are also a means by which continuity and change are registered, placed and understood.

This article is predicated on the view that children are more knowing, active, perceptive and fantasising beings than is generally understood. The narratives produced in the pilot study showed children struggling to understand themselves as both separate from and connected to others: at times their stories centred on a narrative based on them standing alone with seemingly no reference to others. At other times it seemed as if their narratives were based on internalised family narratives in relation to which the child had no separate existence. It is a complex nexus of self, other, family, peer and wider cultural forces that impact on, forge and form, these childrens' narratives.

Within this nexus the children are involved in gaining their own sense of self, and developing an autobiography which both recognises the importance of other people in their lives and enables them to develop a more independent narrative. Psychic health centres on a recognition of one's past, the past of the family and of one's community. Critically, it centres on a recognition, to return to Bollas's argument, that one has a mind that fantasises and thinks. As children struggle to narrate and to make sense of their own and other lives, they pick through fantasies and memories in order to reach some equable position based on recognising the complexity of becoming. The central insight of psychoanalysis and of Bollas's article is that this does not come easy.

The influences on children's narratives are multiple. Children draw on their families, peer groups, the media and their own internal psychic lives in order to create them. But these narratives matter in two ways: they have substance and they are important to children themselves. In his essay on the *Wizard of Oz*, Rusdie argues that a task for all of us is to move towards the realisation that we end up in a different place from where we began. Critically, this argument is not based on the homily that 'there is no place like home' but more that the place, internal and external, is always in the process of being made and lived. Children are moving towards this complex realisation and forming their own narratives, to make sense, and gain deeper knowledge of their lives.

Acknowledgments

I owe special thanks to Phil Cohen for the energy, thought and creativity that contributed to the project discussed in this chapter, and also to the staff and pupils of George Orwell School, Brixton.

Notes

1. The ESRC has recently set up a Childhood Initiative to encourage research on children aged between 5 and 14. In their document inviting research proposals they make clear the dearth of research and understanding of this age group. The research fund is intended to make good this theoretical absence.
2. Working-through is commonly used as a clinical term, to describe the endeavour by both analyst and analysand to make insight more effective and change possible. I am using the term here to indicate that children express their conflicts, anxieties and relationships to others through play, in order to reach some resolution.
3. Phil Cohen is Director of the Centre for New Ethnicities Research and co-founder of the Centre for Adoption Studies, both at the University of East London.
4. I gained information for this section on child development from a number of sources, including the Tavistock Clinic series *Understanding Your Child* (London: Tavistock Clinic and Rosendale Press and Steinberg and Meyer (1995)).

5. Melanie Klein elaborated the concept of splitting. She argued that the infant, overwhelmed by anxiety and terror, deals with these fantasies and feelings by splitting the maternal object into part objects, as a way of separating the 'good' aspects from the 'bad'. For the struggling infant, this primitive fantasy ensures that the two aspects – nice and horrid – are separate and do not contaminate each other. As the infant develops, it shifts from what has been termed the paranoid-schizoid position, into the depressive position, in which part objects can be brought together and experienced as whole.

6. The different spellings of phantasy and fantasy indicate different usages and theoretical inclinations. The Kleinians use the spelling *phantasy* to distinguish between an unconscious process and the semi-conscious daydreams that can be referred to as fantasies.

Bibliography

Alldred, Pam (1998), 'Ethnography, Discourse Analysis and Representation: Dilemmas in Research Work with Children', in Jane Ribbens and Rosalind Edwards, (eds),
Dilemmas of Feminist Research: Public Knowledge and Private Lives, London: Sage.

Bollas, Christopher (1993), 'Why Oedipus', in Bollas, Christopher, *Being a Character*, London: Routledge.

Bradley, Jonathan (1993), *Understanding Your 10 Year Old*, London: Rosendale Press.

Brannen, Julia and O'Brien, Margaret (1995), 'Childhood and the Sociological Gaze: Paradigms and Paradoxes', *Sociology*, Vol. 29, No.4, pp.729–37.

Byng-Hall, John (1995), *Re-writing Family Scripts*, Guildford Press.

Freud, Sigmund (1899), 'Screen Memories', in *The Standard Edition of the Complete Works of Sigmund Freud*, ed. and trans. James Strachey, London: Hogarth Press and the Institute of Psychoanalysis 1953–73, vol 3, 301–23.

Freud, Sigmund (1977) [1909], 'Family Romances', *On Sexuality*, Pelican Freud Library
volume 7, Harmondsworth: Penguin.

Frosh, Stephen (1989), *Psychoanalysis and Psychology: Minding the Gap*, London: Macmillan.

Henry, Gianna (1986), 'The Internal World of the Child', *Bridge Foundation for Psychotherapy and the Arts,* Occasional Paper No.2, Bristol.

Hinshelwood, Robert (1991), *A Dictionary of Kleinian Thought*, London: Free Association Press.

Lush, Dorothy (1993), *Understanding Your 9 Year Old*, London: Rosendale Press.

McDougall, Joyce (1996), 'Female Sexualisations', Freud Annual Lecture, London.

Meadows, Sara (1993), *The Child as Thinker*, London: Routledge.

Miller, Lisa (1993), *Understanding Your 8 Year Old, Old*, London: Rosendale Press.

Phillips, Adam (1994), 'Freud and the Uses of Forgetting', in *On Flirtation*, London: Faber & Faber.

Rose, Steven (1995), *The Making of Memory*, London: Bantam Books.

Rushdie, Salman (1992), *The Wizard of Oz*, London: British Film Institute.

Solnit, Arthur (1983), 'Memory as Preparation', Freud Annual Lecture, London.

Steedman, Carolyn (1982), *The Tidy House*, London: Virago.

Steedman, Carolyn (1995), *Strange Dislocations: Childhood & The Idea of Human Interiority 1780–1930*, London : Virago.

Steinberg, Laurence and Meyer, Roberta (1995), *Childhood,* New York: McGraw Hill.

Urwin, Cathy (1986), 'Developmental psychology and psychoanalysis: splitting the difference', in Martin Richards and Paul Light, (eds), *Children of Social Worlds,* Cambridge: Polity Press.

Winnicott, Donald (1996), *Thinking About Children*, London: Karnac Books.

Memory Work: the Key to Women's Anxiety

Frigga Haug

I shall begin with a commonplace. Every woman knows from her own experience what anxiety is, how it feels and when it starts.[1] The physical symptoms are breaking into a sweat, a beating heart, trembling legs, gasping for breath, etc. Her perception becomes both too sharp and too narrow, and the ability to act is inhibited. Although we know that a difficult situation can be handled better without fear, we have no control over this feeling. Anxiety takes us unawares, lies in wait for us, mesmerises us. Thus far anxiety is a universal human feeling, an index of danger – whether imagined or not. Even though people assume that there is a fundamental connection between anxiety and being human, it is widely known that women experience far more anxieties than men, and that they are even thought of as the 'anxious sex'.

The known gender bias of this feeling is not matched by a comparable knowledge of how it comes about. If we assume that the feeling of anxiety is a response to contradictory situations from which the individual cannot escape on her own,[2] a gender-specific investigation of anxiety finds itself confronted by a series of strategic questions:

1. What are the ordinary conditions to which women in our societies respond with anxiety? (A socio-economic question about women's situation);
2. How do women appropriate the social conditions of their lives? (A socio-psychological question about the socialisation process, the ways in which they are assimilated into society);
3. What social openings are available to women that give concrete sense and meaning to their attempts to make their way in society and yet simultaneously give rise to anxiety? (This is a cultural question that is concerned with the cultural patterns in society as well as individual modes of acquisition – to that extent it overlaps with the question about socialisation).

As is mostly the case with questions about the specific forms and possibilities open to the female sex, a glance at the extensive literature on anxiety leaves you with feeling empty. The majority of texts tackle the question from a 'universal human' standpoint and then proceed in such a male-centred way that even the would-be critic is left with a feeling of despair. If we wish to learn about women's anxiety we must investigate it ourselves. The only source available to us is women's *experiences* and their deposits in the *memory*. This research calls for its own methodology.

Memory work as a sociological method was developed in response to a complex set of problems. In the first place the object was to appropriate that empty space in the dominant theories which should have existed to accommodate women's experiences. At the same time, however, and going far beyond that, it was essential to develop a method that was itself developing and open to development. Finally, the question of experience implies that we are dealing with matters that are ideologically determined, with products that have been integrated into dominant structures; a process that has been endowed with meaning, smoothed over, free of contradictions and made liveable. It follows, therefore, that as a source of knowledge experiences are highly deceptive. They are themselves a product, a botched job, nothing 'authentic' or valid in themselves. On the other hand, there is no alternative reliable source of that production process that constitutes the historical self, identity, apart from the experiences of the individual. Experiences are both the quicksand on which we cannot build and the material with which we do build. We cannot therefore simply rest content with collecting experiences and claiming that these are women's socialisation, or pretending that they in themselves are our knowledge of the laws governing the production of femininity. The problem is much more difficult. A method has to be found that makes it possible to work on experiences, and to learn from them. It is from this consideration that the proposal to work with memories arises.

This method stands in stark contrast to the usual empirical approach. It does not look at experiences and memory as separated from their subjects and as things that can be interrogated without them. Instead it draws the objects of study, the 'experienced' women into the process of investigation as subjects. It is they themselves who possess a 'knowledge' that has still to be made into genuine knowledge that is publicly available. As experts on their own experience the individual women are both 'producers of ideology' and the only ones who 'know' how they did it. Their memories have stored up the information that explains how they came to choose a particular path and why, what meaning they were looking for, what compromises they acquiesced in and what alternatives might have existed. Our task is to reconstruct this process. This calls for the destruction of existing meanings. The underlying assumption is that beneath the scraps of memory that have been assembled so as to create a specific meaning, other meanings, paths and possibilities become visible. They become manifest as contradictions, as disharmony, as rupture, as incongruities or inconsistency, etc. In agreement with Leontjew we assume that personality has a memory. This means that an individual constantly constructs herself anew from history; she privileges certain experiences as relevant, creates herself from them and discards everything else as irrelevant. Our task is to use memory work to disrupt this process, to enable a different past to emerge in order to make possible a different present and with it a different course of action in the future. Hence memory work is both a sociological method that is designed to produce knowledge about women's socialisation and at the same time a method that will enable individual women who have been drawn into the research process to live in a more conscious manner and to make them more capable of acting for themselves. It should make the critique of theory both possible and practical and it should also organise the critique of their perceptions.

Let us take as an instance a scene from our work on women's anxiety. Two preliminary theoretical observations are necessary. First, unlike biographical research we do not write linear histories or whole-life stories, since they would only reveal the construction whose decoding we are concerned with in their overall effect, not in the way they were produced. We concentrate instead on scenes, events, particular stories and hope that by reproducing them in detail it will be possible to subvert the self-censorship that creates harmony in a whole-life story. Second, unlike consciousness-raising groups we do not rely on narration, but write the stories up, so that what we analyse is texts, not people. This acts as a possible corrective to the commonsense psychologising that would otherwise replace analysis; it also enables us to carry out the process of deconstruction with the assistance of textual analysis and discourse analysis.

The following scene was written by a woman in response to the general theme: *An occasion when I was afraid.*[3] The question was put in such general terms because the 'right' question can only be formulated as the consequence of a long investigatory process, but must nevertheless by put at the very outset. At the same time the question has to be put at the level of ordinary experience if it is to provoke experiences in response. Hence the vagueness of this general formulation is a comment on the uncertainty felt about the object of research.

The passage in the Underground

She[4] had recently moved to the city and was on her way home after a concert. She liked going out on her own in the evening, but today she felt bad about going home unaccompanied since it was already very late and the streets were almost empty.

The women in the audience had dispersed in different directions, and none of them seemed to be on the same tube train as she.

She stood alone in front of the entrance to the Tube and was afraid to go down the stairs. Up on the street she could see what lay ahead of her and could keep looking around. In the Tube tunnel she would not know what was round the next corner. Moreover, her retreat could easily be blocked.

She was furious because she did not feel she was in control. In fact she did not move from the spot. She did not want to wait for other people to come with whom she might have gone down to the platform. So she pulled herself together and went down the steps.

It was a ghastly feeling to walk along the brightly lit passage, coming closer and closer to the corner. She felt more and more helpless, the further away she went from the entrance. Once she had turned the corner no-one would be able to see her and come to her assistance. She was afraid of that first second of terror, the second that it would take her to gain an overview of the passage round the corner. To see whether the way was clear or whether there was a man lurking, leaning against the wall. And what if there really was a man leaning against the wall?

She knew the feeling she had when a man came towards her on the street at night, or a drunk accosted her. Your heart stops for a moment. The thought of that moment made her feel panic. She felt helpless and alone, like a cornered animal.

If there were other people nearby or she was together with a woman friend she did not allow herself to be molested. She swore or shouted back. She hated having to lower her gaze just to be on the safe side.

When there were other people present in the Tube she practised testing her own strength. If a man stared at her, she stared back until he looked away. Sometimes men smiled as they tried to out-stare her. She did not smile back. That was not always easy and so she would formulate some insult in her mind to remind herself that she was not playing a game.

Just before she reached the corner her anxiety was so great that she turned round and ran back to the entrance as fast as she could. As she ran, her anxiety increased still further. She now felt she really was being followed. At the same time, she felt that she was involved in an insane, self-induced panic.

Back in the street she thought for a moment that she would only get home again if she took a taxi. But she did not want to take a taxi. If she did not manage to get home in the ordinary way, she would never manage it again. She would think twice about going out alone again.

She was still unfamiliar with the bus system in Hamburg. So she just walked round where she was, in search of a bus stop. When she found one, she saw by the timetable that the last bus had gone. She felt desperate. While she stood wondering what to do she saw a group of men and women walking in the direction of the Tube station. She followed them in the hope of being able to walk along the passage at the same time as them. In fact they were all going the same way. With a feeling of relief she went down the steps with them. There were a lot of people on the platform. She felt happy and was scarcely able to believe that a few minutes earlier she had been in the street alone and in despair.

At all events she would buy some CS gas. On straight roads it was reassuring to have her finger on the trigger and know that she could spray it at someone. But she still felt anxiety when approaching the corner in the Tube. The moment of terror remained.

Before analysing such a scene it is important to discover the common-sense reactions of the group so that if necessary they too can become the subject of discussion. If this is not done views that derive from common-sense, but whose assumptions have not been examined, try to impose themselves by the back door. Moreover, if this is not done, we pass up the opportunity to learn something from ideas that are commonly held about cultural hegemony and perhaps also the power of dominant theories in everyday life. In the case of the scene under discussion we can be sure that in every women's group there will be a consensus that women are afraid of men, of male violence, of encountering them in the dark, of their loud voices, their dominating demeanour. This feeling is so powerful that it seems almost superfluous to study such anxiety, to be astonished by it, and even to appeal to women to overcome their fears. After all every woman knows that in Germany a woman is raped every four minutes – in the USA the time gap is even shorter. In other words, this anxiety is real; dealing with it successfully can only result from the re-education of men or training women in self-defence or in forming women's groups. Women's anxieties are related to the badness of men and women's greater physical weakness. Accordingly when we decided to investigate women's anxieties we were not surprised to discover that many anxieties – like those described in the scene above – are inscribed in this space in which women are at the mercy of men. But on the other hand, there were problems in persuading people that such anxieties were worthy of study. Precisely because we all recognised that it is realistic to be afraid of men, especially in the dark, further questions and analysis seemed beside the point. Covertly, then, we had assumed that anxiety could only be theorised if it was a fantasy, something imagined, exaggerated, unrealistic – if, in short, it were itself a theoretical construct. The fact that the perception and analysis of a reality might itself be the source for the further theoretical understanding of dominance, was overlooked. This was something we now had to relearn. In order to avoid the pitfalls of empathy, simply re-experiencing the experiences of others we begin by creating a distance. This is achieved by simple questions directed at the story. This does not mean that we try to read meanings and interpretations into it, but instead to take note of what has actually been written. The analysis of the text by means of various questions is the actual process of deconstruction. The aim is to clear a path and not simply to follow the suggested meaning that the writer has conveyed in the text and which we can easily supplement for ourselves. Instead to look at the different elements that go to make up the story in a different light, to reassemble them in different ways, if necessary, of else to make visible any gaps, ruptures or contradictions. The analysis of the text by reading against the intended meaning in response to specific questions also serves a further purpose. It means that the various constructs that the writer creates about herself, other people or the subject matter of her story can themselves be made visible by any halfway intelligent questioning.

In the present case the first question was: what does the writer describe as anxiety, alternatively, what does she claim to be afraid of? Even this simple question has the effect of making something she had taken for granted – her fear of men – seem a little less clear cut: she is afraid to go round a corner, and she is afraid of this fear, of the moment of terror. The two anxieties overlap and together they are so great that she fails to describe what she might find round the corner. All we hear is that a man might be lurking, but not what she expected him to do. She is at far greater pains to describe the brightly lit passage and the approach of that corner behind which there waited she knew not what. We established that we knew this scene from countless horror movies; and that this playing on people's nerves was familiar among film-makers. Even if such images do not necessarily trigger feelings of anxiety, they may well intensify them, and since they are familiar from films, fairy tales or television, we concluded that it was important for our research into anxiety to look at the ways in which the imaginary is produced, illustrated and reinforced by the mass media. In other words, anxiety has to be understood *inter alia* as a cultural product.

Our second question asked what is anxiety connected with, what social construction of anxiety has the writer produced? The answer to this question yields a world picture that is not conscious for the most part, but is no less effective in governing the author's actions. She describes anxiety in the context of loneliness, or more exactly, of non-sociability. This anxiety is directed at men as soon as they are not together in groups. She feels safe in every group, either of concertgoers whom she does not know, or of 'young people' whom she also does not know. She explicitly describes men in groups as neutral (as men and women); the group is on the lookout to keep danger at bay. As soon as men appear in anonymous crowds – in the bus, for instance – the element of control is extinguished – this is what we learn from the interpolated scene – and she becomes the target of arrogant, violent glances. As long as she is protected by the crowd she can play at resistance and return their gaze. This act is one that prevents any misdemeanour. It is itself asocial, a mode of defence, and not a peaceful communication. If a man and a woman meet, the writer tells us, this does not lead to an innocuous social interchange, but to violence. Thus the words a 'man or a drunk' are juxtaposed interchangeably, a proof that we are dealing with beings not in control of their senses, if they are not controlled by their peers. As a woman she is quite at their mercy. And she too is mere nature as soon as she lowers her gaze; for she abandons control of her body, or, alternatively, is defenceless and at the mercy of the masculine gaze. The fact that here nature encounters nature condemns the woman to passivity; it prevents her from describing what the lurking man wants from her. Her expectation of what awaits her round the corner is not based on direct experience and is therefore not susceptible to interventions at the level of experience. Instead it feeds on the other experience in which arrogant men gaze at her aggressively. By experiencing every glance from every man as a potential act of violence, she intensifies her own fear of the unknown man at whose mercy she finds herself. However inclined we may be to sympathise with her imaginative construct, we cannot blind ourselves to the fact that there is something monstrous about thinking of the place of men in the social world exclusively in terms of protection and control, and also of thinking of the encounter between the sexes as entirely a matter of brute force.

The third question about the construction of other people in the field of action has already been answered in our discussion of the second question. The fourth question relates to the construction of the self. Anyone who has been concerned with memory work over a long period will have found that the search for the construction of the writer always produces surprises; if only because the majority of writers who participate in the process of deconstruction do not realise that they were going to produce such an elaborate image of themselves, let alone the image that actually emerges in the scene they describe. That was also borne out by the present instance. The writer presents herself as a resister and as a woman who takes all sorts of active steps. Nevertheless, her construction of the scene leaves her with no possible course of action in practice. Even her planned purchase of a tear-gas pistol will prove of no avail, since the cause of her panic does not come to meet her on the open street, but is lurking round the corner. Moreover, the fear of fear cannot be combated in this way. The strategy of going round the corner with other people is not one that will conquer fear, but only an evasion – indeed she foresees that if things go on like this, she will soon not be able to go out alone again.

This construction of an unnamed evil that emanates somehow or other from individual men and renders women incapable of action is one that we found in a number of scenes. In it women experience themselves as sexual beings, as nature, rather than as human beings encountering other human beings. In the scenes imagined this is achieved by reducing each individual man to mere nature and hence to violence. The scenes are intensified by the elaboration of women's own inability to act. In the scene described above one of the ways this is achieved is by the idea that the man is not only lurking behind the corner, but that once she has gone down the stairs, he could also cut off her retreat. In another scene a woman is lying in bed in her own room, imagining what might happen if she were to go to work in an office in an as yet unfinished and hence isolated floor of an office building. In her mind she runs through every possible escape route from a man she has imagined. She pictures herself just managing to reach a door, but the corridor is too long or the door cannot be opened quickly enough or she cannot negotiate the stairs fast enough, etc., until she ends up lying in bed, trembling, bathed in perspiration and her heart racing, quite unable to go to work at all.

In the course of our discussions we have also tried to formulate more general theses that then have the status of theoretical statements. These are then refined in the course of analysing other scenes, and are confronted with statements from traditional theories of anxiety. The insertion of these theses into the social context in which women act requires a further analysis before we finally advance to the point where we can sketch a theory of women's anxiety (or rather, anxieties).

After the analysis of a number of scenes it seemed important to us to explore the way in which women experience and assimilate the relations between the sexes. Since the sexes encounter each other, and indeed live together, in a multiplicity of social situations, this fear of masculine nature has to be restrained, if women are not to be reduced to complete passivity. But by the same token, such fears may be intensified at any moment, to the point where they can threaten women's entire social existence.

Taking a second step we attempted to shed more light on this unspeakable threat by concretising the question more precisely. Everyone knew from their own experience that the worst anxieties about men arose in the dark. In scenes about *Anxiety in the dark* we hoped to fill a gap in the earlier series in a more specific and precise way.[5]

Almost any woman could write these scenes about the dark. Surprisingly they were all very similar, and nowhere was the degree of subjective identification as great. But even though people knew exactly what it is like in the dark, the analysis still produced some surprising results. In one scene, for example, a woman talked about escaping from a constricting social situation into the freedom of nature. But almost at once the trees seemed too tall, the wind was tremendously blustery, the rain beat down, the fog was uncanny, etc.

From the confusion between nature without men and the fear of masculine nature we were able to arrive at the following theoretical formulations:

For women in our society there is no social space in which they can be free, and this is why they develop anxiety. This leads them to search for freedom in nature, a freedom which they then find is too much for them.[6] A new anxiety overwhelms them. Resistance drives them on to an individual quest for a suitable living space that turns out to be outside society. We had assumed that the fear of darkness would lead us to statements about fears of masculine violence. And although everyone was quite certain that even scenes about the fear of nature were 'basically' anxieties about men, that in the darkness that was described a man was lurking, and that trees, wind and fog were merely signs for him, we began to realise that we were not so much concerned here with individual men, but with men as the agents of a social structure, a model of civilisation, in which women have been assigned an unacceptable position in sexual relations.

Further scenes about fear of the dark also contain men, or the idea of men lurking. At their centre there is the fear-stricken woman whose death is certain but who for that very reason is not ready to fight for her life. Instead we find attempts to achieve sexual neutrality – a woman conceals her hair beneath a boy's cap and strides around with a masculine gait; another tries to appear manly in a sleeping bag: a third thinks of herself as plain and hopes to escape notice by appearing unattractive and hence not truly feminine. In all these scenes nature becomes a woman's fate which she can only escape by becoming disembodied. Since these scenes contain no society, no social space worth aspiring to, there are also no possible partners. In society women are as lost as they are in nature – in every case it is her own nature that is her existential problem, one that restricts her scope for action and in which numerous extraordinary incidents disempower her.

One difficulty with working with such scenes about womens' anxieties is that our societies actually contain men who rape and murder women. With such images before their eyes, images that the mass media constantly add further fuel to, it seems to us that it is normal for women to feel anxiety when they meet men – and to feel greater anxiety, the more men have the opportunity to act free from supervision by others of their kind. This convenient coincidence conceals the fact that the real process is much more complex. In every social situation women can feel themselves reduced to their bodies and attempt to use their anxieties to help them escape from the realm of the social. The problem turns out to be much more deeply anchored in sexual relations in general and in the ways in which women are positioned in them.

It frequently happens in the course of memory work that you reach a point where the analysis of the scenes points beyond the horizon of what has been thought up to then, but that you somehow seem unable to make any progress – as is the case here with the question of the *fear of men* that seems constantly to slip from one's grasp. In my experience it is often helpful at such moments to move onto a different terrain. One option is to look at additional theories on the same topic in the hope that criticism will enable us to make a breakthrough. Another is to interrupt the process of collecting individual testimony and insert a phase in which we explore the socio-economic conditions in which women experience anxiety. A third possibility is to have a look at fairy tales, myths and images, in short, the material of which the imaginary is made. Basically, every path leads somewhere useful. In the present instance we asked what role is played in our society by womens' bodies and women's nature, both of which are crucially the starting point, the source and the heart of anxiety?

In Critical Psychology[7] the decisive distinction between animals and humans has been identified in the fact that in mankind the development of the species no longer occurs at the expense of the individuals, but on the contrary, the more successful survival of the species itself depends on the development of individuals. This is explained by the ability of human beings to make history, to create their own world. This arises from the fact of objectified labour, language, concepts, etc., in other words, from the fact that every individual faces the task of appropriating his/her own human essence in order that mankind as a whole should survive in a human fashion. Even these basic notions manage to skate elegantly over the question of the natural reproduction of human beings. Although all the statements about essential human energies are undoubtedly valid, they bypass the question of how the reproduction of the species is to be regulated in a specifically human manner. At this point our theories maintain a curious silence, even though it is obvious that this aspect of humanisation is acted out at the expense of women: physically, morally and above all as far as the 'acquisition of essential human energies' is concerned. Women 'know' this, but since they also perceive themselves as human beings, they simultaneously deny it. They have to meet the various social and historical demands of life and have to maintain and protect their body for this task, to keep it clean, healthy and in readiness. That means also that for a certain period at least they also have to prevent reproduction and live with the countless signals unconsciously and semiconsciously inscribed in society. One such relevant social value system is morality in its significance for women.[8] But even though the prevention of reproduction is one of the aspects of women's behaviour that is simply taken for granted and even though it determines women's emotional world, by the same token women must also be absolutely prepared and willing to accept the task of becoming enthusiastic mothers with all the consequences that this entails for their lives and their life-plans. For example, they may always act on the assumption that real life will begin afterwards, that in effect they have a number of lives. We may perhaps describe the position accurately by saying that women find themselves subject to their own bodies. It is their duty to act as overseers over their bodies and at the same time, they realise that these overseers have almost no power – either with regard to physical pleasure or their own protection, or even their role in the reproduction of mankind. Hence they incur guilt on every side.

Women's fear of men as a fear about their own bodies must be enormous; what it expresses is that womens' entire bodies, their senses and their whole lives are at the mercy of this reproductive task. Furthermore, it means that they have no control over the conditions governing their lives. They neither take collective action to achieve such control, nor can they do so in the situation prevailing in our societies. We can readily see that the task of reproduction is one that they must both desire and fear, and that they live within a system full of contradictory signals. It is not thought to be human to have all too many children in what may well be deprived social circumstances, nor is it held to be feminine to have absolutely no children at all. Society continues to uphold the social rules that assert that sexual behaviour outside certain specified conditions is indecent and depraved, and simultaneously that in other specified circumstances the same behaviour is special and wonderful. (More could be learnt about these contradictory expectations from a study of the social and individual attitudes to both male and female homosexuality. Similarly, the bigoted discussion about the abortion laws should also be re-examined in this context.) Light could also be shed on the vulgar-psychoanalytic thesis that has once again gained currency among men and according to which womens' sexual anxieties or fear of rape spring from their intense desire and longing for the very things they resist. The force of this thesis can be understood as an expectation imposed on women, not as a desire they really possess.

In the history of mankind the contradiction about womens' bodies sketched here points both to immutable constraints, and also to socio-political and cultural deficiencies in the historical relations between the sexes. The problem of human reproduction calls for self-evident values that need to be fought for culturally. They require, among many other things, the overthrow of our system of morals. In our situation the development of society as a patriarchy implies a huge waste of natural resources; in this process women are among those wasted resources. At the stage reached by our civilisation the efforts to develop a human way of reproducing the species seem to have been thought of as individual problems and hence have been delegated to individual women, while on the cultural level expectations are safeguarded by a network of contradictions that itself drives the anxieties that reproduce the system. The anxiety that women are forced to develop becomes existential and thus prevents them from recognising their individual problems as problems of humanity as a whole. They are thereby prevented from even thinking of alternative approaches.

Let us change course once again and return to the anxiety actually experienced by women in sexual relationships and in a cultural system which semi-consciously fuels this anxiety in a contradictory fashion in the service of its own reproduction.

We now encounter the problem not only that men can represent a threat to women in reality, but that women themselves grow into society in such a way that they learn to fear men at the same time as they learn to come closer to them and to submit to them. They thus acquire a kind of ability to act that simultaneously blocks off every escape route.

On this point here is a scene from the responses to the question about *Anxiety about myself*. This new formula derives from the impression that grew from our work hitherto and from the conviction that when people express anxieties about their body, it is really the entire person that is at stake.

Memory Work

A Midnight Cycle Ride

It was immediately after the Currency Reform in 1948. She was 11 years old at the time, and her sister was 13. In Leipzig the first Fair was being put on and her mother wanted to take the opportunity to travel through all the Allied Zones to visit her parents in Berlin, since she had not seen them for years. There was no way of travelling from the village she was living in. But a bus left at midnight from one of the neighbouring villages. To get there took over half-an-hour on foot – too far in the dark and with luggage. So the plan was that their mother would take the luggage on one bicycle and she and her sister would ride on a second one. On the way back the two girls could have a bicycle each. Of course, they would ride back quickly – it was already very late and their two small brothers were left sleeping alone at home. She was very proud that she was so indispensable to this plan, something that seldom happened, since usually her mother worked out her plans just with her sister.

The journey there went quite smoothly. They rode in the pitch-black darkness through puddles and potholes in the road – the carrier on which she was riding was as hard as ever, and she longed for the moment when she would at long last be able to ride on her own. Together with their mother they waited for the bus at the chestnut tree in the other village. But there were a few drunks wandering around who pestered them. Their mother became uneasy and so sent them off on the return journey before the bus came, at a moment when the men were not looking. They raced off – the thrill of the dark and the importance of their excursion had now shrunk somewhat, thanks to the danger they felt pressing in on them from behind. She kept looking back. As she did so she caught sight of some bicycle lights and heard voices, swearing at them – the voices of the men they had eluded. They were now in full flight; the men raced after them and despite their drunken state they caught them up quickly, making a lot of noise. The girls pushed down on the pedals as hard as they could – they ought to put their lamps out, since they were just illumin-ated targets. But the distance between them was already so small that they would never have managed to stop, undo the dynamos and still make their getaway. They could already hear them panting behind them and she felt that she was both moving weightlessly and that she could not go on. 'Quick, get into the ditch,' her sister cried – and disappeared from her side. She also threw her bicycle into the ditch on the other side and jumped in after it. It was all wet and she was holding on to the nettle above her for protection when she heard the furious voices of the men above her. They had stopped, having lost sight of their quarry. She pressed against the ground and held her breath although she wanted to scream from fear, and was also afraid for her sister since she somehow imagined that they were after her because she herself was still too small.

Much later she heard her sister calling her quietly. Stinging from the nettles, her feet soaked, she clambered out, pulling the bicycle behind her. The physical pains filled her with tentative pride for having managed to escape. They decided to ride back into the village either to look for their mother or to seek out the smith whom they knew. Somehow or other he had expected them, since the men had been seen chasing them. He loaded them and the bicycles into his delivery van and drove them home. She felt bad that she could no longer prove that she was grown-up and could cycle in the dark, and at the same time, felt there was some justice because she was not allowed to go in a car.

As we have shown above, we normally start our work on such scenes with the sort of interrogation that you might find with teaching the study of texts in school. That is to say, we design a set of questions and apply them to the text. These questions can be justified, rejected and extended by the group deconstructing the text. An effective method has been to start by compiling lists in columns with very simple pieces of information about, for example, the actions of the narrator, actions of others, feelings,[9] and interests. At the second stage we move on to more complex issues dealing with the construction of the self, the construction of others or the objects concerned, questions that involve some measure of synthesising. In the case of the initial questions we just enter words that occur in the text, while at the second stage the actual words used are to be avoided, in other words, there should be a higher degree of abstraction. The breakdown of the scene into such columns normally brings an immediate insight. For example, you can see at a glance how someone can be completely immersed in a multiplicity of emotional situations, or alternatively describes no feelings at all. Or you can see the extent to which someone takes action or whether the other participants in the scene behave passively, and so forth. The breakdown of the text into columns is simply a tool, though one that precedes the creation of an analytic, reconstructive text about the scene. It is also very illuminating to carry out analysis of the language used in the scene, something which at this stage has barely been tried with these scenes about anxiety. Our twelve-year-long experience with memory work enables us to conclude tentatively that for the majority of their experiences most women only have a borrowed language at their disposal. Moreover, even on the subject of feelings, which are supposed to be the special terrain of women, there is a huge linguistic deficiency. Clichés are common, a kind of prefabricated set of linguistic expressions that destroys knowledge instead of increasing it. Memory work is itself a kind of school of language, an opportunity to try out, to seek out and discover words with which to describe one's own experiences.

Perhaps because of its unusual immersion in postwar German history, the preceding scene confronted us rather sharply with issues raised by the socialisation of girls.

In 1948, shortly after the Second World War, order was far from being restored. Travel possibilities were very inadequate. That forced people to adopt unconventional methods, such as bicycle rides at midnight with children who should have long since been in bed, as indeed their brothers were already. The author describes all of this as a welcome adventure that gives her added importance as an individual, indeed makes her seem useful, even indispensable, and credits her with other abilities. This means that she does not just strike out into the hitherto forbidden world of the night; she also sheds her place of relative insignificance in the hierarchy of siblings. After all, unlike her brothers, she is able to take part in carrying out a plan, even though it is one her older sister has worked out with her mother. The world of order is left behind; she grows up.

Unlike the scenes with older girls or women danger here does not manifest itself initially as a subjective feeling, but as a perception on the part of her mother, more or less as a kind of infectious uneasiness. The author also conveys this linguistically: she is not threatened by darkness or strangeness. Instead 'a few drunks were wandering around' and they 'pestered' the family group. Nothing indicates that the words 'drunken', 'pestered', meant anything particular to the author; indeed, the fact that her mother sends them away quickly seems at first to be a continuation of the adventure; racing off on the bicycles seems as if it were part of a game.

But the newly constructed collective 'we' of the action soon gives way to the isolated 'I' that is pursued by danger. Her body begins to speak to her: the danger is 'pressing in' on them, her eyes signal 'light', her ears 'voices', 'panting'. When the men pass by as she hides in the ditch, she can imagine what danger might be awaiting her. Oddly enough, the original hierarchy is now reinstated itself: the men were 'after' her sister, because she herself was still 'too small'. In this way the growing girl's fear of men is not extinguished – on the contrary, she is out of her mind with fear – but it is explained as being part of growing up. In contrast she soon learns the lesson: *you have to enlist the protection of men whom you know. The bigger you become, the more important that is.*

At the same time the little girl's anxiety is immediately comprehensible. She mobilises paternalist feelings, including resentment towards her mother who sends her daughters 'home' under such conditions. But empathy can do no more than convey the insight that children – especially female ones – should not be allowed out on the streets after dark, particularly when drunks (men not in control of their senses) are out and about. From the standpoint of analysis we learn a little more about how ideas of men enter the feminine imaginary. They appear self-explanatory so that further questions are otiose, and seem to call for associating with anxiety rather than with men (men are just being to escape from). These ideas are formed on the one hand through a sort of emotional infectiousness: the mother is obviously afraid, whereas the daughter only sees an adventure. But the mother represents order, so that her own violation of customary behaviour – which promised taking unusual steps, new significance, usefulness and growing up – was at the same time transmitted to the girl as extremely problematic. Escape from men is at the same time a leave-taking from her mother, indeed it abandoned her to a danger that her mother had herself drawn attention to. The pursuit of the girls is in a sense a liberation of the mother; the privileges of the older sister also mean endangering her. In short, the author finds herself in a tangle of contradictory signals that necessarily inhibit any accurate account of and search for the real danger.

This leads us to the following contradiction: to leave the world of childhood and extend your ability to act also means trying to escape from the protection and accustomed order of the child's world. The early lesson is: *girls need a new protector when they grow out of the old one.* Where then would be the satisfaction of growing up? But at the same time growing up is known to be unavoidable. What additional reserves of curiosity are needed to picture to oneself the future dangers men seem to represent, when at the same time men are supposed to be the source of protection? Can a girl escape from this contradiction simply by ignoring it?[10] Or conversely, what efforts must she make to achieve adulthood in an energetic and self-confident way? How can she live out this contradiction that seems to be an inherent part of male images without submitting to them? A preliminary finding seems to be that the vacant space obscurely occupied by the dangers posed by men can be filled by prefabricated images taken from a variety of sources. In the scene at present under consideration the narrator's perception is influenced by adventure stories from childhood in which cops and robbers, hot pursuit and games of hide-and-seek enrich our imagination. This would be a possible way of extending our project. We ourselves opted for a different route. We examined the literature that gives adolescent girls advice on how to deal with such problems. We also referred back to fairy tales, a cultural building-block that has an impact on our imagination. Here, for example, we discover one solution to the paradox according to which masculinity simultaneously represents threat and protection. Even the examples that appear at first glance to resist such classification often turn into protective beings if only you share your bed or table with them. They cast off their hedgehog quills or lion-skin and slip out of their frog-shape, if only a woman takes them seriously. Sometimes, however, they fail to change and persist as nasty dragons. In that event you just have to wait for the arrival of the good man to provide protection and salvation. In every case women's activity remains confined to selfless devotion, and the additional piece of advice is '*Don't trust your senses*'.

Let us take a step back to girls of pre-school age. A further way of overcoming the contradiction of paradoxical masculinity is the introduction of the 'wicked uncle'. We assume that the efforts of parents and teachers to create a mysterious aura of unnamed sexuality around men with sweets and hence to stop girls from being too trustful towards strange men, do not really help girls survive, but instead lead to anxiety and an inability to act. This lesson about the 'wicked uncle' still occupies a place in the curriculum of the first years at school, even though the treat of sexual abuse is far more likely to come from a trusted member of the family than from strangers in the street.

It is understandable that one of our scenes should portray this as the author's chief problem: 'What would her parents say if she accepted presents from strange men?' She ends up throwing her chocolate bunnies away because she found even her parents' questions 'unpleasant' and 'they should on no account learn that her uncle had picked her up and carried her'. The event crystallises in her mind into a kind of crime which is her fault – she is afraid that 'everything might come out'. This is fertile soil for the guides that warn against strange uncles. It is possible to train modes of perception that result in insulating people from the world through fear. The lesson is that *it is dangerous to become involved with unknown people*. This attitude is inscribed in relations between the sexes.

The contradiction about the wicked uncle described by our author lies in her relationship with such men, alternatively, in her parents' injunction to beware of strange men. In order to recognise the uncle as a treat, she has to be close to him. But that is the very danger her parents have warned her to avoid. She incurs guilt if she informs herself. Her chosen strategy of perceiving her uncle's various actions as threatening is itself a violation of their warnings. The contradiction then is that she should avoid coming into contact with any possible evil, but that she must come into contact with it in order to recognise it for what it is. The solution can only lie in an early-warning system that springs into action long before any danger comes on the scene.

Preliminary Conclusion

What we have achieved is a preliminary insight into a highly contradictory process of socialisation which in practice recommends a retreat into self-denial, domesticity and submission at every stage in the growing-up process. Contradictions block the path of development and place taboos on the world in an almost archaic manner. They begin with the twofold riddle that men – having been endowed with sexuality long before sexuality has become a real issue – oscillate between familiarity and an alienness that cannot be interrogated. It is inappropriate to explore the badness that is thus intimated. This mindset persists and propagates itself in the world. The world is so bad and full of dangers that a girl should not venture into it and a woman would be well advised to stay at home. The next contradiction concerns adulthood as such. The desire for liberation, the wish to escape from parental protection, is frustrated by the insight that this can only be achieved at the cost of a new protective custody. We thus find that women in a sexual relationship are caught up in a contradictory identity in the sense that they cannot develop their personality without losing it. The desire for spaces controlled by one's own man is self-denial in the cloak of freedom. There is no experience to which women can appeal that would enable them to find their way without anxiety around a world they have appropriated in theory. Indeed their knowledge of the wickedness of the world stands menacingly in their way to prevent them from setting foot in it.

For our initial question about anxiety in sexual relations and about its paradigmatic power in our society we learned that anxiety about the body is not restricted to the process of reproduction and women's role in it. On the contrary, the subjugation of the female sex to this social function seems to press both womens' bodies and the mysterious male figures into service. Women's acceptance of modesty, of retreat, their loss of curiosity and adventurousness, indeed their renunciation of inquiry and knowledge seem to have been purchased by this anxiety about the body, with the consequence that physical anxiety becomes the synthesis of all these experiences. At the same time, it becomes impossible for women to obtain any understanding about these relationships. How can you want to learn about dangers when knowledge itself seems to be a danger?

Curiously in almost every scene other women stand as guards blocking the entrance into the world, knowledge and autonomous action. They include sisters, girlfriends and strangers. And nowhere do they join forces in search of solutions, or enable them to recognise obstructive contradictions together or to discover new modes of living and acting. On the contrary, the danger perceived as coming from men drives women to men for protection. So this complex of dangers ensures that heterosexual relationships develop in a way that entails the renunciation of any development at all. This goes along with the worldwide practice of leaving the conduct of public affairs to men, in so far as they are conducted at all. Anxiety prevents women from reversing the defeat of the female sex and this brings further anxiety in its wake. Thus anxiety makes a double appearance at a strategically significant point; it is both the sign of awakening and the guardian of the different points at which women (as individuals) might break out of the framework that society assigns them to. It is the emotion that both signals an awakening and also impedes and retracts it. This is a vicious circle which we have to break.

Postscript on Memory Work as Sociological Method

In this text I have not tried to present the method of memory work either as a set of dogmas or as a collection of rules, but as part of an ongoing project. This may mean that some aspects have been insufficiently emphasised while others were totally overlooked. I should like at this point to add a few points, so far as seems necessary, and at the same time to present them as unresolved problems.

Michel Foucault proceeded from the assumption that language is a battlefield on which the dominant culture acquires its hegemony. By speaking, i.e. giving linguistic expression to our feelings, sensations and wishes, we are also spoken by the dominant normality. There is no escape from this. We can go along with these ideas to a certain extent and it is part of our own assumptions that such 'alien' speaking or the fact that women have no language 'of their own' is accentuated in patriarchal culture. However, such a view when followed through consistently leads to an infinite process of deconstruction, and there is no solid base or vantage point from which to resist or from which it might be possible to gain a home of one's own. We may generalise the point for memory work and inquire from what standpoint do we deconstruct the meanings that are constituted in a narrative, and what value do we assign to the apparently casual components of such a scene, and with what right?

We can doubtless reckon on general agreement if we assume that every author of a scene from everday life must, if she wishes to be understood, write in the dominant language, at an appropriate emotional pitch, in a generally comprehensible fashion, logically and without obvious self-contradiction, and produce a coherent narrative with a beginning, a climax and an end. We are experimenting with an exemplary method designed to enable people to present themselves in the dominant language as the appropriators of dominant cultural patterns. What is conveyed is the experience of fitting into society. The experience imparted then is that of a political disciplinary process that was undertaken independently and was then confirmed through the act of communication. But no one apart from the individuals concerned is in a position to regard this process as one of cutting them down to size, and not merely as the experience, if not the description, of achieving a social class goal. We assume then that these experiences contain deposits of what has been left behind, semi-conscious elements, both of awakening and resistance. These are articulated in the reports as inappropriate words, nonsensical passages, unexplained silences, contradictory statements. They too are experience, but experience that is in conflict with the experience that has been made meaningful. The paradoxical criterion by which the individual bits of experience, both those that just emerge little by little and those we have fragmented for analytical purposes, have to be measured is the individual's ability to act. It seems possible to work on the assumption that every individual has the need not to be at the mercy of the conditions in which she operates, and to be able to achieve competence, autonomy and co-determination in all relevant matters. This assumption has a political dimension, one critical of domination, as well as a methodological one. The individual women in the research group could see in their own texts how they made compromises, how they adapted and subordinated themselves in order to preserve some scope for action in contradictory structures. Lifestyles, attitudes, and ways of dealing with conflicts can be decoded as solutions that once seemed plausible. At the same time the desire for an expanded ability to act, for more wide-ranging solutions, for the ability to develop a lifestyle in which to deal with contradictions, to be equal to them rather than being paralysed – this desire becomes the material out of which more liberated life opportunities become viable and hence to be regarded as vision, as genuine option and as something once wanted or imagined. This search is a collective activity, during which the requisite language comes to light, whose materials were lying around undiscovered in the narrated experiences. This process remains open-ended.

It may help to explain why it is better for memory work to be performed in a group, rather than alone. It is not just that it is important to have the imaginations of a number of people at one's disposal. What is even more significant is their lack of respect for the surface meaning, and the way their grasp of the various tactics is clarified by the public nature of the process. The similarities of women's experience go hand in hand with their great variety and diversity and this makes it possible not only to see one's own experience in that of others, but also through a process of comparison to recognise inconsistencies and omissions, as well as new awakenings and solutions. This is particularly in evidence when women from quite different cultures come together. (For example, it is possible at points where certain individuals get stuck for other women to continue writing the scene. This has the double effect of highlighting the common features of female socialisation and culture patterns and of discovering a language for the contradictory narrative of one's 'own' story.) It is a laborious process, but even so the best way forward up to now has always seemed to us to follow up the initial collective deconstruction of a scene with its questions and tasks, by asking the author to produce a second version. Gaps need to be filled in, contradictions spelled out, motives further explained. In particular the blatant discrepancy that almost always makes its appearance between the feelings and actions of the narrator must be ironed out in a way that makes sense to the writer. This process of writing the 'new version' is not just a contribution to our knowledge of female socialisation; it is also always an important learning experience for the writer. Normally she cannot simply fill in gaps or clarify contradictions without placing a question mark over the initial narrative. In other words, she experiences herself as a person who has to cast doubt on herself and her interpretation of her past in order to appear 'credible' to herself. This process of changing oneself cannot occur without a crisis. It loosens up what was previously held to be self-evident and ties the individual into a relationship with herself and the world that we can perhaps best describe as 'theorised']*theorieförnig*]. At first glance such a term has negative connotations, but they vanish when we recollect that before all else theories are tied to experiences. In other words, theories are being put back on their feet.

Translated by Rodney Livingstone

Notes

1. '*Angst*' has traditionally presented a problem to the translator (as indeed the use of the German term in English suggests). In German it is found in common usage and just means 'fear'. '*Ich habe Angst*' means 'I am afraid'. But in psychoanalytical contexts it has acquired a semi-technical meaning. In consequence starting with the standard translation of Freud, it has customarily been translated as 'anxiety'. I have adhered to this practice here, but have occasionally used 'fear' or other synonyms where the syntax made it desirable. James Strachey has observed that when Freud wrote in French he used the synonyms '*angoisse*'

and '*anxiété*'. For his discussion of the question, see the Appendix 'The Term "*Angst*" and its English Translation', *The Standard Edition of the Complete Psychological Works of Sigmund Freud*, James Strachey (ed.), Hogarth Press 1962, Volume 3, pp. 116–17. (Translator's Note)

2. We owe this view to Sigmund Freud. The study of his writings is stimulating even though his works have rightly attracted the anger of feminist researchers on account of their male-centred and family-orientated hypotheses about 'the nature of women'. In his studies of anxiety there is a radical change from his early view (cf. 'On the grounds for detaching a particular syndrome from neurasthenia under the description "anxiety neurosis"' (1895). See *The Pelican Freud Library*, Volume 10, pp. 53–60) to his later writings ('Inhibitions, Symptoms and Anxiety' (1926), ibid. pp. 229–333). Initially he thought that anxiety was triggered by the widespread practice of coitus inter-ruptus, whereas later on it was birth that figured as the traumatic background against which anxieties were repeatedly re-enacted. In this context one conclusion that he reaches is that anxiety is a feeling that springs from conflicting desires. Without accepting his arguments in their entirety, I have accepted this hypothesis for my work on women's anxiety. In so doing I remove it from the context of ego and id and generalise it to conflict situations as such.

3. The research project on anxiety began with fifty women aged between 20 and 60. The majority were students. But the group also contained women from different occupations, including local housewives, who had volunteered for the four-year research group that was part of the Adult Education programme put on by the University. As is still customary in Hamburg the group did not include any black women. In all seventy-four scenes were written up and analysed; in addition there were twenty-eight essays from 11-year-old schoolchildren of both sexes.

4. We have discovered that when women talk about themselves in the first person, they tend to make excessively brief, laconic statements, simply because they do not think they are very important. Since memory work is recollecting as many details as possible, and regarding them as of sufficient importance to make them worth recording, we have decided to ask women to write in the third person, in other words, to see themselves as historical personages. This does not mean the nega-tion of the explicit demand in the Women's Movement that women should learn to say 'I'. It just means that this demand is not necessarily appropriate for the work undertaken here.

5. This 'concretisation' of the question after the first major part of the study does not mean that all of women's anxiety are to be set in the

context of physical sexual relationships. In further projects and with different questions we explored the problem of anxiety in political situations (including the fear of acting or speaking in public) and anxieties about the normal experiences at the workplace. It would take us too far to go into all these issues here.

6. Margaret Atwood has used this syndrome in one of her novels. The main character stays in the forests in the expectation that she will gradually grow the fur that will enable her to survive in the wilds. (*Surfacing*. Bloomsbury 1972.)

7. Critical Psychology is the name adopted by a group that has arisen out of the work of Leontjew, Sèves and Marx's Feuerbach Theses and has attempted to ground the whole of psychology on materialist foundations. Its chief exponent is Klaus Holzkamp. Critical Psychology has been active for the last twenty years; it has numerous publications to its credit and has its own journal: *Forum Kritische Psychologie*. An essential feature of the school is that its methods are historical and developmental, that is to say, after tracing the development of living creatures it attempts to define the social as the specific characteristic of humanity and attempts on this basis to reformulate psychology as a whole.

8. Cf. the study 'Morals also have two genders' in F. Haug, *Beyond Female Masochism*, Verso 1992.

9. We found it very useful, particularly in the case of research into anxiety, to list not just the explicit feelings, but also separately to specify anticipated feelings and actions.

10. We have repeatedly found this strange connection between women's anxieties and the fear of knowledge in widely differing contexts, at different ages and social position. When we read Christa Wolf's story about the nuclear acident at Chernobyl (*Störfall*) we found the same link between anxiety and the fear of knowledge. It seemed important enough to us to warrant making further research into the relationship a major priority.

Bibliography

Atwood, Margaret (1972), *Surfacing*, Bloomsbury.
Blum, Ulrike (1990), *Feministische Psychotherapie*, unpublished talk for the Congress of the German Society for Behavioural Therapy, Berlin.

Eichenbaum, Luise and Susie Orbach (1992), *Outside in, inside out*, Penguin.

Foucault, Michel, (1970), *The Order of Things*, New York.

—— (1972), *The Archeology of Knowledge*, New York.

—— (1978), *The History of Sexuality*, New York.

Freud, Sigmund (1895), 'On the grounds for detaching a particular syndrome from neurasthenia under the description "anxiety neurosis"', *The Pelican Freud Library*, Volume 10, pp. 31–63.

—— (1925), 'Some psychical consequences of the anatomical distinction between the sexes', *The Pelican Freud Library*, Volume 7, pp. 323–43.

—— *Introductory Lectures on Psycho-Analysis, The Pelican Freud Library*, Volume 1.

—— (1926), 'Inhibitions, Symptons and Anxiety', *The Pelican Freud Library*, Volume 10, pp. 229–333.

—— (1933), 'Anxiety and Instinctual Life' in the *New Introductory Lectures on Psychoanalysis, The Pelican Freud Library*, Volume 2, pp. 113–44.

—— (1895), 'First Steps towards a Theory of Anxiety Neurosis', *The Pelican Freud Library*, Volume 10, pp. 53–60.

Haug, Frigga and Hauser, Kornelia (1991), *Die andere Angst*, Berlin and Hamburg.

—— (ed.) (1983, 1991), *Sexualisierung der Körper*, Berlin.

–8–

A Journey Through Memory
Annette Kuhn

Not long ago, I wrote a book in which I used personal memory materials – artefacts such as photographs and films, as well as remembered events in my own life – to explore some of the ways in which memory, the activities and the products of remembering – can bring together the personal, the social and the historical; and to look at memory's place in making identities that place us as members both of families and of wider communities – communities of class, gender, nation, for instance. The book *Family Secrets* (Kuhn 1995)[1] was a number of years in the making; and working on it was truly a voyage of discovery, with the doldrums and setbacks, as well as the thrills, of a journey into the unknown. I set out on my adventure under the guidance of earlier travellers along the way, but soon found myself turning off in new directions, onto unfamiliar pathways whose destinations lay beyond my sight. And if finishing a book and seeing it appear in print was a conclusion of a sort, it was by no means the end of my journey through memory. This chapter tells the story so far of a voyage that turned into an odyssey of the heart as much as of the intellect.

Revisionist Autobiography, Visual Autobiography, and Memory Work

Family Secrets is not a work of autobiography; but it is rooted in a critical interest in a variant of autobiographical writing that I call 'revisionist autobiography'. In the mid-1980s, a number of books of a broadly autobiographical nature, written by intellectuals of my own generation, were published in Britain. My introduction to these works was *Truth, Dare or Promise* (Heron 1985), a collection of essays by and about girls growing up in the 1950s. These stories attracted me not just because of the 'what' (they resonate powerfully with memories of my own childhood); but also because of the 'how', the way the tales are told. The writers for the most part appear to be uncomfortable with the idea of an 'autobiographical self', to the degree at least that this self carries connotations of the transcendent ego of bourgeois and patriarchal individualism and of the power of the authorial voice. Given that all the book's contributors are feminists, and many of them also socialists, this is hardly surprising. But how can these women write about their own lives without setting up those lives, those selves, as unique, special, or exemplary?[2]

For autobiography – the writing of one's own life – is exactly that, a type of *writing*. A literary genre like any other, autobiography has formal conventions of its own. Traditionally, autobiographies are written life stories organised as narratives: beginning, middle, and end are held together in the telling of an ordered sequence of events. The time of the story has ready-made shape in the chronology of the writer's life: the story opens with his birth or early childhood, proceeds through various life stages, and ends at or near the time of writing. This sort of life story is characteristically presented, or read, as evoking a *Bildung*: it is an account of the development of the central character (the writer) over time. The present, the time of writing, is set up from the outset as the goal towards which the story will inexorably direct itself. Autobiography differs from fictional forms of storytelling in two main ways: events narrated make a claim to actuality (they 'really' happened); and the narrator, the writing I, is set up in a relation of identity with the central protagonist, the written I. Writer and subject purport to be one; the writer in the moment of writing being the same as, or a logical extension of, the self of the earlier years of the real life being written about.

This, of course, is itself a kind of fiction. The linear narrative of conventional autobiography, its production of the narrator as a unitary ego, is the outcome of a considerable reworking of the rough raw materials of an identity and a life story. A kind of causal logic is taken for granted: the adult who is writing 'now' is contained within the child he writes about; events are ordered retrospectively from the standpoint of the present, the moment of telling, which is often also the moment of narrative closure. In consequence, the story is ordered and read as if this life could have been lived in no other way.

The source materials of the written life story are subjected to what psychoanalysis calls secondary revision. And in welding together the writing I and the written I – in producing narration, narrator and protagonist as indivisibly one – the conventional autobiography constructs a powerful central organising ego for its own story.[3] But if autobiography is a specific writing strategy, one through which a certain self, a particular identity, is constructed and made public, it can equally well be deconstructed: not only through criticism, but also through 'other' practices – stories of different lives, told differently.

A critical deconstruction would attend to the narrative strategies and rhetorical devices at work in autobiographical texts, and with the ways in which the autobiographical self is textually constructed. How, for example, might 'femininity' become an attribute of the self produced in women's (and men's?) autobiographical writing? How do writers construct themselves, or become textually produced, as belonging to a particular gender group or social class or generation or nationality or ethnic group? To what extent might autobiographies 'write' their writers (and indeed their readers) across a range of different social, cultural and psychical categories, to produce complex and even contradictory subject positions, hybrid or fragmented identities?

The texts which fuelled my own interest in autobiographical writing are revisionist in the sense that they incorporate into their writing implicit or explicit critiques, even deconstructions, of traditional modes of autobiographical writing. Their feminist and socialist authors come from a variety of class backgrounds, though almost all of them are white. The formation of many such British intellectuals of their generation ensures that most of these texts are informed in one way or another by psychoanalytic, mostly Freudian and post-Freudian, thinking. And the circumstances of their production combine to produce in these writings a scepticism about the reliability of memory and also an awareness of the pitfalls of an ego which sets itself up as transcendent.

Is 'theoretical selfconsciousness and an explicit critique of the idea that individual stories can be "simply" evidential or authentic' (Marcus 1987: 78) compatible with the idea of any sort of autobiographical identity? And what, if any, is the relationship between on the one hand this self-reflexive writing by contemporary socialist and feminist intellectuals and on the other an older tradition of 'outsider' life stories, stories produced by members of social groups whose stories have traditionally been untold, hidden, or silenced? How do life stories 'from below' – by women, by former slaves, by working-class men and women, for example – handle the relationship between life events, the narration of these events, and the narrating subject? Significantly, such autobiographers, for whom 'being a significant agent worthy of the regard of others, a human subject, as well as an individuated "ego" for oneself' (Gagnier 1991: 141) is not necessarily easy or to be taken for granted, tend also – though not as a rule self-consciously – to shun the 'great I' of conventional or bourgeois autobiography. Does this attitude come with the territory of social, cultural or political marginality, whatever its form? Can a questioning of bourgeois or patriarchal notions of identity and a desire to redress social and historical injustices be reconciled in autobiographical writing? If so, how? Revisionist autobiography certainly attempts such a rapprochement: usually by insisting, within the writing itself, on a gap between the I that writes and the I (or perhaps better the me) that is written about; and/or by drawing explicitly on formal bodies of knowledge or theories as frameworks within which to explore the I or the me, and its place in history, its contingency.

The rationale for revisionist autobiography has not purely, nor indeed at all, to do with the life and times of particular individuals, but rather with the relationship between the personal, the individual, and the social; or, to put it another way, between experience and history. The self might be constructed, for example, as a product of patriarchal, psychic or social relations such as, say, class. In this sense, identity is seen as not merely 'in process', but as a potential battleground, too. In these terms, the subject/object of the story cannot possibly be regarded as an exceptional, or even as a fully-formed, individual. These writings also subvert assumptions about the transparency, authenticity, or 'truth' of memory; and materials not ordinarily considered pertinent to autobiography may be brought into play in the writing. Among the most interesting examples of work in this vein are Ronald Fraser's *In Search of a Past* (Fraser: 1984) and Carolyn Steedman's *Landscape for a Good Woman* (Steedman 1986). Fraser uses psychoanalysis as both theoretical model and narrational device; while Steedman draws on social history as a source of material to illuminate her own life and that of her mother. In both books, the narrating 'I' is in consequence fragmented, dispersed across different discourses.

In *Truth, Dare or Promise*, each essay includes a photograph of the writer as a child: this is usually a family snap or school photo. As I recall, in none of the essays is the photograph commented upon: it appears to be present simply as illustration. What is the function of images like this in relation to written accounts of these particular girlhoods? Are they making some claim for the authenticity of the authors' childhood selves – evidence, in other words, of some 'truth' about the past? If this is so, it is surprising that writings so self-conscious about their own discursive strategies should fail to take on board the discursive operations of the photographic image. Images are just as much productions of meaning as words, even if the 'language' is different.

This raises a number of questions about how images like this – personal photographs of the kind preserved in family albums -- are used by the people who make or own them (Holland 1991). Personal photos have a particular, and a very special, place in the production of memories about our own lives. In the twentieth century, countless millions have been offered a new kind of access to the past through the democracy of family photography: in our time, family photos are foremost among the mementoes we treasure. As part of a vast industry devoted largely to the cultivation of ideal images of the family, family photography constrains our remembering, tries to funnel our memories into particular channels. But it also has more subversive potential. It is possible to take a critical and questioning look at family photographs, and this can generate hitherto unsuspected, sometimes painful, knowledge and new understanding about the past and the present, helping raise critical consciousness not only about our individual lives and our own families, but about 'the family' in general and even, too, about the times and the places we inhabit.

In touching on memory production, personal photographs have something in common with autobiographical writing: though if the activities of looking at and talking about photographs also involve a putting into discourse of memory, they lack the dimension of writing and thus perhaps the more revised public productions of self characteristic of conventional autobiography and even, in a different way, of revisionist autobiography. Personal photographs are commonly taken as evidence that this or that event really happened, this or that person was actually present at a particular time and place: they seem, in other words, to stand as guarantors of the past actuality of some person or event. In everyday terms, the meanings of photographs are more often than not taken as self-evident.

But as a cultural theorist I am concerned with how images make meanings. For me, every photograph contains a range of possible meanings, from those relating to cultural conventions of image production to those that have to do with the social and cultural contexts in which the image has been produced and is being used. I find that these meanings seldom yield themselves fully to a surface reading. I start out with the assumption that photographic images, far from being transparent renderings of a pre-existing reality, embody coded references to, and even help construct, realities. To unpick their meanings, photographs have to be deconstructed, too. Both personal photographs and autobiographical writing have a part in the production of memories, offering us pasts which in one way or another reach into the present, into the moment of looking at a picture, of writing or reading a text.

In her 'political, personal, and photographic autobiography' *Putting Myself in the Picture* (Spence 1986), Jo Spence uses her own photographs as source material, in much the way Ronald Fraser and Carolyn Steedman, in *In Search of a Past* and in *Landscape for a Good Woman*, draw on their own memories and dreams as material for interpretation.[4] In a practice she calls 'visual autobiography', Spence uses her photographs as a set of texts to be 'read' – deconstructed and interpreted. Refusing the transparency commonly attributed to photographic images, Spence acknowledges their status as cultural artefacts, sometimes suggesting that her photographs tell lies – or at least carry meanings which have as much to do with aesthetic and cultural conventions as with any unsullied 'truth' about their subject, 'Jo Spence', past or present.

It is but the shortest step from this to acknowledging that photographs may 'speak' silence, absence, and contradiction as much as, indeed more than, presence, truth or authenticity; and that while in the production of memory they might often repress this knowledge, photographs can also be used as a means of questioning identities and memories and generating new ones. A 'visual autobiography' grounded in this premiss has this much at least in common with revisionist autobiographical writings. There is no 'peeling away of layers to reveal a "real" self', says Spence (Spence 1986: 97), but rather a constant reworking of memory and identity.

In these images and these texts, these writings and these readings, a staging of memory is taking place. In *In Search of a Past*, Ronald Fraser's recourse to psychoanalytic inquiry allows him to show that the relationship between past events and our memories of them is far from imitative, that we cannot access the past event in any unmediated form. The past is unavoidably rewritten, revised, through memory; and memory is partial: things get forgotten, misremembered, repressed. Memory, in any case, is always already secondary revision: even the memories we run and rerun inside our heads are residues of psychical processes, often unconscious ones; and their (re)telling – putting subjective memory-images into some communicable form – always involves ordering and organising them in one way or another. In their staging of memory, revisionist autobiography and visual autobiography can encompass a therapeutic aspiration. These practices often embody, though not always explicitly, a wish and a conviction that the wounds of the past be healed in the very activity of rescuing memory from the oblivion of forgetfulness and repression.

My own journey through memory was inspired and guided by these examples: revisionist autobiography's radical reworking of the written life story and visual anthropology's passionately questioning attitude towards personal photographs. I was led to look closely at the source materials for both practices – personal memories, photographic images and 'formal' bodies of knowledge – and their possible uses. Eventually, attention to materials, methods and uses was to overtake my original fascination with strategies of writing and reading. It was at this point that my venture was brought up against an impasse: critical analysis, while opening up important and intriguing areas of investigation, seemed to be taking me only a certain distance along my path. Partly because of an affective, almost a visceral, engagement with the material I was working on – I was experiencing a clear and forceful sense of what can only be called gut recognition – the distanced standpoint of the critic began to feel less and less adequate to my material, incapable of addressing such powerful responses to my critical objects. I am captivated, intrigued, moved, by Fraser's, Steedman's, Spence's, and all the other stories: they speak to me in the most compelling way, engaging my own past, my own memories. Getting to grips with this response demanded that I should not stifle it by insisting upon a critical distance, but rather acknowledge it and bring it into play by embracing my own past and its representation through memory. This takes me beyond intellectual engagement (which I have never, however, relinquished). It promises to help me think and speak adequately of histories, of lives, of which I too feel a part. It gives voice to a sense of belonging that is both strange and familiar, forgotten and remembered.

Allowing myself to pursue this path less travelled proved a crucial turning point in my journey through memory. Admitting and addressing my own memory material was what made possible, in fact *necessary*, the writing of *Family Secrets*. This new direction also turned out to be the start of an adventure that has taken me far beyond any personal history to which I might lay claim: into familial, cultural, national, and many other manifestations of collectively shared memory. Along the way, I have made some discoveries about how memory works, and observed in action some of the psychical and cultural processes through which memory organises not only our inner worlds but the outer ones of public expression and circulation of memory-stories as well. I believe, too, that I have identified a set of cultural products which, while inhabiting diverse media and forms of expression, share key characteristics in common: these I have named 'memory texts'. If my journeyings have been, on occasion, frustratingly directionless, they have given me a more profound and fully lived understanding of the activity of remembering, of how remembering binds us as individuals into shared subjectivities and collectivities.

Memory has many uses, individual and social. At one extreme, to paraphrase Freud on hysteria, when there is too much of it and it is too compulsive, memory can be appallingly crippling. To extend the psychical outwards to the collective, we have only to call to mind the oftentimes bloody consequences of that hyper-remembering, that unremitting rehearsal of distant pasts, that marks the sectarian tribal imagination. If the certainties of sectarian memory inhabit one pole of a continuum at whose midpoint perhaps lie inert forms of memory such as nostalgia and heritage consciousness, at its other extreme are found forms of radical remembering that work actively and consciously to bring to light the repressed or the forgotten, whilst sustaining a critical and questioning attitude towards the past and towards memory and its uses.

This is my definition of 'memory work': an active practice of remembering which takes an inquiring attitude towards the past and the activity of its (re)construction through memory. Memory work undercuts assumptions about the transparency or the authenticity of what is remembered, treating it not as 'truth' but as evidence of a particular sort: material for interpretation, to be interrogated, mined for its meanings and its possibilities. Memory work is a conscious and purposeful staging of memory. Memory work, then:

1. Involves an active staging of memory
2. Takes a questioning attitude to the past and its (re)construction through memory
3. Questions the transparency of what is remembered
4. Takes what is remembered as material for interpretation.

Memory work stages memory through words, spoken and written, in images of many kinds, and also in sounds: the multifaceted quality of memory-expressions is reflected in different practices of memory work. Word-memories, image-memories, even sound-memories have all been important in my own memory work. In doing this work I have taken to heart a number of lessons about memory: that the relationship between actual events and our memories of them is by no means mimetic; that memory never provides access to or represents the past 'as it was'; that the past is always mediated – rewritten, revised – through memory; and that as an activity remembering is consequently itself far from neutral. I have learned that memory does not simply *involve* forgetting, misremembering, repression – that would be to suggest there is some fixed 'truth' of past events: memory actually *is* these processes, is always already secondary revision. But, disdaining bleak agnosticism, the radical remembering of memory work will not let matters rest there.

In acknowledging the performative nature of remembering, memory work takes on board its productivity and encourages the practitioner to use the pretexts of memory, the traces of the past that remain in the present, as raw material in the production of new stories about the past. These stories may, as I have indicated, heal the wounds of the past. They may also transform the ways individuals and communities live in and relate to the present and the future. For the practitioner of memory work, then, it is not merely a question of *what* we choose to keep in our 'memory boxes' – which bits and pieces, which traces of our own pasts, we lovingly or not so lovingly preserve – but of what we do with them: *how* we use these relics to make memories, and how we then make use of the stories they generate to give deeper meaning to, and if necessary to change, our lives now.

Some Theses on Memory

In the course of doing my memory work, I noticed several patterns and regularities: in the ways memory is produced and constructed in memory texts; in formal and other textual characteristics of memory texts across media, matters of expression and genre; in the subjectivities memory texts produce for their users – rememberers and 'recipients'; in the ways memory texts manage the tension between personal memory and the collective imagination, between the selfhood of the remembering subject and the the contexts in which memories are produced, textualised and used; in how the *mise-en-scène* of memories is characteristically imaged; in how sound figures in memory texts; in how narrative time is organised in memory-stories.

What follows is a summation, in six theses, of observations on memory and memory texts which emerged from the intimate acquaintance with many and varied memory texts called for in my efforts to do some memory work on my own account. These theses are a very provisional attempt to give some form to what are really quite shapeless observations, and to explore the links and the discontinuities between personal and collective memory:

1. Memory orders our inner worlds
2. Memory is an active production of meanings
3. Memory texts have their own formal conventions
4. Memory texts voice a collective imagination
5. In modernity, memory embodies both union and fragmentation
6. Memory is formative of communities of nationhood.

1. *Memory Shapes our Inner Worlds.* Memory inhabits, colours – even forms – our inner worlds. In psychical terms, remembering (and, equally importantly, forgetting) is part of the properly human quest for origins which finds its most elemental expression in primal scene fantasies. You are present at your own conception or birth: you observe the scene; you are yourself, the child; you are one of your parents; you are both your parents; you occupy all these positions at once. Primal scene fantasies are expressions of a wish not just to be there at the scene of your own emergence into the world, but to author yourself, to be your own progenitor; and so to take command over the past, over a world in which you were not yet present. That you may assume any or all of the roles in the primal scenario answers a wish to be everywhere at once, to see, experience, know and remember all. Do such fantasies of total power afford some compensation for (or disavowal of) the losses – beginning with separation from the mother's body – that are the lot of humankind? Does a wish to return to a familiar and yet, once lost, *other*, place offer a pattern for desires which surface in acts of memory?

Might the insistence on *place* in memory, for instance, not be a mirroring of the *mise-en-scène* of the primal scene fantasy, in which one is in a place, in a scene, and at the same time in any number of places within that scene? And does memory share the imagistic quality of unconscious productions like dreams and fantasies – for 'the Unconscious does not operate with the language of logic, but with images' (Martin and Spence 1988: 16), functioning in much the same way as the dreamwork, with its condensations, its displacements – gaps, non-causal logic, discontinous scenes. The language of memory does seem to be above all a language of images. And if there is a connection between memory and the unconscious, might this not also shed light upon the commonly unstraightforward relationship between memories and the 'real' past events to which they purportedly refer? Might the often inexplicable feeling of familiarity attaching to many of the less tangible pre-texts of memory (places, sights, sounds, smells) not speak of a fantasy of union with the mother's body, a wish to return to that safe place? Because many of these psychical processes are in some degree unconscious, acts of remembering often bring forth thoughts and feelings that seem hard to explain in any rational way. You have a sense, perhaps, that something has been irretrievably lost, but you don't know what it is; or if you do it is nameable only in the vaguest terms ('happier days', 'home').

Perhaps you yearn for the completeness, the security of days and places gone by, while you know you cannot retrieve them; know indeed that they might never ever have been, while yet disavowing that knowledge. And so memory is tinged with the bittersweet, death-defying sadness of nostalgia. Mourning is another kind of remembering, one that involves a repeated recalling to memory of the lost object in a reality process that, unlike nostalgia, will end with letting go. Perhaps being 'moved', as

Barthes, writing in *Camera Lucida* (Barthes 1981) tells us he was on finding the photograph of his mother as a girl, has something to do with a recognition of some thing, some moment, some feeling, that is close and familiar but which we can do nothing but accept is gone forever.

2. *Memory is an Active Production of Meanings.* Once voiced, even in 'inner speech', memory is shaped by secondary revision: it is always already a text, a signifying system. This is the first stage at which memory produces meanings. For while it might refer to past events and experiences, memory is neither pure experience nor pure event. Memory is an account, always discursive, always already textual. At the same time, memory can be articulated through a wide range of media and contexts. There is a world of difference, is there not, between the memory-sharing among members of a family looking through the family snaps for the hundredth time and the remembering provoked by the oral historian? Between the written memoir and the autobiographical film? Between an exhibition of old photographs and any of those countless radio or television programmes that promise to tell us about 'the way we were'? Some of these offer themselves quite openly as occasions for personal or collective reminiscence (books and exhibits of old photos of local scenes). Or published cultural commentaries might include personal reminiscences among their source materials (Richard Hoggart's book *The Uses of Literacy*) (Hoggart 1957). Other memory texts call up, in words, or with the directness and apparent purity of sounds or images, a sense of what remembering actually feels like (the film *Distant Voices, Still Lives*) (Terence Davies, GB, 1988). How much do these diverse memory texts have in common?

3. *Memory Texts have their own Formal Conventions.* Memory texts of all kinds and in all media appear to share certain formal attributes; though these are less apparent in texts (such as written and published memoirs) that have undergone considerable revision at a conscious level and may move towards certain literary conventions. Particularly prominent, though, among the peculiar characteristics of memory texts is a quite distinctive organisation of time. In memory texts, time rarely comes across as fully continuous or sequential. Literally, formally, or simply in terms of atmosphere created, the tenses of the memory text do not fix events to specific moments of time or temporal sequences. Events are repetitive or cyclical ('at one time . . .'); or seem to be set apart from fixed orders of time ('once upon a time . . .'). Relatedly, events narrated or portrayed in memory texts often telescope or merge into one another in the telling; so that a single recounted memory might fuse together a series of possibly discrete events. Or events might follow one another in no apparent temporal sequence, or have no obvious logical connection with one another. The memory text is typically a montage of vignettes, anecdotes, fragments, 'snapshots', flashes.

All this produces a sense of synchrony, as if remembered events are somehow pulled out of a linear time-frame, or refuse to be anchored in real historical time. Memory texts are metaphorical rather than analogical: as such, they have more in common with poetry than with classical narrative. Events in the memory text seem often to have been plucked at random from a paradigm of memories and wrought into a 'telling' that is by its nature linear, syntagmatic. For the Formalist literary theorist Roman Jakobson (Jacobson 1972), poetic language was precisely this twisting of paradigm onto syntagm; and in similar vein the pioneering experimental film-maker Maya Deren (Deren 1963) spoke of poetry in film as a vertical exploration – an investigation, through the particular temporality of this time-based medium, of a moment, image, or idea. And to borrow once more from Formalist language, the memory text stresses plot over story: that is to say, the formal structure and organisation of the account are typically of as much, if not greater, salience than its content. Often, too, memory texts will deliver abrupt and quite vertiginous shifts of scene and/or of narrative viewpoint. The metaphoric quality, the foregrounding of formal devices, the tendency to rapid shifts of setting or point of view: all of these produce the characteristically collagist, fragmentary, timeless, even musical, quality of the memory text.

The film *Distant Voices, Still Lives* presents virtually all of these formal properties: significantly, not so much through the spoken or the written word as in images and sounds. Although clearly 'about' a working-class childhood in Liverpool (place is crucial – though much more important than the city is the intimate space of the family house, laid out and explored on the screen in lovingly intense detail), the film is impossible – without being perversely auteurist – to label autobiographical in any conventional sense. Of any narrating autobiographical 'I' there is no trace; there is no enunciative voice capable of attribution to any particular individual narrator or character. And the pastness of the film's obviously highly invested *mise-en-scène* declines to let itself be attached to specific dates. While the events shown appear to span a period of time between the early war years and the mid to late 1950s, they are not narrated in any linear order of time, and there is no discernible 'classical' flashback structure.

Revealingly, the mother – the very epitome of the martyred, enduring working-class mum – looks exactly the same throughout the entire film.

Events are often presented in apparent isolation from, as if temporally or causally unrelated to, one another. Other modes of association are at work: episodes are narrated in the manner of a series of anecdotes or family stories honed by years of repetition, or else they appear on the screen as visual/audial memory-flashes – music and songs are especially prominent. Elsewhere, recurrent scenes – of pub singsongs and family get-togethers and rituals in particular (*Distant Voices, Still Lives* could with accuracy be renamed 'two weddings, a christening and a funeral') – produce a sense of time as cyclical: a version of 'timelessness' in which life's peak events, the rituals of birth, marriage and death, inexorably repeat themselves, but never change.

Although, no, *because* – *Distant Voices, Still Lives* offers no obvious single point of identification, it induces a certain sense of recognition. This is not because the remembered places and events of, say, my own childhood, resemble those in the film: if there is authenticity here, it is not that of naturalism, nor even of realism. It is more that the film contrives to convey the affect, the structure of feeling, that clings to my, possibly to everyone's, childhood memories. Though perhaps this is not quite universal. Writing about *Distant Voices, Still Lives*, Carolyn Steedman confesses to being moved (despite herself, for she finds the film's 'working-class romance' distasteful) by a scene in which a young man leaves the family house during a wedding party and stands in the doorway, weeping. 'I know exactly [sic] and for what purpose he weeps . . . it is *my* feeling, *my* moment. The young man cries because he knows that *it will go on like this*, that nothing will change; that the endless streets, the marriages made like his parents', the begetting of sons and daughters, all will stretch on forever, no end in sight' (Steedman 1989: 27). One of the formal qualities of the memory text – its organisation of time as cyclical rather than as sequential – captures something of what it feels like to live, or rather to remember living, in a particular family and a certain class setting. This example serves, if nothing else, to show that even the most apparently 'personal' and concrete contents and forms of remembering may have a purchase in the intersubjective domain of shared meanings, shared feelings, shared memories.

4. *Memory Texts Voice a Collective Imagination.* What links personal memory with its shared, collective, counterparts, and how do the formal properties of memory texts figure in this encounter? Assuming that all memory is in any case secondary revision, and that all memory texts are shaped by conventions that are in their nature collectively held, should we not straight away dismiss as a false dichotomy the distinction between personal and collective memory? Or would this be reductive? Do my observations not simply point to the fact that the psychical and the social, if formally distinct, are in practice always intertwined?

But if memory texts will have little truck with the conventions of classic realist narrative, they do tell stories of another sort. One type of memory text, for example – raw oral history interview material – frequently combines historical, poetic and legendary forms of speech, whilst still expressing both personal truths and a collective imagination. As Alessandro Portelli observes of oral history life stories, 'The degree of presence of "formalised materials" like proverbs, songs, formulaic language, stereo-types, can be a measure of the degree of presence of "collective viewpoint"' (Portelli 1981). Such memory texts create, rework, repeat and recontext-ualise the stories people tell each other about the kinds of lives they lead. In the process, the stories often take on a timeless, mythic quality which grows with each retelling. This mythicisation works at the levels of both personal and collective memory and is key in the production, through memory, of collective identities. (A story my brother tells of a time of traumatic abandonment in his childhood has much the same narrative structure and draws on a similar plot – the hazardous journey from danger to safety – as the mythic Dunkirk evacuation story embedded in the popular memory of World War II. The personal and national myth cele-brated by such stories is that of the underdog's triumph over adversity.)

'You'll eat a peck of dirt before you die.'
'Hard work never did anybody any harm.'

These sayings punctuated my mother's tales of her own childhood, and call to mind the formulaic, even clichéd, utterances which oral historians have noted in their informants' stories. Telling and retelling their memories is one of the strategies people use not just to make sense of the world, but actually to create their own world and give themselves and each other a place, a place of some dignity and worth, within it. In her sayings, my mother casts herself not merely as the victim of a poverty-stricken youth, but as heir to a proud tradition of endurance: 'we' are the people who are ennobled as well as toughened by hard work. The *communitas* affirmed by these formulae is one of class and generation. With these sayings, my mother merges her own identity into a collective one – perhaps in much the same way the working-class authors of the life stories discussed by Regenia Gagnier (Gagnier 1991) avoid the transcendent 'I' in their narra-tives, so instating a continuity of individuality and community. Other working-class life stories, especially those produced by individuals (like

Terence Davies and Richard Hoggart) who have left their class of origin
behind, might be narrated – necessarily from the point of view of the
'present' – in terms of the marginality, the not-belonging, the struggle
for identity of an 'uprooted' narrator.

Thus: in making sense of, we also imagine, and make, a shared world.
Memory texts translate the psychical activity of warding off loss into the
domain of the social. A compulsion to tell and retell the same stories, to
the point indeed that they become formulaic, has about it the air of a
desire to forestall death. Exactly: a group seeks to hand on the contents
of its memory-bank to future generations – and so to ensure collective
immortality for itself.

5. *In Modernity, Memory Embodies both Union and Fragmentation.*
Memory texts are made, shared and remade in many different contexts:
but it is perhaps the family that provides the model for every other
memory-community. Every family has its stories – its cast of characters,
its anecdotes about what so-and-so did when, its 'we used tos' (not to
mention its amnesias and secrets). Stories like this are obviously not
confined to families; but the shared remembering and complicit forgetting
that goes on in families provide the model for other communities – most
especially for the idea of nation as family, with its assumption of a past
held in common by all its members, a past that binds them together today
and will continue to do so into the future.

The condition of modernity, though, has wrought considerable changes
in how we relate to, how we produce, memory. As a modern individual, I
regard what I remember as the source of my own singular identity. Yet at
the same time, the era of mechanical reproduction and electronic simulation offers not merely new media for the circulation of collective memory
(sound recordings, photographs, televison programmes, films of and from
the past are part of the currency of everyday life), but completely new
ways of imagining a past that, as almost everyone alive today cannot fail
to see and hear, transcends the life of the individual. Memory texts
proliferate – there are more of them, across more media – as memory-
communities overlap, merge, fragment. (Does the girl born in Bradford
to Bengali parents, for example, belong to the community of Islam or of
Yorkshirewomen, or to both, or to an altogether new community?) In
modernity, collective remembering can divide, fragment, hybridise, unite,
enrich.

How can this be so? In the psyche, the drive that powers acts of memory
would seem to exert a specific pull: the desire, often only partly conscious,
for a lost 'home' grounds the work of memory as quest for union,

re-union, wholeness. The timeless quality of memory texts; their extreme investment in place, in the *scene* of memory; their repetitive, formulaic, quality; their characteristic emotional tone: all add up to an impetus towards not fragmentation but fusion. In the collective domain, this translates as a search for common imaginings of a shared past. If memory's desire runs in harness with the condition of modernity, public memory may be comprised of a mélange of smaller collective memory-stories, always in flux and always potentially in contradiction. Remembering can be the occasion for cultural difference, or even conflict, as well as for solidarity.

Everyday historical consciousness and collective memory do overlap, however, in stories about the recent past, that past which falls within the timespan of our parents' and our grandparents' memories. Here, remembering of the kind that goes on in families feeds into a consciousness of a history that transcends the memory of any individual or family:

> the period of the past experienced by means of
> family stories . . . differs qualitatively from times
> previous to it. Here, historical imagination is
> entangled with one's particular social origin and this
> differs from the way one imagines other, even earlier
> epochs and their struggles (Lindner 1986: 43).[5]

Memory's imaginings accrete in formulae, clichés, stereotypes, that come to function as a shorthand for clusters of shared memory-meanings.

6. *Memory is Formative of Communities of Nationhood.* With its foothold in both the psyche and in the shared worlds of everyday historical consciousness and collective imagination, memory has a crucial part to play in any national imaginary. Significantly, the word 'nation', with its roots in the Latin *nasci* (to be born), is defined in terms of both common culture and history and also shared space or territory.[6] When associated with ideas of nationhood, memory feeds into a conception of a history that is 'ours', and that belongs to all of 'us'. The historical imagination of nationhood then has something about it of the acts of remembering shared by families and other communities, and also of that desire for union, for wholeness, that powers the psychical dimensions of remembering. In the idea of the homeland, and even more clearly in that of the 'motherland', all of these aspects of the national imaginary are condensed. That the 'imagined communities' of nationhood are fictions in no way detracts from their power.

My voyage through memory continues. I have no idea where it may eventually lead, nor do I want it to end just yet. As recounted here, my story of the journey so far aims to convey something of how I got started and what I took with me on setting out; turnings taken, and what I discarded; and, finally, some insights gathered along the way. All of it is offered in a spirit of continuing inquiry.

Notes

1. The methods I used, which are quite straightforward, are outlined on p.4 of the book.
2. My thinking on revisionist autobiography was developed in conjunction with students on 'Autobiography and Female Identity', a course I taught in 1987–8 at the City Literary Institute in London.
3. For some criticisms of such writing from a feminist standpoint, see Haug et al. (1987).
4. See also Spence (1996).
5. See also Wright (1985).
6. The *Shorter Oxford Dictionary*'s principal definition of 'nation' is: 'A large aggregate of people so closely associated with each other by factors such as common descent, language, culture, history and occupation of the same territory, as to be identified as a distinct people'. See also Anderson (1983).

Bibliography

Anderson, Benedict (1983), *Imagined Communities: Reflections on the Origins and Spread of Nationalism*, London: Verso.

Barthes, Roland (1981), *Camera Lucida: Reflections on Photography*, New York: Hill and Wang.

Deren, Maya (1963), contribution to 'Poetry and the film: a sympsium', *Film Culture*, no 29.

Fraser, Ronald (1984), *In Search of a Past*, London: Verso.

Gagnier, Regenia, (1991), *Subjectivities: A History of Self-Representation in Britain, 1832-1920*, Oxford University Press.

Haug, Frigga et al. (1987), *Female Sexualisation*, London: Verso.

Heron, Liz (ed.) (1985), *Truth, Dare or Promise: Girls growing Up in the Fifties*, London: Virago Press.

Hoggart, Richard (1957), *The Uses of Literacy*, London: Chatto and Windus.

Holland, Patricia (1991), 'Introduction: History, memory and the family album', in Jo Spence and Patricia Holland (eds), *Family Snaps: The Meanings of Domestic Photography*, London: Virago Press.

Jakobson, Roman (1972), 'Linguistics and poetics', in Richard and Fernande de George (eds), *The Structuralists: from Marx to Levi-Strauss*. New York: Anchor Books.

Kuhn, Annette (1995), *Family Secrets: Acts of Memory and Imagination*, London: Verso.

Lindner, Burkhardt (1986), 'The *Passagenwerk* the *Berliner Kindheit*, and the archaeology of the "recent past"', *New German Critique* no. 39.

Marcus, Laura (1987), ' "Enough about you, Let's Talk About Me": Recent Autobiographical Writing', *New Formations* 1, 77–94.

Martin, Rosy and Spence, Jo (1988), 'Phototherapy: psychic realism as a healing art?' *Ten-8*, no. 30, Autumn.

Passerini, Luisa (1983), 'Memory', *History Workshop Journal*, no. 15, 195–6.

Portelli, Alessandro (1981), 'The peculiarities of oral history', *History Workshop Journal*, no 12.

Spence, Jo (1986), *Putting Myself in the Picture: A Political, Personal and Photographic Autobiography*, London: Camden Press.

Spence, Jo (1996), *Cultural Sniping: The Art of Transgression*, London: Routledge.

Steedman, Carolyn, (1986), *Landscape for a Good Woman: A Story of Two Lives*, London: Virago Press.

Steedman, Carolyn (1989), 'Class of heroes', *New Statesman and Society*, 14 April, 27.

Wright, Patrick (1985), *On Living in an Old Country: the National Past in Contemporary Britain*, London: Verso.

Method in Our Madness? Identity and Power in a Memory Work Method

Mariette Clare and Richard Johnson

This chapter recovers and reflects upon a method of inquiry called 'Memory Work'. It was adopted by a group of seven postgraduate students and one teacher, based in the then Centre for Contemporary Cultural Studies (CCCS) at Birmingham University. The group met between 1982 and 1986.[1] No work was published under its collective authorship Before its project – a collective book – was completed, the group broke up. This break-up has implications for the writing of this chapter and our representations of the group's work. Neither of us, for different reasons, feels that we own the project in any simple way, or that we can represent the writings and the views of others (c.f., however, Dawson (1994); Johnson (1987), (1991), (1993a), (1993b) and for unpublished work, Clare and Johnson (1986); Dawson (1991); Weinroth (1989); West (1987)). Accordingly, as the starting point for this essay, we each wrote our own account of the reasons why we adopted memory work in 1984. We have also limited our use of the original (1980s) material to the memory work pieces which we wrote ourselves.[2]

The initial focus of the 1980s project was the popularity of nationalism. For several years, a group with changing composition had been working around 'popular memory': in sum, the ways in which private memories and identities come to be connected with public versions of history, those of the Conservative nation for example. In what follows, however, we concentrate on questions of method and practice rather than on the substance of the collective argument. As we experienced it, memory work involved not only a technique, but the much wider and more problematic issues of knowledge, power and the academy; the development of a fully self-reflexive way of working; and recognition of the emotional dimensions of intellectual discovery and collaboration. In the course of this chapter we trace our experience of memory work as a practice – its aims, principles and rules – and explore the reasons why we chose it – its appropriateness to our aims. It is clear, in retrospect, however, that starting out on memory work set in train unpredictable processes which were intellectually generative but personally troubling and destabilising. These included the splitting up of the group with major and unequal consequences for individual careers and prospects. Paradoxically, however, the break-up of the group taught us further lessons in the dynamics of knowledge/power and in the formation of social identities. In the later sections of this chapter we draw out our own main lessons from the work of the group, especially those concerning issues of method and the formation of social identities.

What's the Method?

The rules of memory work as we practised it can be simply described. The group chooses a theme and each member undertakes to recall a personal episode associated with the theme. The next task is to write an account of this episode with as much particularity as possible and with the detail not overwhelmed by pre-emptive interpretations. In theory these autobiographical fragments are to be written at some speed, preferably within an hour. The speed is important because it seems to minimise the opportunities for self-censorship and self-editing, making the contradictions of everyday life more available for analysis. The material this method produces is rich and many-layered, but is limited enough in length and ambition for one fragment to be read and discussed in a working session of about two hours.

To exemplify the method, we both produced, for this chapter, our written memories of how the group came to use memory work.

Mariette wrote, without a title:

> It's hard for me to recall/reconstruct/remember why it was so important to me, personally, intellectually, politically, to argue for the use of memory work in the Pop. Mem. group.

Richard boldly wrote a title at the top of the page: 'Why We Adopted Memory Work'.

Our accounts agreed on the pivotal significance of a visit to the CCCS of a group of women from Berlin who had written a book using what they called 'Memory Work' (see Haug 1987).

Mariette:

> I remember that some of the women from the group in Berlin came to the CCCS to talk about the project on female sexualisation and to describe their memory work method. I remember very little of the actual seminar except a vague sense of three or four of them sitting at the curved, hollow ring of tables in the seminar room.
>
> I think what attracted me to their ideas was that they valorised the private, the everyday, the personal and carved out a space for aspects of experience that, as a mother of three, were of immediate, daily interest to me. Did the interest in narrative come before or after? I can't remember.

Richard:

> Was it about the same time that the women's group around the journal *Das Argument* from Berlin came to Birmingham? Did they include Frigga Haug? What was the contact here? Anyway, I remember this sort of broke the logjam around method. I also remember sitting the other side of the table to 3 women from Germany, learning about their work. Was there more than one meeting then? Anyway, previously we had thought of autobiography in terms of quite long narrative accounts of the self, over time. Now we had suggested to us a method that was much more flexible, in effect the production and analysis of autobiographical fragments, with quite a lot of emphasis on the analysis stage.

It is important to note that we both recalled some of the *same* circumstances of the adoption of memory work, and of its attraction for us. It is possible, of course, to use memory work as evidence - in this case to construct an 'historical' account of how memory work came to be adopted. We will return to a more factual account of this kind later.

In the process of memory, however, the 'now' is as important as the 'then'. Memory is a relationship between pasts and a particular present. Autobiographical fragments of this kind certainly provide evidence about events, feelings and meanings in the past. They also reveal through their formal features and choice of instances much about the writer's current identities and trajectories.

To read memory work in these two ways – at the second analytical stage of the method – is to attempt to disentangle the conditions which govern the possibilities and forms of remembering. Such conditions include the complex relay between a particular past and the present – our memory of the past as shaped by present conditions and our life in the present as shaped by our memory of the past. Our own accounts of the origins of memory work differ, for example, both because we were placed differently in the past and because we are placed differently today.

The *differences* between the two extracts (and the larger fragments they are taken from) reveal our different positionings and frameworks, now and in the past. Mariette produces her memory work today in terms of an individual self, shown as much in the privatised domain of mother-hood as in the public world of the academy. Her memory work is an account of how she realises that it is possible to have what she wants: to assert the value of excluded, local knowledges – here, those of caring and the domestic – and to insist on their presence in the public. As she wrote later in the same fragment:

> The stories were my bids for recognition, and for a stake in the public. I not only wanted a voice, but for my voice to be heard . . . I wanted to make central to the group project, the individual, the intimate, and to make public the private anchorage points of my own self. I wanted to put in those aspects of experience kept out of public (?male ?white ?middle-class) discourse, and to affirm and have affirmed their importance.

Richard's account is in terms of a more public and collective 'we', with a long-term project and a set of intellectual and practical problems which memory work helps to solve. It is only later in his fragment that he looks at the implications of memory work for personal relationships and his own 'patterns of intimacy'. The fragment as a whole moves from a public 'we' – for whom Richard feels he can speak – to an account of memory work as a solution to personal problems. His difficulty is, in a sense, the opposite to Mariette's. Plentifully recognised in the public domain, this work-based identity disrupts and constrains in many different ways, patterns of friendship, caring and domesticity:

> So memory work was also adopted – by me – because it was a way to intimacy, emotional explicitness, close friendships and supportive political-personal dialogue with co-authors - something I had always wanted . . .

One reading of the two extracts suggests that at that time the authors' emotional investments were both shifting. Schematically it would appear that Richard was moving from public to private and Mariette from private to public. What this conceals, however, is that, in their inner spaces, public and private were defined and experienced in radically different ways.

A crucial dimension of difference between the two accounts is the matter of ownership. For Richard the history of memory work is incor-porated into his identity and practice as an academic, especially as a teacher. This has involved the need to construct, on many occasions, some account of memory work as a method, including its derivation.[3] Teaching and practicing memory work has produced a continuous narrative which predates the Berlin women's visit and extends to his current work. This ownership is qualified by the collective origins of the work and his sense that he cannot use it in individual research and writing. Nonetheless the continuity has produced a sense of ownership, conveyed in his account by its professional/'intellectual' character and its rehearsed confidence.

> The problem that emerged was that we didn't have a way of getting at the more private or personal investments or disinvestments in the nation. That such disinvestments/investments were active was clear enough from our experience of the [Falklands/Malvinas] War which was quite traumatic. So my memory is that we were looking for ways of getting at the personal to supplement or transform previous work, which was quite extensive in the old group, on public discourses of Englishness.

The givens in this account are related to an academic identity and practice and to knowledge of the public sphere. Knowledge of 'public discourses of Englishness' is already in place. What the account problematises is 'getting at the more private and personal investments' as though these were not present or foregrounded already. This dichotomy only works in so far as Richard can present his own centrality in the academic as the stance of the group as a whole. Once again the 'we' in the sentence is treacherous. Discussion between the two of us highlighted key differences which blew this 'we' apart. The injunction to write memory work at some speed means that there is little time for self-censorship or reflection. As writers in these circumstances we reach for the habitual and most readily available formulations. In the course of our analytical dialogue, Richard realised with a shock how his 'memory' spoke not only of the past, but of a residual self, all too active in the present. Mariette's account, which well exemplifies the memory work 'rule' to remember a concrete episode and recover the associated feelings, is marked by phrases that represent her as a tentative and unreliable narrator: 'it's hard for me to recall/ reconstruct/ remember . . . I remember very little . . . a vague sense . . . I can't remember . . . I seem to remember'. This uncertainty or ambivalence is also constructed by her use of double negatives: 'I was not uninterested in public/political questions' and 'I can't be sure that I got through mine [reading the first piece of memory work] without crying'. 'We' is only used twice in the whole fragment, in each case to refer to specific group agreements. For example:

> Once the idea of memory work was adopted the ideas for topics seemed easy to find – we had to choose from dozens.

On the whole Mariette speaks only for herself and her private memories and refers not to the group as a whole but to its individual members, each of whom is named in the account. Her memories are not of a consensual 'we' but of her experience of conflict and a struggle to be heard within the group: she writes 'I kind of remember "winning" the argument, not alone', then goes on to offer her version of the stances of others.

Counterposed to the uncertainty of memory is Mariette's insistent emphasis on wanting and desire:

> The stories were my bids for recognition and for a stake in the public. I not only wanted a voice but for my voice to be heard . . . I wanted to restore a different form [from academic writing]; I wanted to make central to the group project the individual, the intimate, and to make public the private anchorage points of my own self. I wanted . . .

The repeated 'I wanted's in this passage testify to the intensity of desire at the time and suggest the depth of the subsequent losses. These features of the extract can be understood in terms of the formal failure of the Popular Memory project and its unequal consequences. For Mariette the failure of the project blocked one collective route to academic recognition. Despite a successful career, her relationship to the project, and all the desires it carried, has been marked by discontinuity, grief and loss. This difficult, complex, painful and largely unrecognised relation to the past is expressed in the hesitancies of memory and the emotional resonances which mark her memory work. The bitter paradox remains that it was the real life process of power across the public/private division that blocked the route to academic research, writing and publication about these very same processes.[4]

It is important to distinguish memory work, as we are practicing it now, from other forms of autobiographical writing. Fragments are written expressly to be presented to an other or group of others. Simultaneously each reader is also writing and presenting their own memory work. This is the basic condition of the practice and its consequences resonate through all aspects of the process.

We both experience remembering and writing as an intensely personal and 'inner' process. It is the part of the method that most resembles autobiographical introspection. It is hard not to feel possessive and protective towards these fragments. This feeling is heightened, however, in the second phase, when these 'precious' stories encounter the scrutiny of others. Most disturbing, moreover, is the realisation that others' analyses are producing meanings of which we, as authors, were originally unaware.

The stories cease to be (even apparently) our own, or under our own control. This sense of dispossession can be very threatening. All this perturbation may be fed back into the writing of subsequent stories.

Practicing once again this intensely autobiographical method reminded us how stories that represent personal memories are inescapably inter-personal and social. In this method, autobiography is deeply qualified by the presences of others as readers and critics. The individual control which the single autobiographer seems to exercise is transferred to the reading group and its unpredictable dynamics. Whereas, in classical autobio-graphy, the reader remains implicit, here the critical and analytical pres-ences of others and of all their social differences is built into the method. The key value of the method, indeed, is this dialogue of different perspect-ives on the meanings of memories, a dialogue which (if it can be sustained) accentuates the differences within the reading/research group, denatural-izes the storytelling itself, makes strange the familiar ordinariness of our lives and induces in the writer further self-reflection.

In-Disciplinary Concerns: Why We Adopted Memory Work

When we looked at the documentation of the time, in our individual 'archives', we noticed the absences in our memory work accounts. We also realised, however, how faithfully the differences of memory and conflicts of analysis in our current memory work replay some of the issues and conflicts of 1982–84. Early plans for the group book and our notes on presentations and discussions reveal a process of discord, negotiation and compromise. The experience of the Falklands/Malvinas conflict made more urgent previous work by group members on the popularity of Conservative nationalism. The recycling of World War II images and narratives heightened the issues around the political deployment of public memory and its place in hegemonic constructions of the nation. At the same time as this war had its impacts, a longer and more uneven process of struggle around the group and its project was being waged.

In many ways the lines of conflict here were those we sought to expose in our analysis of the differences between our current memories. On the one side was an already articulated project to understand conservative nationalism primarily, by *adding* ways of researching the private. On the other side was an emergent and fundamental challenge, harder to articulate than the dominant version even today, to the underlying public, masculine agenda. In particular the challenge was about the invisibility and uncon-sciousness of masculinity and the exclusion and hence the devaluing of the work of women in reproducing social life.

So far as we can see from today, there was a complex interaction between the longer struggle and the lessons of the war. We were all opposed to the war and its dominant narratives. Was this the basis of a temporary unity and sense of common purpose in the group as a whole? Certainly the war brought home to Richard the marginalisation (under 'Thatcherism') of the social categories he belonged to (e.g. public sector radical professional, critical intellectual) and of social projects with which he identified (the hope of a non-militaristic, socialist and feminist future). This sidelining of his forms of masculinity during the war and after was similar to but also very different from Mariette's more structural gender and class-based marginalisation. For her the war had nothing like the salience of the ferment of (different) feminisms, the socialism she learned from her father and the daily need to pit herself against what was powerful and was supposed to be known.

In retrospect it is clear that the war sharpened awareness among members of the group of particular key issues: the contradictions of Thatcherite Conservatism; the ambiguities of a 'Left nationalist' response; the gendered nature of both militarism and the peace movements of the time; the global nature of the conflict; the issue of justice for the Majority World. All members reported that, during the war itself, they had felt excluded, marginalised and powerless, unable to recognise themselves in the dominant representations. The narrowed and polarized scripts of gender and heterosexuality, the combinations of conventional romance and military adventure ('Wars and Weddings') repelled and alienated us all. If this was the Nation, in its finest hour, even those with a claim to it did not want to belong. These concerns, deriving from outside the academy, gave urgency to the existing agenda of the group to understand the popular purchase of conservative nationalist forms. Today, it is also very clear that our apparently common marginalisation and opposition had very different contents and proceeded from unequal structural positions. In particular the framework which we identified in Richard's memory work was also present in the precedence given at the time to the problem of Conservative hegemony in the public sphere. Within this framework the private is positioned only as a resource for understanding movements within the public political space. It thus continues to be subordinated. By contrast the emergent framework starts from valuing the privatized work of women in knitting together the social world and uses these values to challenge the reinforcing complicities between formal politics and academic knowledge and power. It is through processes such as these that public histories can subordinate private memories, but are also vulnerable to challenge by them once they can be expressed.

So for different reasons, we all wanted to get our own back. We remember our shared and different exclusions as a founding moment of the group project, a partly imaginary unity which, as we have shown, hid many major differences. We imagined an ambitious project: to grasp the cultural formation of the nation, layer upon layer, and see how it could be changed.

The history of the group up until the adoption of memory work can be seen as a series of compromises, struck usually in the terms of the 'old analysis'. It was indeed easy enough to reconstruct the field of the most public meanings. This was a matter of reading critically mainstream media representations and the speeches of politicians. It was true that the difficulty, from this perspective, was to understand their popular purchase. Given the validity of the question, we did not wish to *assume* either their popularity or a popular scepticism about them. It seemed that we needed to research popular responses empirically. Since this involved engagement with local and personal experiences, extending the original project in this way also seemed to meet the emergent demands.

One solution of this negotiated kind was to make the further move of analysing the links between Thatcherism and existing popular discourses, especially as articulated through representations of everyday life. 'Everyday life' here included food, the countryside, childhood games and fantasies, familial and sexual relations, and leisure and entertainment, including popular representations of the past. There were clearly points of entry here for an analysis of the daily work of women and a critique of heterosexuality. Already, before the adoption of memory work, our book plan included studies of 'wars and weddings'; masculinity, war and boy culture; the staging of popular pageants (especially the 1938 coronation); Warwick Castle as a commercial heritage site; ruralism and nature; commemorative rituals; the meaning of place and location; nation, past and present in food advertisements. Practices such as these were available for analysis through their own forms of public representation, although not so 'universally' as the forms of mainstream media. For example, in establishing the links between food and nationalism, Mariette looked at contemporary advertisements, women's magazines and recipe books. What this work confirmed was that projects like the ideological waging of the Falklands/Malvinas conflict, depend as much on everyday life constructions as on formal political processes and mainstream media representations. Crucial to the conduct of war is the construction of relations of Us and Others through everyday practices and their representation.

A second set of arguments about the popular, nearer to the terms of the emergent framework, was developed before the adoption of memory work. Established arguments about gender and literary genres were converted into a thesis about gendered identity and imaginary life in general.[5] Most of the work here focussed on the genres of adventure and romance. In the Falklands/Malvinas conflict the news media constantly deployed these genres, even conjoining them in the romantic familial welcome home given to returning soldier heroes. According to this thesis, nationalist rhetorics are successful when they connect with the social identities produced in the most familiar popular genres.

Although these daily discourses and narratives are highly visible and can be critically analysed, they still leave unanswered the question of popular readings. How do individuals and different social groups position themselves in relation to such narratives and discourses? What sort of evidence could be produced to answer this question? We wanted answers not only 'in theory', but through close engagement with the particular, neglected messiness of everyday life.

Memory work offered itself as a solution. Unlike an elaborated autobiographical practice, it allowed us to focus not on 'the life' but on the episode, the theme and the telling. Unlike published autobiographies or oral history transcripts,[6] the author was there to answer further questions, to provide contexts for both past and present moments and to participate in the analysis of the cultural formation of the self or selves. Because of the intensely personal nature of the enquiry there was a strong uneasiness about making the subjectivity of others into an object of academic research. The obvious resource was to use ourselves as the objects and subjects of research, adopting the method described by the Berlin women. Our own sense of inspiration at the time meant that we did not fully recognise how the unresolved differences within the group would constantly interact with the research process itself.

Memory work was not adopted for narrowly disciplinary or academic reasons. For Richard the development of cultural studies politically as well as intellectually was a major motive, but so too was the negotiation with feminism. For Mariette the pleasure of 'thinking new things' was much more important than the development of an academic discipline of whose social foundations she was anyway critical. The impulses to adopt memory work, as we reconstruct them, came mainly from outside the academy, in searches for solutions to personal and political difficulties. The different experiences of disempowerment during the Falkland/ Malvinas conflict made sense of the project of deconstructing the public/ private boundaries and their policing. The academic location and the resources of CCCS made it possible to believe that voices, marginalised as private or silenced altogether, could make themselves heard. Memory work as a method challenged many of the conventional distinctions between the public and private domains.

Among the perpetual fascinations and frustrations of this project were the ways that the methods we adopted reproduced, in different forms and on a smaller scale, the very relations of power they were meant to investigate. Because of the implications of the break-up of the group, it is difficult for us to specify exactly how these relations of power were composed in the actions and inactions of members of the group. Even now, in writing this chapter, we are constrained by our understanding of the power of making local and personal events more public, of the power of public definition. It would be unacceptable for us to offer unilateral definitions of what was at stake for other members of the group. We try to speak only for ourselves and the differences and conflicts between us. Of course, this cannot produce a complete account of the other positions and conflicts within the group. The most we can do is to sketch in some of the probable grounds for some of the more persistent conflicts within the group, or of those of which we are aware.

Adopting the Method

Addressing the *processes* of memory work underlines the generative and reflexive nature of methods of this kind. As it turned out memory work was not just a way of answering our original questions but produced a whole new agenda. This also involved new emotional investments and relationships of power within the group. In our experience, work in collaborative groups always has this potential for enrichment, elaboration and personal change. The adoption of memory work, however, intensified these processes. As Mariette put it:

> It [memory work] became a deeply absorbing, deeply disturbing, exciting, dangerous, reckless game. It was threatening and exhilarating.

Indeed the struggle over whether or not to do memory work was itself a transformative moment, intensified by the fact that seven members of the group had retreated to the Cotswolds for a week's concentrated work on our proposed book.

One aspect of this transformation was around power relations in the group. According to Richard's memory work:

> Perhaps it would be truer to say that the prospect and actuality of memory work threatened to change the terms of alliance and recognition in the group

... I also remember that the eventual adoption of the method was tied up in complex ways with my control as a teacher and more personal struggles, so it seemed to me at the time ... Shifting alliances! Anyway, the adoption of memory work was very much for me an experience of disenthronement as the teacher of you all, and represented a moment of maximum vulnerability. I did in fact feel I had lost my use in the group, which is why the offered friendships ... were so enabling.

In Mariette's memory the shift was not simply that of Richard's 'disenthronement' as a teacher. For one thing, her experience as an adult educator led her to separate Richard's power as an established academic from his rather unselfreflective practice as a teacher. For another, the conflict for her was about reshaping the project to embed a feminist method and agenda.

In discussing the episode today we had difficulty in disentangling various aspects of the struggle over whether to adopt memory work or not. We agreed that gender and sexual politics were central and took very individual forms, not coinciding with the male/female division within the group. All group members had been critical of the heterosexual and stereotypically gendered forms through which the Falklands/Malvinas war had been narrated. This did not mean, however, that in a group of four women and four men, issues of gender power were resolved or that lesbian and gay knowledges and experiences within the group were fully recognised. On the contrary these issues were to be constantly contested.

Because of the academic context, the politics of the group often came back to the patriarchal and class nature of academic knowledges and relations of power, and the different personal investments in these formations. Academic power included the ability to set the agenda of study, to legitimate a method of inquiry and to access or modify the dominant forms of language and modes of publication. In an educational system as hierarchical as the English one is, relations to academic forms are also strongly articulated to class origins, positions and trajectories. Class impacts in other ways too, in discrepancies between individuals in their inner senses of entitlement to social privileges. In a group embracing different nationalities, the focus on Britishness (usually Englishness) was already an element in the matrix of power relations in the group. It placed some members as more knowledgeable about the nationalist repertoire than others – or seemed to. All these relations and others[7] were constantly in play. Differences of age/stage, for example, intersected with differences in the gendered relations of caring for dependants, producing particular patterns of misunderstanding within the group.

Because Richard was in a position to offer significant recognitions and practical support to the individual academic projects and identities of other members of the group, the different power relations within the group were often condensed in the teacher/taught relation. Previous alliances around the project had had a somewhat homosocial and patriarchal character. This was challenged by the enthusiasm for memory work and what it implied: changing the cultural capital and intellectual currencies and redistributing insecurities in the group.

For example the conventions of the new method challenged the accepted styles of academic writing, as indeed it was designed to. Less consciously, it undercut the hard-won acquisition of ordinary academic competencies. Memory work forced a re-evaluation of existing criteria of academic recognition. Acceptability now depended on learning a whole new set of writing skills. As we will argue later, the writing of such stories involves the risky business of producing versions of the self for others. In effect, memory work changed the rules for self-production in an academic setting. It was not that academic self-production had been safe and comfortable before for all members of the group. As we have seen, the scripts for academic membership, unless consciously challenged, tend to favour some social identifications and marginalise others. Memory work produced some striking reversals here, centre-ing some of those previously marginalised and marginalising some of those previously dominant. Though the positions of members could shift, structural inequalities remained within the different public/private divides. Though new rules of self-representation were now in play, prioritising for example, personal experience and private (e.g. sexual) identities, the old rules, hugely reinforced by the wider context, remained. All negotiations therefore became more complex.

A second aspect of the transformation concerned the agenda of the project. In part, the adoption of memory work shifted the emphasis from public history to private memory, and further away from a state-centred view of politics and closer to the personal, the local and the daily. But much more was involved as soon as we started the practice of memory work. A new object of enquiry emerged: the production of collective and individual identities in the processes of remembering and of story-telling themselves. The original agenda had been to provide an account of local and private attachments to the Nation. The new agenda, which only started to become clear in the course of doing memory work, prioritised an understanding of identity formation, viewed as a process. From this point of view the memory work method itself could be understood as a microcosm of the larger social formation of individual and collective identities.

National identity could remain one theme within this new agenda but there was a pressure too to pursue the understanding of self-production free from questions of national belonging. This was in part because only some identities, some of the time, get to be articulated to the Nation. It was also because some members of the group, ourselves included, became totally beguiled by the fascinating practice of collective critical auto/ biography. Ideally the two projects went together, memory work being a way of recasting our understanding of state and nation. In practice, however, the doubled agenda created multiple opportunities for mutual mis-ascriptions: inveterate navel gazing on the one side, intransigent state-centrism on the other! In these ways not only the adoption of memory work, but also its practice, reproduced the founding but shadowy antagonisms within the group.

Another set of shifts were involved in the new agenda. It reframed the old understandings of history and memory. Initially we planned to use memory work to provide evidence of our past investments in nationalist forms. Using memories as evidence, however, forces a re-examination of the relationships between past and present identities, personal and public/historical. The analysis of memory work pieces could not be confined simply to what they revealed of the past. Memory is also a construction of identity in the present. Equally, the struggle to produce an identity under present conditions involves reconstructing the meanings of past events, and provides a new agenda for remembering.

In the sections that follow we go through each stage of the 1980s process with particular questions in mind. How did the differences we have described intersect with the memory work process? How did the memory work process itself further shift the agenda of the group and how was this related to changes in persons, identities and relationships? Finally, what was learned in the course of these processes – and when?

Choosing the Theme

Choosing the theme, like analysing the stories but unlike writing them, was a collective activity. Like the decision to adopt memory work itself, it gave scope for further contestation, producing oscillations in the choice of themes and the agenda of analysis. Themes within the older framework of nationalism included the Falkands, World War II, the Monarchy, School History, the Countryside and Castles. Others could be approached in the terms of this agenda but also opened out to new questions. Such themes included Romance, Heroes/Heroines/Models (fact and fiction), Girl/Boy Fantasy, Food. Further choices explored the usually private sense of exclusion or opposition to the dominant public forms: Political Dissidence, Experience of Difference, First Political Experience, Transformative Moments, Utopia. Finally there was a cluster of themes which represented the growing fascination with the processes of self-narration and with identity: New Strange Places, Nostalgia – Old Places, Waged Work, and Girl/Boy Fantasies. We also wrote stories about storytelling itself and even about doing memory work, one piece anwering the other in a present-day dialogue.[8] This was to cross the boundary between 'objective' academic practice and using our own subjectivity as a resource. It also offered examples of the daily processes of self-composure in the present, unavailable from relatively frozen memory work sketches.

Choosing a theme was never free of risk. The first two themes were 'Heroes/Heroines/Models' and 'Days Out'. The theme of Heroes and Heroines was chosen to explore the relationships between the adventure narrative and everyday gendered identities. The reporting of the Falklands/Malvinas conflict was dominated by heroic accounts of the 'Task Force' in which young soldier heroes went out 'boys' and came back 'men'. How, then, did we ourselves relate to such narratives? If these and other military heroes had no appeal, then who *were* our heroes and heroines? What was the nature of our private attachments to such figures?

By drawing our theme so widely we opened the way to very different forms of storytelling. The stories we actually told took us a long way away from the familiar nationalist narratives. Mariette, for example, wrote a story about a passionate reading, aged 19, of Doris Lessing's *The Golden Notebook*. In 1965 she found this book revelatory, dealing as it does, with themes of women's sexuality, political engagement, creativity and madness: hardly the typical traits of a model Englishwoman. Richard wrote about his relationship to his history teacher and about learning how to be an intellectual: a category in the English case not easily 'nationalised', even in a left-wing version. In neither case were we writing directly about heroes/heroines who figured in the Conservative Nation's pantheon. What was fascinating (at the stage of analysis) were the processes of identification and self-production – the ways we 'wrote' ourselves by finding a form for these memories, nationalist or (most commonly) not. Already the practice of memory work was subverting and transforming the original project.

The 'innocent' Heroes and Heroines turned out dramatically to marginalise some members of the group. We learned one of the most important lessons of memory work: how the absence of positive public versions of some important aspect of the self produces great personal anguish and hunger. Again, it was the memory work practice which made this lesson so personal, direct and concrete. Being obliged to remember and then to re-enact this absence replays these difficult feelings. The private pain was not necessarily visible to others. Yet the group, having collectively chosen the theme was responsible for recreating the hurtful exclusions. Such exclusions occurred wherever the group failed to grasp its own differences and its power to recognise. The expression of feelings of exclusion in the group always created turning points: where they were heard and responded to, new avenues opened up; where they were refused, personal and intellectual possibilities were closed down. It was in response to the trauma of Heroes and Heroines, that the happy, up-beat and apparently 'safe' topic of 'Days Out' was chosen.

Writing the Stories: Reviewing, Selecting, Remembering and Writing

When Mariette sat down to write her story on this theme she did not intend emotional exposure. She was as startled as the rest of the group by her tears at the memory, unbidden it seemed, of an unsuccessful day out in her teenage years, not long before her father's untimely death:

> Days out as a family didn't happen much for me . . . The summer of 1963, I think . . . I wanted my Dad to come to Stratford to share with him my pleasure, my absorption in the magic of the theatre. I think he wanted to come too, although I knew and he knew, that Shakespeare was not much in his line. Our tickets were up in the gods and I think it was on that day that I both realised and suppressed the realisation that he was indeed very ill. It took him a long time to struggle up all those stairs, his legs stiff and his breathing difficult. He made some semi-humourous comment about it and too, later, about his difficulty in hearing. The play was *Cymbeline*. What I remember of it now is . . . the mood of melancholy captured by the soft blues, greys and purples of the stage set, the words of the play's famous song – 'Fear no more the heat of the sun'. The grief in the play resonated with my own unacknowledged grief. For my Dad didn't enjoy the day out. Like me his daughter, he meant well, but in our good intentions we fatally missed each other . . . Neither of us knew any way of transcending that situation. I know I felt guilty. So I think did he. I turned away from it as he left, back to my holiday and to my own life. It was not long before he died.

Writing stories like this consists of several different activities, all of them tasks for the individual rather than the group.

The first task is to review a range of possible memories relevant to the theme. This amounts to a rehearsal of what is known about the self in this particular respect. Scanning your memory for possible stories to tell involves complex emotional evaluations; nor is this process wholly under conscious control. Some rehearsals go badly wrong when some half-forgotten or actively repressed episode demands to be heard. Mariette's Days Out story was one of these. It is at this point too that the rememberer may be faced with a more or less dramatic mismatch between her own life and the theme the group (or the more general culture) has chosen – an absence of heroes and heroines for instance. Finally there is the writer's anxiety about how any of the rehearsed stories will be received by the group. Will a story, like Mariette's Days Out with its strong emotional charge, be accepted or will it be refused, leaving her feeling exposed, isolated and foolish?

One story must now be selected. Some stories, however insistent and urgent their demands, can be rejected: they are too risky. They threaten the hard-won coherence of the self; they testify to unfinished business. The most dangerous may never have been told before. They may also be rejected because the writer fears that the experiences and feelings involved will not gain recognition in the group. Selecting a troublesome story opens up possibilities of personal change and shifts in the dynamics of the group. Other memories do not seem risky at all: they present themselves as pleasurable and safe. Some have already assumed the form of familiar stories, friendly old anecdotes often told with apparently predictable consequences. Some are 'treasured memories' that anchor existing identities in a reassuring way. Selecting which story to tell is to negotiate all these possibilities.

Although it may also occur in the course of writing, remembering is a practice with its own difficulties and delights. There are two related aspects of the process. Some form of recovery of the past is essential. The memory work method's emphasis on remembering in detail seemed to trigger memories not recently revisited. Initially, remembering is hard work: it requires a definite intention to remember and a sharp focus on the detail of the chosen episode. Under these conditions it is surprising how much can be recovered. This effort to remember and its productiveness are themselves evidence of the dependence of memory on past events, of the historical givenness of memory. Memories, however, must also always be composed, 'written'. Although a memory may be born as a fleeting image or other sensuous experience, it can only be fully present, even to the memory worker, when it acquires a more elaborated form: written, spoken or visualised. In this sense remembering is dependent on the means of representation available in the present.

Memory work also brought us both up against the limits of remembering.

Sometimes there are memories that seem particularly hard to recover; sometimes there are memories that cannot be recovered at all. Sometimes there is no memory trace. Working against memory are many forces of forgetfulness. Sometimes the distress of past events demands that a memory is repressed, lest recovery breach our current defences against the pain. In memory work about going to boarding school, for instance, Richard was unable to recover detail or feelings about the first time he left home. Sometimes events are so far removed from an agenda of contemporary significance, then and now, that they fade from consciousness.

Both dynamics illustrate the social as well as the psychic nature of the process. Mariette's story, for example, had to be remembered, selected, and written against the dominant social definition of Days Out, with its implicit expectations of pleasure. Because it was about dying and bereavement, this never had felt like a story that would be welcomed: it had no cultural place. Memories without social support tend to disappear from public expression and therefore from overt social identities. They tend also to dwindle in the individual consciousness. They are 'forgotten'.

The actual writing of the story, often accompanied by further remembering, was both exhilarating and disturbing. The exhilaration we both experienced in the writing itself stemmed from our power to define our own experience, to own and recognise it. By formally writing accounts of ourselves for others, we were explicitly enacting the everyday process through which personal and social identities are produced. Writing ourselves in this way was to exercise real agency and control – whatever came afterwards.

Discovering the connections between memory and the production of personal identity led to an increased interest in the written, spoken and visual forms through which self-composition is achieved. Part of the pleasure we both felt in writing our stories was to do with this sense of finding a form. Memory work privileged narrative as the way to encode experience. This preferring of narrative was part of the conflicts over the gendered, power-laden nature of academic forms of writing. Reflecting on the structures and uses of narrative, however, we realised how central this form must be in composing versions of the self in everyday social interaction. In order for a sequence of events to become a narrative they must be ordered and told from a particular point of view. They require what Labov calls a 'so-whatness', an answer to the sceptical listener's question 'so what?' (Labov 1972: 366) A story must have a point, moral or meaning. This is what satisfies the listener, but it also positions and defines the story-teller. It constitutes the story-teller as the holder of particular values, attitudes and perspectives. In telling the story of your own life, this formal or structural positioning is accompanied by the processes of making sense of its contingencies, past, present and future. Depending on the circumstances, especially those of others' readings, composing yourself in this way can feel exhilarating and enabling or put the self in deepest jeopardy. If we are to put into the world any version of ourselves such risks are inevitable. It seems possible that narrative as a cultural form and narration as a practice are the basic means of self-composition, both inner and outer, private and public.

Composing the self involves not only creative work but also rules, conventions and conditions. Forms of narrative enable but also constrain. This became clearest where the group recovered an earlier interest, less in narrative and identity in general, more in narrative genre and gender. Even as self-narrators we are not free to make ourselves up according to any storyline. We are dependent on the socially available repertoire of stories and the way they are ascribed to existing social identities. Originally we had identified genre like adventure and romance as part of conservative, nationalist discourse, perhaps as the means by which it became popular. From the perspective of memory work, the problem appeared the other way round: whether we could narrate ourselves as men and women at all without some recourse to adventure, heroism, romance or true love. Even to write ourselves against some generic form, or in a hyper-, parodic or ironic version of it, is to acknowledge the ineluctability of these conventions.

Analysing the Stories

Initially each story was read aloud and discussed in detail. Each author commented first on the context of the past episode and its significance today. Beyond this the group had few guidelines. The group started off with good intentions, but as stories accumulated, differences of power showed themselves in discrepancies of attention and in exclusions. Even with an agreed framework, the process of analysis would have been troublesome. It felt as if your story would be alienated, become unrecognisable, in the readings of others.

Richard's first memory work piece was about 'a man who taught me history for two years'.

> I think he became, in some respects, a model because he was very different from the whole cultural milieu in which he was discovered. Long-jawed, high-foreheaded, intensely earnest, he spoke so fast, so excitedly, he spluttered. He was very different from the teams of house-masters and head-masters whom

one was supposed to emulate. Moreover, he was ostensibly married, in a way that most of the others were ostensibly not. He lived in a separate house, off school premises . . . His wife was intellectual too, and there seemed to be a kind of equality between them . . . Both were fresh from college (Oxford), though she was already borne down, I think, by childcare and domestic demands. I remember hazily, a baby, or was it two? Still, in this place, they produced an oppositional space: domestic not institutional, intellectual not muscular, 'feminine' but only in opposition to an all-male world of exaggerated masculinities, dominated by sporting heroes, homosexual attachments, 'responsible positions' ambiguously accepted, and a grind of examination-orientated study.

Richard noted how this story was written as an 'affirmative memory', one of the few about his school-days. The story was subtitled 'How I became an "intellectual"' – 'I definitely wanted to be not only like him in some ways, but *better* than him.' It was also written as a story about a dissenting identity. Richard's hero was a scholarship boy, Yorkshire and working-class who recognised his and his friends' enthusiasms for *The Uses of Literacy* and 'the Angry Young Men'. From this point of view the story provided evidence for the place of 'heroes/models' in the construction of identity.

It became clear that the story was being read by members of the group not as a story of rebellion but as a story about the reproduction of intellectual masculinity; not as a story about solving problems for the self but about creating them for others. Originally 'safe', the story became decidedly risky in the process of analysis. The collective reading was disquieting for the author; but it also gave him opportunities for rethinking his previous identifications.

Later, Mariette did a piece on 'Experiences of Difference/Dissidence'.

Reading Richard's piece on the countryside, his utopian family excursion, I was hit by one of the momentary flashes of overwhelming envy that assail me from time to time. My family, and especially in ventures into the wide world, is never and can never be utopian . . . Having a handicapped child changes the simplest and most taken-for-granted events of domestic life into mountainous obstacle races . . . It's the most obvious experience of difference in my life that mostly I take good care never to think about . . . It changes irrecoverably the nature of daily life.

I remember walking down through the village late one November afternoon to see a friend . . . with N and B in the twin buggy. The sun was behind me in the west, the eastern sky was green, the first star was out. There were narrow ragged clouds blowing across the sky, and it was dark enough for the trees to look black . . . It was during the time that the medical profession thought N had . . . a rare metabolic disorder leading to slow degeneration and certain death . . . and since he had it there was a high probability that B did too. They were cheerful, well-wrapped up in their pushchair, rosy, fat, fairhaired toddlers, for whom I felt that intense physical passion of parent for infant. But I also knew what it is actually insanity to know – that there was no magic screen round me to stop the impossible and unthinkable things that only happened to other people from happening to me. I was sure that my children were going to die, and that I was going to have to watch it happening and there was no way out of that.

The rest of this memory work piece was not about the past, but about the daily reality of bringing up a child with what was eventually correctly diagnosed as cerebral palsy. In a strict sense this story was not 'memory work'; it stemmed from contemporary experiences. This made it risky in a particular way: it was not possible for Mariette to hide behind some identity that could be put behind her – a past self. It was also risky because of the resistance of all those currently regarded as able-bodied to accepting issues around disability as of major concern. Telling this story also opened up the possibility of a renewed neglect of the labour of caring, recognition of which had been a strong motive in Mariette's initial advocacy of memory work.

The writing and reception of both these stories illustrate the way the group came to function as a small-scale version of larger public domains. Just as mainstream media feed off and assign new meanings to the private local lives of individuals and groups, so we savoured, consumed and sometimes spat out these constructed fragments of each other's lives. All members of the group, as writers and as readers experienced these gratifications and perils. These experiences, unequally shared, soon became the basis for some provisional theorisations of the relationship between composition of the self through the stories and the ratifications or disqualifications awarded in the small public of the group.

Some stories met with very little recognition from the group. Such experiences converged with our reading of psychoanalytic literatures, especially Jessica Benjamin's reading of the erotic dimensions of domination and subordination (Benjamin 1980, later 1990). 'Recognition' in her usage illuminated the dependence of our attempts at self-composition on a power-laden relation to social and psychic others. As Benjamin puts it:

In order to exist for oneself, one has to exist for an other. It would seem there is no way out of this dependency. If I destroy the other, there is no one to recognise me, for if I allow him no independent consciousness, I become enmeshed with a dead, not-conscious being. If the other denies me recognition, my acts have no meaning; if he is so far above me that nothing I can do can alter his attitude toward me, I can only submit. My desire and agency can find no outlet, except in the form of obedience.

We might call this the dialectic of control: If I completely control the other, then the other ceases to exist, and if the other completely controls me, then I cease to exist. A condition of our own independent existence is recognising the other. (Benjamin, 1990: 53)

Benjamin's version of recognition, however, is not limited to overtly erotic relationships. The basis of her theory is a general account of how human (culturally specific?) individuality is inevitably formed in social interactions, from those between the infant and the carer to those of adult life.

Not to have your story recognised in the group created the sense that your 'acts [had] no meaning'. That aspect of the self that the story represented could only have a shadowy existence in the group. This had consequences not only for the group's collective story but also for the author's self-narrations. An unrecognised story fails to achieve the social presence of a fully circulating public form. The author may consciously disavow or even repress the story, or cling to it more tenaciously in her inner speech with a hope of future recognition. But the failure of recognition in her own case may affect her ability or willingness to recognise the stories of others. She may also not recognise what is offered *as* recognition. In the Popular Memory work, refusal of a story at the group level depleted the resources of the project and also created a kind of group unconscious, an accumulation of untold/unheard self-narrations. By the untimely end of the project the tangle of such mutually unrecognised stories had become so complex that it was hard for anyone to unravel them. The most intractable knots were tied to the many social differences and relations of power within the group which we have already analysed: a criss-cross of mutual non-recognitions and consequent and uneven blockings of stories and identities.

Richard's story and its reception is an example of one form of misrecognition. Here the story was heard but in terms different from those in which it was first formulated. Recognition is offered but only on condition that the author reframes the meaning of the experience. Misrecognition presents the author with a dilemma. He must either cut or stretch his story and therefore some aspect of himself to fit the forms of (mis)recognition; or, unable to relinquish what seems a central aspect of himself, he may insist on maintaining the original story, at least internally.

Where the weight of power is against the misrecognised, holding to your story is a necessary form of resistance, retaining the power of self-definition and subjective 'authenticity'. One contemporary example is 'coming out' in lesbian and gay politics; risking this, making public a formerly private identity has the potential to transform the self and all the surrounding social relationships.

In the case of Richard's story, initial misrecognition provided an opportunity for the author to reposition himself in social relationships by re-interpreting an old storyline. This self-re-recognition (as a particular kind of man) also offered recognitions to the critical readers of the original text by accepting their meanings. This is an example of a positive instance of 'misrecognition' which worked *against* the balance of power relations.

More commonly, misrecognitions are perpetrated by dominant groups over those they seek to subordinate and are less open to positive correction. Misrecognition is certainly about social difference and power. It also has a psychic dimension. The emotional life of the recogniser is important here: recognition can be afforded, offered on conditions, or withheld according to *her* identifications and the degree to which *she* has found recognition. The psychic and the social dimensions continually interact: we have found it especially difficult as readers, for example, to admit stories of others where they threaten to reveal our complicity in privilege and power.

Mutual recognition can only ever be incomplete. Any recognition, any version of the other, occurs through imaginary or psychic means. We can only internalize versions of others by imagining them, and this imagining is infused by feelings derived from our own inner history. Indeed the self that (mis)recognises the other has only come to be through the acceptance of an other's autonomy. Only when both 'Others' are not overwhelmed by their own psychic dynamics can they mutually recognise themselves and each other.

> A condition of our own independent existence is recognising the other. True independence means sustaining the essential tension of these contradictory impulses; that is, both asserting the self and recognizing the other. (Benjamin 1990: 53)

In Benjamin's argument the possibility of mutual recognition is always affected by relations of domination and submission. Recognition is always partial. Recognition from the other – individuals, groups or the larger society – must be struggled for within unequal social relationships.

Within any particular public, large or small, there is always a political struggle over the terms of recognition. The struggle within the Popular Memory Group over the adoption of memory work is a good example. The terms of intellectual recognition – of what constituted good and relevant work – were challenged and the balance of recognitions changed. The production of an agreed version of a publishable text required a pattern of mutual recognitions, good enough for the purpose. 'The book' would not only have 'written up' the project but also have written the group, as an achieved collective identity of some kind. To realise the group identity in this way would have required the successful negotiation of a point – or points – of view from which the group's process and conclusions could be narrated. Without such a resolution, the adoption of memory work redistributed the difficulties, contradictions and levels of ownership within the group. This was deeply paradoxical in a group that had struggled self-reflexively over academic and other forms of power and had made a study of nationalist and other exclusions. How could we end up reproducing these patterns?

Conclusion

Memory work as process showed us how the construction of a collective identity under conditions where power relations are untransformed, always involves the differential recognition of identities. Some identities are recognised as exemplary, some are recognised as long as they 'behave' and stay in their place, and others are marginalised, subordinated or expelled to become the demonic/desired Other. The dynamics of the group itself can now be understood as manifestations of the dialectic of identity and recognition.

These insights also throw light on our original topic – the nation. All the representations of the nation put the subjects/citizens in their places. Nations are not so much unities but structures of differences and inequities. Like the terms of recognition within the Popular Memory Group, nationalist discourse works as a meta-narrative of identity, rooting itself in other social identities and regulating them. It is precisely emotional investment in these other social identities – in forms of ethnicity or masculinity for example – that enables interpellation by the dominant discourses. In this sense all nationalisms are composite, articulated, and have a particular social politics. But disarticulation and resistance are equally possible: we did not recognise our selves or our stories in the dominant Falklands representations. We set about to produce a critical public of our own – and showed in the process that criticism is not enough.

Criticism is not enough because of the emotional weight and charge involved in all work on identity. The resolution of differences within the group was always complicated by these psychic processes. For all individuals such investments and their implications for Self and Others are always partly unconscious, and contain strongly imaginary elements. To work directly on such material is to generate emotional turbulences which are hard to predict in advance. Some of these unconscious processes were uncovered and negotiated in our memory work project; but some have only become clearer to us in retrospect; and others no doubt remain obscure. Certainly we were aware in sitting down to write this article of much unfinished business between and within our selves and with our (real and imaginary) Others.

Despite bruising experiences, we are clear that memory work has a great deal to offer as a method of inquiry. It makes available the actual forms through which identities are composed: stories or images which encode memories; the genres of inner speech which constitute subordinated or emerging selves. It reveals the centrality of memory to the processes of continuity and change, themselves at the heart of individual and collective identity. Without the effort to remember and without cultural forms to remember with, there is no continuity; without the effort of reworking versions of the past, there can be no change. Memory work also shows the dependence of this work of identity on the social processes of recognition and misrecognition, whether embedded in intimate relations and small groups, or mirrored in the larger screens of powerful media and political discourses. It illuminates the obscure relationship between memory, individualised psyches and social/political processes.

Recognition and misrecognition are intrinsic to practices like memory work. Always demanding, they can be handled in more or less productive or damaging ways. For instance, it is important not to foreground judgements of the material in the discussion/analysis phase, but rather to recognise and help to extend the purposes and meanings of a story. Each author should be able to rely on a fair share of attention. This may involve some check on the overproduction of stories and clarity about how many a group can digest. The method generates much insight from a limited amount of material, especially if attention is paid to process as well as to product. It is difficult to prescribe general rules for group members because of the ever-presence and asymmetry of power relations in all such groups. The need will always arise for some members, especially the most powerful, to reframe their memories and identities in the light of the commentaries of others. The group dynamics will replicate but, if consciously examined, also challenge the operation of the social forms of power. This is why reflection on the group's own processes can always produce knowledge of larger fields of power and meanings.

We now value memory work not simply as an extension of intellectual or academic disciplines but as a personal and political resource. At best it provides a method of giving proper weight to the experiences and identities of others. It can make transparent the operation and encoding of cultural power. It foregrounds the hard work of producing identities under pressure; of remembering and asserting the self against the cultural grain. It reminds us, daily, that the most publicly recognised forms are often the most unrecognising: subordinating memories, enforcing forgetfulness and making identities unrecognisable, both to others and to self.

Notes

1. There were earlier groups in CCCS with the same name, and some overlapping membership and themes. See, for example, Popular Memory Group (1982); Bommes and Wright (1982); Dawson and West (1984).
2. We have also limited our account, in this chapter, to the work of the group itself. We have not tried to relate it to the explosion of work, subsequently, on issues of memory, narrative, auto/biography, subjectivity and identity. Nor have we addressed explictly the whole 'postpositivist' (and especially feminist) turn in method of which the work of the group was clearly a part. Or indeed the flood of work on 'heritage' and national identity, the early phases of which formed an immediate context for the project. References are limited to texts which influenced us at the time.
3. e.g. in BA and MA teaching and in advice on research practice to Ph.D. students.
4. Though she too used memory work insights in a successful career as an adult education teacher and in research on self-advocacy and a critical self-reflexive professionalism. See, for example, Clare (1990).
5. In these moves we were influenced by the work of the English Studies Group in CCCS and by the Media Group and Romance Groups of which some of us were also members. cf. Batsleer et al. (1985) and CCCS Media Group (1982).
6. Previous Popular Memory Groups had engaged critically with the practice of oral history especially as represented at that time in the work of Paul Thompson (Thompson 1978 and cf. Popular Memory Group (1982).
7. In retrospect we were often tripped up by these 'other' relationships, which neither we nor contemporary sociology, had theorised. Many

significant differences in the group remained largely undiscussed – e.g. parenthood/non-parenthood in general or the difference it made that both Mariette and Richard were adoptive parents.

8. For example Richard and Mariette both wrote about 'stories I tell myself when I wake up in the morning'.

Bibliography

Batsleer, Janet et al. (1985), *Rewriting English: Cultural Politics of Gender and Class*, London: Methuen.

Benjamin, Jessica, (1980), 'Master and Slave: the Fantasy of Erotic Domination' in Ann Snitow et al. (eds), *Powers of Desire: The Politics of Sexuality*. New York: Monthly Review Press.

Benjamin, Jessica (1990), *The Bonds of Love: Psychoanalysis, Feminism and the Problem of Domination*. London: Virago.

Bommes, Michael and Wright, Patrick (1982), '"Charms of Residence": The Public and the Past' in Centre for Contemporary Cultural Studies, *Making Histories: Studies in History, Writing and Politics*, London: Hutchinson.

Centre for Contemporary Cultural Studies Media Group (1982), 'Fighting Over Peace: Representations of CND in the Media in 1981', *CCCS Stencilled Occasional Paper* No. 72.

Clare, Mariette (1990), *Developing Self Advocacy Skills with Adults with Disabilities* London: Further Education Unit.

Clare, Mariette and Johnson, Richard (1986), 'Nationalism, Narrative and Identity', unpublished paper presented to the Conference of the Association of Cultural Studies, 22 March.

Dawson, Graham, (1991), 'Soldier Heroes and Adventure Narratives: Case Studies in English Masculine Identities from the Victorian Empire to Post-Imperial Britain', (Unpublished Ph.D. thesis, University of Birmingham).

Dawson, Graham, (1994), *Soldier Heroes: British Adventure, Empire and the Imagining of Masculinities,* London: Routledge.

Dawson, Graham, and West, Bob (1984), '"Our Finest Hour?" The Popular Memory of World War II and the Struggle Over National Identity' in G. Hurd (ed.), *National Fictions: World War II on Film and Television*, London: British Film Institute.

Haug, Frigga (ed.) (1987), *Female Sexualisation: A Collective Work of Memory*, London: Verso.

Johnson, Richard (1987), 'Cultural Studies and English Studies: Approaches to Nationalism, Narrative and Identity, *Hard Times*, No. 31, (Berlin).

Johnson, Richard (1991), 'Two Ways to Remember: Exploring Memory as Identity', in *Nothing Bloody Stands Still*, Annual Magazine of the European Network of Cultural and Media Studies, Amsterdam: Cultural Studies Foundation.

Johnson, Richard (1993a), 'Everyday Life – National and Other Identities' in Ute Bechdolf et al. (eds), *Watching Europe: A Media and Cultural Studies Reader*, Amsterdam and Tübingen: Amsterdam Cultural Studies Foundation and Tübinger Vereinigung Für Volkskunde E.V.

Johnson, Richard (1993b), 'Towards a Cultural Theory of the Nation: A British-Dutch Dialogue' in A. Galema, B. Henkes and H. Te Velde (eds), *Images of the Nation: Different Meanings of Dutchness 1870–1940*, Amsterdam: Rodopi.

Labov, William (1972), *Language in the Inner City*, Philadelphia: University of Pennsylvania Press.

Popular Memory Group (1982), 'Popular Memory: Theory, Politics and Method' in Centre for Contemporary Cultural Studies, *Making Histories: Studies in History-Writing and Politics*, London: Hutchinson.

Thompson, Paul (1978), *The Voice of the Past: Oral History*, Oxford: Oxford University Press.

Weinroth, Michelle (1989), 'Communist Polemic and the Legacy of William Morris: An Impasse in a Revolutionary Aesthetic' (Unpublished Ph.D. Thesis, University of Birmingham), subsequently published as *Reclaiming William Morris: Englishness, Sublimity and the Rhetoric of Dissent*, Montreal and Kingston: McGill-Queen's University Press 1996.

West, Robert (1987), 'English Ruralism and Nationalism in Britain 1920–1945', (Unpublished Ph.D. thesis, University of Birmingham).

Index

Index

Index

CPSIA information can be obtained at www.ICGtesting.com
Printed in the USA
LVOW010944281112

309128LV00008B/393/A